DEMOCRACY BEYOND BORDERS

About the Author

Dr. Andrew Kuper is a Managing Director at Ashoka—Innovators for the Public, which supports and connects social entrepreneurs in over sixty countries. He is also a Fellow of Trinity College, Cambridge University.

Born and raised in South Africa, Dr. Kuper holds his PhD from Cambridge. He has been a visiting scholar at both Harvard and Columbia. As Senior Associate at the Carnegie Council on Ethics and International Affairs, he directed the project on multilateral strategies to promote democracy. He is also Co-Director of Kuper Research, a media and sociopolitical consultancy based in South Africa.

Dr. Kuper has published on the media and democracy, charity and global poverty relief, globalization and the role of corporations in development. He is the editor of *Global Responsibilities: Who Must Deliver on Human Rights?*

DEMOCRACY BEYOND BORDERS

JUSTICE AND REPRESENTATION IN GLOBAL INSTITUTIONS

ANDREW KUPER

OXFORD

UNIVERSITY PRESS

OXFORD

UNIVERSITY PRESS

Great Clarendon Street, Oxford OX2 6DP

Oxford University Press is a department of the University of Oxford.
It furthers the University's objective of excellence in research, scholarship,
and education by publishing worldwide in

Oxford New York

Auckland Cape Town Dar es Salaam Hong Kong Karachi
Kuala Lumpur Madrid Melbourne Mexico City Nairobi
New Delhi Shanghai Taipei Toronto

With offices in

Argentina Austria Brazil Chile Czech Republic France Greece
Guatemala Hungary Italy Japan Poland Portugal Singapore
South Korea Switzerland Thailand Turkey Ukraine Vietnam

Oxford is a registered trade mark of Oxford University Press
in the UK and in certain other countries

Published in the United States
by Oxford University Press Inc., New York

British Library Cataloguing in Publication Data
Data available

Library of Congress Cataloging in Publication Data
Data available

Typeset by Newgen Imaging Systems (P) Ltd., Chennai, India
Printed in Great Britain
on acid-free paper by
Biddles Ltd., King's Lynn

ISBN 0–19–927490–8   978–0–19–927490–1
ISBN 0–19–929165–9 (Pbk.)   978–0–19–929165–6 (Pbk.)

3 5 7 9 10 8 6 4 2

For Jos, Laurance, and Kate Kuper
Whose love and clear-eyed approaches to change
are the inspirations for this work, and this life

Contents

Acknowledgements

My most important intellectual debt is to Onora O'Neill, whose incisive comments and *Menschlichkeit* improved my thinking and well-being at every turn. Amartya Sen helped me to integrate key normative and empirical concerns. John Dunn, David Held, and Istvan Hont vigorously exposed my weaknesses, and then strengthened my grasp of the context and contentions of the text. Thomas Pogge lent me his ear and his air-conditioned office, both of which proved indispensable to surviving summers in New York. Raymond Geuss, John Tasioulas, and three anonymous reviewers offered inspiring challenges in the home stretch.

During my year at Harvard, made possible by the trustees of the Henry Fellowship, I profited greatly from regular discussions with Sandra Badin, Seyla Benhabib, Bryan Garsten, Michael Sandel, and Tim Scanlon. The rest of the research was funded entirely by Trinity College, Cambridge, where my fellow Fellows and my students provided an immensely stimulating home and work environment.

Some lifelong friends provided not only emotional but also intellectual and logistical support. Thank you to Lucy Delap, Jackie Dugard, Michael Pitman, Jimmy Roth, Simon Stacey, and Nir Tsuk. For empathy and exhilaration, I also thank Jude Browne, Adam Freudenheim, Fredrik Galtung, the other Kupers, Karen Lewis-Enright, Fiona Melrose, Annie Moser, the Oppenheimers, Adina Oskowitz, Robin and Tricia Pearse, Thiru and Ashika Pillay, Ornit Shani, and Sigal Spigel. Finally, I owe unique debts to Nim Geva, for laughter in the dark, to Zeev Emmerich, for daily illumination, and to Gordon Kuper, for devotion beyond borders.

I have dedicated the book to my family, who have crossed continents, actual and emotional, to be with me in the ways that matter.

All these generous people shaped the book and its author. However, according to the universal principles of academic justice, the author alone is responsible for every deficiency.

An earlier version of Chapter 1 appeared as 'Rawlsian Global Justice: Beyond *The Law of Peoples* to a Cosmopolitan Law of Persons', in *Political Theory*, Vol. 28, No. 5 (2000), 640–74.

An earlier version of Chapter 2 appeared as 'Why Deliberation Cannot Tame Globalisation: The Impossibility of a Deliberative Democrat,' in *Analyse & Kritik*, Vol. 25, No. 2 (2003), 176–98.

Introduction: Walking the Tightrope

> To live is to build a ship and a harbor
> at the same time. And to complete the harbor
> long after the ship was drowned.
>
> Yehuda Amichai

1. Context

Liberalism and modern democracy are now the most widely accepted forms of official justification for political rule. Both doctrines were developed largely in and for nation-states. Yet, in the face of what is bluntly called globalisation, it is arguable that an international political system based on states will be unable to meet some of the most daunting political challenges that confront our world. Is it possible to develop an institutional framework that is not based primarily on states, one that would enable justifiable and effective rule? In particular, can the principles and practices of liberal justice and representative democracy be extended, to positive effect, beyond the state contexts for which they were devised? I argue in this book that we should end our dubious romance with the nation-state and that we can do so in favour of a more suitable prospect: not a world state, nor a system of superstates, but a multiform global system that I shall call Responsive Democracy.

The book does not—I should stress—seek to explain at length the complex processes and phenomena that fall under the rubric of globalisation.[1] I accept from the outset that there has been a massive

---

[1] However malleable and abused, the term captures a widespread perception about our era. Here are some early prominent examples: human individuals and communities are enmeshed in a network of 'accelerating interdependence'; 'time-space

growth in the extent, intensity, velocity, and scope of impact of cross-border human social relations and transactions.[2] My concern is with the glaring absence of a corresponding increase in our capacities to exercise political control over this enmeshed world. This deficit is partly due to a peculiar way in which our practical imagination is constrained.

If liberalism and democracy are seen as ineradicably tied to the state form, and yet the state is failing to fulfil important governmental tasks, we are in deep trouble. We are left then with only two alternatives: a system of liberal democratic states that would often be unstable and ineffective, or some form of non-state global order that would be illiberal and undemocratic. (We might well get a fitful combination of the two.) Neither is an appealing prospect. While liberalism and democracy are far from flawless guides to political organisation and human conduct, both have had significant advantages over the major ideological and practical competitors. The need to retain these advantages on its own would provide sufficient justification for attempting to develop a non-statist account of liberalism and democracy. But I shall provide a stronger justification—to wit, that many of the flaws in current liberal democratic thought and practice are in fact the result of the two doctrines being conceived in statist terms and affixed to state structures. Our best hope lies in reconstructing the theory and practice of liberal justice and democratic representation on foundations that are *neither nationalist nor statist*.

To this end, the book presents the core components of (1) a theory of global justice that arises out of a critique of the influential political philosophy of John Rawls; (2) a theory of democratic representation that constitutes an alternative to the approach taken by Jürgen Habermas and his deliberative democratic followers; and (3) a theory

---

compression' occurs 'as interaction accelerates', making the world a far smaller and more immediately reactive place; and, as the range and depth of shared activities increase, the impact of 'action at a distance' is greater than ever before (see, respectively, K. Ohmae, *The Borderless World* (London: Collins, 1990); D. Harvey, *The Condition of Postmodernity* (Oxford: Blackwell, 1989); and A. Giddens, *The Consequences of Modernity* (Cambridge: Polity, 1990)).

[2] Here I follow D. Held, A. McGrew, D. Goldblatt, and J. Perraton, *Global Transformations: Politics, Economics and Culture* (Cambridge: Polity Press, 1999). This descriptive account of globalisation is superior to many others of its kind partly because, together, the co-authors are able to traverse traditional disciplinary boundaries.

of how political and moral ideals that are necessarily framed in abstract terms can help orient practice in messy, non-ideal conditions. Together, these three currents of the text form a novel, non-state theory of global justice and democracy.

I am aware, all too aware, that these are large promises on which to deliver. Partly for this reason, I do not ask the reader to rest content with highly abstract reflections, but illustrate how my approach enables us to specify beneficial and feasible reforms to four rather different global institutions: the International Criminal Court, the International Court of Justice, the United Nations General Assembly and Security Council, and Transparency International.

The guiding insight that makes these theories plausible, practicable, and indeed compatible is that it is possible to generalise and carry to a higher order of abstraction the traditional idea of the separation of powers. I free this idea from its usual moorings in three ways. First, I show that there is no moral or prudential justification for the claim that political power must be located ultimately at one level of authority (e.g. the state); the capabilities of persons, especially vulnerable persons, are best protected and advanced by dispersing power to several *levels* of authority that operate above and below the state. Second, I show that the classical tripartite separation of powers fails in important respects; further *types* of authoritative powers are also required to compel authorities to check and balance one another. Third, I show that these extensions, properly combined, do more than protect citizens against the might of any one overweening power; the combination also has the effect of improving political inclusion and mobilisation, as well as political judgement. Accordingly, this radically revised idea of the separation of powers forms a practical general framework that could address both liberal and democratic concerns about global order.

2. Justification

What allows, indeed requires, me to make this argument is a certain conception of political legitimacy. Against Rawls, I maintain that liberal conceptions of the person and of toleration are profoundly at odds with any political order that recognises nationalism and statism in its basic structure.[3] I develop a liberal theory of justice that is

---

[3] This is not a historical but a conceptual claim; however, I believe that the history of liberal states is replete with this disruptive (and, I shall argue, avoidable) tension.

termed 'cosmopolitan' because it attaches primary moral significance to individuals considered as free and equal persons, and never merely as members of associations or nation-states. This moral cosmopolitanism leads me to argue—on grounds of both equality and efficiency—for shifting much political authority away from the centralised state and towards a balance of local, regional, and global institutions. I am also led to reject Rawls' attempts to disavow democratic rights and obligations at the global level: the justification for and legal protection of very basic human rights cannot be separated out from wider rights claims nor from a wider normative and institutional framework.

The question then becomes how these joint commitments—to democracy and to *institutional* cosmopolitanism—can be reconciled: How is it possible for individuals to have any control or influence where the political order is so complex and operates at such great scale? Against Habermas, I do not think that individuals are best included in governance if and when the political system maximises various forms of deliberation between citizens. Indeed, I show that the maximising requirements on communication and participation contained in Habermas' theory of 'deliberative democracy' can be met only by making assumptions about human cognitive capacities and about institutional capabilities that are not plausible in any remotely large-scale and pluralistic society. I argue, further, that all attempts to rescue deliberative democracy, through forms of representation that are supposed to 'mirror' participation, must fail. These attempts do not make adequate room for the exercise of discretion by representatives, portray citizens' actual views in distorted ways, and produce poor quality political judgement. Purportedly 'all-inclusive' deliberation in fact would contribute to the exclusion of vulnerable and marginal individuals. However, important lessons can be learnt from these failures, especially concerning the parameters of a 'thicker' theory of representation—a theory that conceives of the function of representatives as quite different from a glorified mirroring, aggregation, or interpretation of citizens' views.

The key to reconciling democracy with institutions of great scope and complexity is to recognise that the notion of an *agent* as representative must be understood as deriving from the more basic notion of a representative *system*. When we ask the general question as to whether citizens ultimately have control over political decisions, our fundamental concern is not whether any one agent or group of agents pursues citizens' interests and articulates citizens' views; rather, we are asking whether there is a systematic causal connection between citizens having certain interests and views (on the one hand) and such interests and views being identified and pursued by their political system (on the other). I argue, however, that existing democratic devices such as elections and party systems fall significantly short in achieving this kind of *responsiveness*. Moreover, there are good reasons to think that 'civil society' cannot compensate adequately for the shortcomings of these formal mechanisms. I propose three kinds of institutional innovation that are required to induce representatives to collectively judge and act in the interests of citizens and with appropriate attention to citizens' views.

The first innovation is to introduce formal institutions with powers that cross some traditional political–juridical divides. These 'advocacy and accountability agencies' would supply relevant information and assistance to various authorities and to a majority of citizens. Advocacy and accountability agencies would also act as professional contesters on behalf of certain vulnerable individuals and minorities. The second innovation is to bring non-state, non-territorial actors—including non-governmental organisations and transnational corporations—carefully into the formal structures of governance, thereby harnessing the benefits of their expertise even while increasing our collective capacity to control their activities. The third and final innovation is to place robust requirements on the dealings between these political actors, by enshrining a 'charter of obligations' in international law—a charter that distinguishes the capabilities of authorities (what they can do) from their competences (what they may do) from their obligations (what they ought to do). The charter would not so much reduce political friction as channel it towards more constructive results. The three innovations together would better balance the distribution of responsibilities, would reduce harmful bureaucratic forms of communication and interaction, and would equip citizens with enhanced means to contest and control political decisions.

None of this is to say that there is no place for the state in governance. But it is to say that we should not continue to conceive of other kinds and levels of political authority as mere band-aids, applied with very limited success to remedy the deficient and detrimental operations of states. Rather, each different authority—the state no less or more than any other—should derive its legitimacy directly from its role in a complex division of political labour. Engaging in recent debates about the two World Courts, the UN, and advocacy agencies such as Transparency International, I illustrate how the current (largely statist) division of global political labour can be reformed feasibly and beneficially. I show how statist and deliberative modes of thought lead to a mischaracterisation of the problems that afflict these institutions and to an impoverished conceptualisation of potential routes to reform.[4]

The integrated normative and institutional framework presented in these pages is inherently speculative: since we live in a world without many strong non-state liberal democratic structures, our basic question is not 'what works best at present?' but rather 'what may we reasonably and realistically hope will work in the future?' None of this implies that a normative theory of liberal justice and democracy can avoid tests of practicability, or that such a theory will not need to be constantly adjusted in light of empirical hazards. Rather, we are interested in a political theory above all because it might supply a coherent and justifiable approach for dealing with the vicissitudes and opportunities of our shared future. No amount of empirical investigation is sufficient to answer such fundamental and forward-looking moral concerns.

In our time, the pressing set of problems becomes not only *what* liberal democracy is and ought to be (content) but also *where* liberal democracy is and ought to be (scope). I have attempted to provide a systematic account of how we might begin to respond to these problems. Still, considering the many promises above, the reader would be wise to be wary at this point. As Wittgenstein put it, with characteristically wry acuity, 'If someone tells me he has bought the outfit of a tightrope walker I am not impressed until I see what he has done with it'.[5]

---

[4] Although there are many important lessons to be learned from federal thought and practice, I am sceptical of both the idea of a world state (Chapter 1), with voting for one federal assembly (Chapters 2 and 4), and the traditional idea of a limited tripartite separation of powers (Chapter 3). As will become evident, Responsive Democracy is not democratic federalism. The global order for which I argue is not world federalism.

[5] R. Monk, *Ludwig Wittgenstein: The Duty of Genius* (London: Vintage, 1991), 464.

1

Global Justice
Beyond *The Law of Peoples* to a Cosmopolitan Law of Persons

John Rawls' *The Law of Peoples* (*LP*) represents a culmination of his reflections on how we might reasonably and peacefully live together in a just world.[6] My aim in this chapter is to show that a theory of global justice can be developed that is more in keeping with the Kantian constructivist procedures Rawls once employed for domestic justice in *Political Liberalism* and *A Theory of Justice*.[7] This result is important because it helps establish that my alternative conception of global justice better realises some fundamental liberal values, even on Rawls' own terms.

Rawls has a strong hold on the imaginations of political theorists, but that is not the main reason I have adopted the approach of reading and responding to his work so closely. Rather, it seems to me that his later work *at once* exemplifies the orthodoxy of 'liberal statism' that dominates the field *and*, along with his earlier work, contains powerful conceptual resources for overcoming that inconsistent and pernicious orthodoxy.

My core argument is that Rawls has begged some of the central questions of global justice by adopting at the outset a 'thin statist' conception of the legitimate divisions between persons who share a world. Once this ungrounded assumption is removed, the nature and

[6] John Rawls, *The Law of Peoples* (Cambridge, MA: Harvard University Press, 1999*a*).

[7] John Rawls, *Political Liberalism* (New York: Columbia University Press, 1993*a*) and *A Theory of Justice* (Oxford: Oxford University Press, 1971). Also see his 'Kantian Constructivism in Moral Theory', *Collected Papers* (Cambridge, MA: Harvard University Press, 1999*b*), 303–59.

boundaries of the basic political units which the principles of global justice coordinate might look quite different, as might the principles themselves. Although my focus is on ideal theory, on formulating a moral vision of justice in a cosmopolitan world order, the closing section does discuss relevant implications for non-ideal theory.

The chapter is structured as follows: The introductory section outlines Rawls' project and constructivist methodology in *LP*, with a view to characterising his thin statism in particular. It briefly articulates four arguments for his position. Each of the next four sections explicates and then criticises one of those four arguments and in so doing further develops an alternative conception of global justice. Sections 1 and 2 consider how widely the scope of liberal moral and political concern ought to be drawn, arguing for representation of persons through a global rather than a two-stage (domestic and then international) original position. Section 3 explores the cosmopolitan institutional implications of this modified Rawlsian procedure and elaborates a politically liberal conception of 'plurarchic sovereignty'. Section 4 defends the relevance of that ideal conception of justice for realistic political action in the decidedly non-ideal conditions of the contemporary world. In closing, I provide brief illustrations of appropriate action in two contested issue-areas: the rules of engagement with illiberal states and the use of force in humanitarian intervention.

The most crucial differences between Rawls and me are the following: (1) he effectively supports a system of unitary nation-states with limited sovereignty, while I reject that whole idea in favour of a more multiform institutional configuration; (2) he disavows democratic rights at the global level, while my argument establishes that the rights to full free speech and democracy are fundamental requirements of global justice. We are thus led to support quite different liberal approaches to the aims and methods of world politics. Indeed, it is the need to reconcile my joint commitments to plurarchic sovereignty and to democracy that makes the argument of the rest of the book necessary: I am compelled to provide a normative theory of democracy for a complex world in which political authority is no longer the predominant preserve of the state.

Prelude: Rawls' Constructivism and Thin States

In *LP*, Rawls attempts to provide 'a particular political conception of right and justice that applies to principles and norms of international law and practice' (*LP* 3). The question to which this conception answers is the following: how can the conception of justice as fairness, elaborated in *Political Liberalism* for a closed and self-sufficient liberal democratic society, be convincingly 'extended' to cover relations between societies, including some non-liberal societies (*LP* 9)? This question emerges since, after the principles of domestic justice have been decided upon, many issues of justice remain to be resolved—namely, those which arise once the assumption of a closed society is dropped. How is a domestically just society to interact with other societies? Rawls thinks the extension of political liberalism to global justice can be achieved by running a second session of the original position.[8]

At this 'second level', the parties in the original position represent *peoples*, with the result that the constructivist procedure models conditions for arriving at terms of cooperation that are 'fair to peoples and not to individual persons' (*LP* 17, n. 9). Persons are not the relevant '(moral) actors' precisely because persons' basic claims to justice have already been taken into account (*LP* 10): the principles of domestic justice are established prior to and independently of the principles of global justice (which are either derivative or compatible), and are given lexical priority. This is the methodological heart of *LP*: Rawls works upwards and 'outwards' from sufficiently just societies (peoples) to a just Society of Peoples (*LP* 3, 23).

A Rawlsian constructivist procedure has three steps. If each step of the procedure can be justified, then the principles chosen will be fair.[9] The first step is to say for whom justice is being derived by answering the question 'what is a people?'; the second is to identify what alterations must be made to the original position if suitable account is to be taken of the change in moral agents at this second level; and

---

[8] The original position is a 'device of representation'. What it ultimately represents is the contractarian conviction that we can derive principles of justice that are fair to all members of a society by asking what all members *would* agree to *if* they were deciding in a way which took everyone else into account equally. Since we are all partial to our own interests and allegiances, however, how do we identify this impartial perspective? In *A Theory of Justice*, Rawls argues for the adoption of a hypothetical situation or thought experiment in which each decision-maker represents a person or group in the society, but also has no knowledge of the race, gender, social class, and the like of those represented. In this original position, a veil of ignorance screens out any knowledge that could bias decision-makers one way or another. Because the parties in the original position could turn out to represent *anybody* in the society, they are driven to take *everybody* into account equally. The principles that the parties would then agree to necessarily aim to be fair to all.

[9] This constructivist procedure relies on the idea of pure procedural justice developed by Rawls (see esp. *Theory*, 83–90).

the third is to determine which principles of global justice would be chosen by representatives of those agents, deliberating under those procedural constraints on argument.

In his 1993 Amnesty Lecture 'The Law of Peoples', which served as a prelude to the book, Rawls initially defined a people as 'persons and their dependants seen as a corporate body and organised by their political institutions, which establish the powers of government'.[10] In the book, he provides a more extensive characterisation of peoples as having, in ideal theory, three basic features—institutional, cultural, and moral. Institutionally, each people has a 'reasonably just . . . government that serves their [a people's] fundamental interests': protecting their territory; preserving their political institutions, culture, independence, and self-respect as a corporate body; and guaranteeing the safety, security, and well-being of their citizens (*LP* 23–9, 34–5). Each people's citizens are also culturally 'united by what Mill called "common sympathies" '; Rawls clearly means by this 'an idea of nationality', generally based on 'a common language and shared historical memories' (*LP* 23–5).[11] Finally, each people has 'a moral nature', in that each is firmly attached to a moral conception of right and justice which is at least not unreasonable (*LP* 23–5, 61–8). Each is prepared—in rationally advancing its fundamental interests—to propose as well as abide by fair terms of cooperation, as long as other peoples do so as well.[12]

This normative idea of a 'not unreasonable' and 'reasonably just' people is less demanding than the idea of a reasonable and fully just society as specified in *Political Liberalism*. Politically liberal societies are certainly included, but so are comprehensive liberal societies (such as that specified in *A Theory of Justice*) and 'decent peoples'. The latter are also schemes of social cooperation, but they are associationist, in that persons are respected not directly as free and equal individuals

---

[10] John Rawls, 'The Law of Peoples', in S. Shute and S. Hurley, eds., *On Human Rights: The Oxford Amnesty Lectures, 1993* (New York: Basic Books, 1993*b*).

[11] '[J. S. Mill] uses an idea of nationality to describe a people's culture' (*LP* 25, n. 20), and 'I think of the idea of nation as distinct from the idea of government or state, and I interpret it as referring to a pattern of cultural values of the kind described by Mill . . . ' (*LP* 23, n. 17). Rawls approvingly quotes *Considerations on Representative Government*, where Mill writes of 'common sympathies, which do not exist between them and any others—which make them cooperate with each other more willingly than with other people, desire to be under the same government, and desire that it should be a government by themselves, or a portion of themselves, exclusively . . . ' (ibid.).

[12] For Rawls' ideas of the reasonable and rational, see *Political Liberalism*, 48–54.

but rather as reasonable and rational 'cooperating members of their respective groups' (*LP* 64). This minimal criterion of respect, which defines a decent people, is derived from the basic idea of a bona fide system of law (and not from the idea of persons as free and equal), as follows: A law-governed scheme of social cooperation differs from a 'scheme of commands imposed by force' precisely because persons are able to recognise, understand, and be moved to act on the law without necessarily being coerced (*LP* 65).[13] Yet without some reassurance that domestic institutions of justice take some account of citizens' important interests—at the very least as members of groups which each cleave to a comprehensive doctrine—a legal system cannot impose such moral duties and obligations for all members of society, since citizens will not be thus (morally) motivated. The pursuit of the common aims of a decent people must thus be constrained by 'a common good idea of justice', which at least takes citizens' important interests into account, thus allowing them all to play a responsible role in public life (pp. 66–8).[14] Most significant among persons' interests are those in having their basic human rights secured, and in having laws non-arbitrarily administered (*LP* 78–81).[15]

The idea of a decent people is a central innovation of *LP*. As with any construct, it is created to serve a particular analytic purpose; Rawls' main aim is to develop *liberal* principles of global justice that are *also tolerant* of peoples with other moral and political traditions. (The idea of toleration in *LP* is the subject of Section 2, below.) In order to generate these liberal principles and ensure their acceptability 'from a decent non-liberal point of view' (*LP* 10), the second session of

---

[13] Here Rawls follows P. Soper's *A Theory of Law* (Cambridge, MA: Harvard University Press, 1984), esp. 125–47. On several problems with Soper's theory, see J. Raz, 'The Morality of Obedience', *Michigan Law Review*, Vol. 83, No. 4 (1985), 732–49.

[14] 'Well-ordered societies with liberal conceptions of political justice also have a common good conception in this sense: namely, the common good of achieving political justice for all its citizens over time and preserving the free culture that justice allows' (*LP* 71, n. 10). The idea of a comprehensive 'common good conception', which includes a 'decent consultation hierarchy', is discussed in Section 2, below.

[15] These claims about interests are examined in Sections 1 and 2, below. In addition to liberal and decent societies, Rawls discusses 'outlaw states' (those which fail even to be decent), 'burdened societies' or 'states suffering from unfavourable conditions' (to which decent and liberal peoples have duties of assistance), and 'benevolent absolutisms' (which honour human rights but in which citizens play no major role in public life) (*LP* 4, 90–112). The principles for dealing with each type are different and important, but my focus is the liberal–decent divide.

the original position is run in two stages—once for liberal peoples, and thereafter for decent non-liberal peoples. As in the case of establishing the fair terms of cooperation for a closed society, parties to each stage are situated symmetrically, behind a veil of ignorance which screens out information (this time it is territory size, level of development, particular common good conception of justice, etc.) which might make them less than impartial in the rational pursuit of the good of those they represent. The strong claim that Rawls makes is that, in virtue of sharing the three minimal features described above, delegates in both stages would independently come up with the *same* law of peoples.

This result may not seem at all intuitively obvious: why should every decent non-liberal people accept a liberal law of peoples? Rawls reminds us that decent peoples are not unreasonable, and so do not engage in aggressive wars or pursue expansionist ends, nor fail to respect the civic order and integrity of other peoples; thus the delegates of decent peoples would accept the symmetrical (equal) situation of the original position as fair (*LP* 69). He also reminds us of the common good conception of justice, which takes account of persons' important interests, ensuring that decent peoples would accept principles honouring basic human rights (*LP* 78–81). Finally, a decent people's fundamental interests—in security, independence, the benefits of trade, and so on—would lead it to accept and adopt the laws of peace (non-intervention, war only in self-defence, restrictions on conduct in war) and duties of contract (observing treaties and undertakings, mutual assistance in times of need) (*LP* 30–43, 89–113).[16] According to Rawls, these are nothing less than liberal principles of global justice.

Notably missing from such a law of peoples are principles for respecting persons as free and equal citizens with constitutional democratic rights; if the latter were included, decent peoples would certainly not accept them. But Rawls wants to draw a clear line between basic human rights ('liberty rights' to bodily integrity, etc.), on the one hand, and more extensive liberal democratic rights, on the other. The primacy of this aim is repeatedly emphasised in *LP* and is based on a stipulation that 'all persons in a decent hierarchical society are not regarded as free and equal citizens, nor as separate individuals deserving equal representation . . . they are seen as decent and rational and as capable of moral learning as recognised in their society' (*LP* 71). He insists that this exclusion of persons in decent societies from treatment as fully free and equal individuals is required by liberal conceptions

---

[16] These are unpacked as eight principles of international justice (Rawls provides a summary at *LP* 37).

themselves: liberal peoples must express toleration for decent non-liberal ways of ordering society. (In Section 2, below, I evaluate and criticise the basis for this stipulation and conclusion.) Drawing the line in this place does allow Rawls to address a major programmatic concern, by identifying what liberals should *not* tolerate: 'We must reformulate the powers of sovereignty in light of a reasonable Law of Peoples and deny to states the traditional rights to war and to unrestricted internal autonomy . . . included in the (positive) international law for the three centuries after the Thirty Years' War' (*LP* 25–7).

This claim needs careful interpretation, lest it appear more radical than it is. Rawls endorses the existence of sovereign states and of an international state system, with the important caveat that such sovereignty is not absolute. When he writes that peoples are not 'states as traditionally conceived', he means only to 'emphasise' that his conception of states is very far from the traditional Realist conception of states as predominantly concerned with power (*LP* 25–7). Realist states pursue their 'rational prudential interests' in power, unconstrained by 'the reasonable', and are thus unmoved by the criterion of reciprocity; Rawlsian peoples have moral conceptions of justice and regimes which 'limit their basic interests as required by the reasonable', but they are still states (*LP* 28–9). Indeed, as we have seen, they are *nation*-states, each with a single independently derived system of law, and a 'so-called monopoly of power' on the enforcement of that law, and on the pursuit of persons' politically important interests, in a particular territory (*LP* 23–6, esp. n. 20 and n. 22). The difference is that in Realist theory the shell of state sovereignty may not be pierced or removed if and when the regime acts unjustly—this exemplifies what I shall call 'thick statism'— whereas in Rawls' theory, the law of peoples reasonably constrains what a state may rightly do to its own people and other states—this exemplifies what I shall call 'thin statism' or 'liberal statism'.

The crucial methodological question, which Rawls himself asks, is why *this* issue of *extension*—from justice within a closed society to international justice—is what a Rawlsian theory of global justice ought to address. Why are peoples assumed to be the politically relevant subjects with which to start? Rawls himself once pointed to much the same question, as follows: 'Wouldn't it be better to start with the world as a whole, with a global original position, so to speak, and discuss the question whether, and in what form, there should be states or peoples at all?'.[17] At the time, he had 'no clear initial answer to this

---

[17] Rawls, 'Law of Peoples', 42. In the book, he writes: 'Why does the Law of Peoples use an original position at the second level that is fair to peoples and not

question'; indeed, he saw no reason why such a starting-point would not result in the adoption of exactly the same principles.[18] In the book, however, his reasons for preferring a thin statist procedure can now be discerned. I term them the arguments from *incorporation, toleration, cohesion,* and *realism*:

1. *Incorporation*—if peoples are stipulated to take members' interests into account, and all persons are members of peoples, then all persons' interests are fully accounted for and given due consideration.
2. *Toleration*—liberal principles require respect for other cultures and ways of ordering society, and so imposing on them a conception of global justice based on the idea of persons as free and equal would be wrong.
3. *Cohesion*—the alternative to a Society of Peoples is an illiberal, strife-torn world state; thus, even if the former involves some injustice, it is preferable.
4. *Realism*—as a practical matter, to best secure the great goods of world peace and respect for human rights, liberal regimes should fully engage decent non-liberal peoples rather than excluding them from international forums and law.

In the ensuing four sections, I explicate and rebut these arguments for liberal statism in turn; in doing so, I show how an alternative conception of global justice might be developed from less unsatisfactory basic assumptions. To put it another way, Rawls has not gone far enough in distancing himself from the Realists; he still tolerates too much.[19] I sketch a theory of global justice that is not statist at the outset, and is, I argue, more in keeping with political liberalism.

1. Incorporation: Different Interests of Persons and States

'In laying out the Law of Peoples, we begin with principles of political justice for the basic structure of a closed and self-contained liberal democratic society' (*LP* 86).

to individual persons? What is it about peoples that gives them the status of the (moral) actors in the Law of Peoples?' (*LP* 17, n. 9).

[18] 'Offhand it is not clear why proceeding in this way should lead to different results than proceeding, as I have done, from separate societies outwards. All things considered, one might reach the same law of peoples in either case' (Rawls, 'Law of Peoples', 54–5).

[19] I use the term 'Realism' to denote schools of power politics in international relations theory; 'realistic' and 'realism' denote practical workability.

Familiarity with Rawls' theory of justice should not mask just how odd it is to take 'society . . . as a closed system,' 'self-contained and . . . having no relations with other societies',[20] as the founding assumption of a theory of *inter*national or, better, *global* justice. As Onora O'Neill points out, this assumption is not the mere 'considerable abstraction' that Rawls claims it is, 'since abstractions (taken strictly) omit or bracket certain predicates true of the matter from which they abstract. Rather the idea of a closed society is an idealisation, that assumes predicates which are false of all existing human societies'.[21]

Now, like the idea of a frictionless surface used in natural science, this idealisation is not necessarily objectionable, so long as there are very strong arguments for why the false construction can, by analogy or resemblance (for no strict inference to a true conclusion is possible), show something useful about cases that are not idealised.[22] Rawls would maintain that the idea of a closed society is a useful device for representing persons' fundamental interest in having basic human rights respected in their own society; the same interest will lead each society to endorse a global legal framework which supports societies' respect for rights, and in this way, all persons of the world can have their rights respected. The underlying idea here is this: if both peoples and persons are stipulated to have a fundamental interest in basic human rights, then their interests coincide. If this were true, persons would in no way be disadvantaged by starting from societies and not persons, and societies could form the basis for a stable global human rights order.[23]

But I now argue that there is a strong presumption against Rawls' idealisation: the assumption of a closed society obscures the fact that

---

[20] Rawls, *Theory*, 8 and *Political Liberalism*, 12.

[21] O. O'Neill, 'Political Liberalism and Public Reason: A Critical Notice of John Rawls *Political Liberalism*', *Philosophical Review*, Vol. 106 (1997), 411–28. O'Neill develops the implications of this distinction in *Towards Justice and Virtue* (Cambridge: Cambridge University Press, 1996).

[22] O'Neill thinks, however, that there are still 'considerable disanalogies between uses of idealisation in practical and theoretical reasoning, because the direction of fit is reversed. In theoretical reasoning idealisations that are wide of the mark will reveal their failure, or are likely to. In practical reasoning we may conclude that we ought to live up to the idealisations' (personal correspondence, but see ibid.).

[23] Rawls could also reply that the idealisation of a closed society is justified because it recognises and represents the existence and value of common sympathies or nationhood, while at the same time it at least forms *a* constructivist basis to secure persons' important interests (especially in human rights). In Section 2, below, I assess this argument and show that Rawls seeks to tolerate common sympathies in the wrong way.

the interests of persons and of peoples do not necessarily coincide. So even if a confederation of peoples secures urgent rights, it may well do so in a less than optimal way; other institutional configurations may *better* secure persons' basic rights *as well as* other rights and fundamental interests.

Do peoples' and persons' interests necessarily coincide? There is good reason to think not: depending on how subjects are divided into sets at the outset, the outcomes of reasonable and rational deliberation—about what their interests are and how best to pursue those interests—will differ. Consider the following example.[24] In a world of two states, U and D (Underdeveloped and Developed), the government of each intends to act rationally so as to secure the interests of persons in their territories to the maximal extent possible. It might be rational for D to restrict immigration because the cost of supporting new residents would result in a slight reduction in standards of living for its current citizens; and it might be rational for U to restrict emigration, because it would deplete the skills base for securing current citizens' rights and well-being.[25] If two parties representing these states, though they did not know which, had to establish a law governing their relations, it would be one that allows for only highly restricted movement of persons between the two from U to D.

Yet it is not true in principle that this law best secures the rights and well-being of all the persons in both countries. It may be the case that allowing some more movement of people between the two would result in a gain for those who are worst off or even in a more extensive scheme of basic liberties for all: a minor worsening of the well-being situation of those who were citizens of D and for those left behind in U might make immigrants from U significantly better off, sufficiently to justify the movement. This is not, however, a consideration which could count for parties representing U and D's respective citizenries separately, but only for parties representing all the persons in U and D at once, as individual persons.

This example evidences a more general point about social choice: what is rational to agree upon at the level of two parties representing

---

[24] This example raises various issues about the status of immigration in Rawls' work, and about the social embeddedness of persons' identities—issues discussed later in the chapter. For the moment I use this example to illustrate a more general point about (grouping for the purposes of) social choice, and the relevance of that point for establishing political boundaries.

[25] Many such scenarios are imaginable; indeed is arguable that US–Mexico and South Africa–Mozambique relations, among others, fit this model (my point is, rather, conceptual).

two sets of persons' interests (that together exhaust the set of existing interests) is not the same as what is rational if it is the interests of each and every person that are being considered. Thus there is no reason to think that what proves—as Rawls put it[26]—'more or less sound' for one domain (justice for persons in a closed society) is appropriate to another (global justice for persons), any more than there is reason to think that the principles for packing eggs into padded boxes are extendable to the principles for packing egg-boxes into a crate. Nor is it apparent that the sequence should be to design egg-boxes first and only later ask questions about how to design the crate. Therefore Rawls' theory of domestic justice might provide tools for the independent construction of global justice, but it cannot simply be incorporated as the first step in that construction. Since the idea of decent peoples as a starting-point embodies two layers of distortion (ascriptive associations, thin states) in representing individuals' interests, liberals—for whom individual persons are the ultimate locus of concern—should be deeply wary.[27]

We have seen that the interests of all human individuals and those of the same persons assumed to be grouped as members of states do not necessarily coincide, and that we may come to have good reason to jettison thin statism in favour of a global original position which represents all the persons of the world. But Rawls might object that my example concerns interests that are not 'fundamental', and so risks impugning a possible global human rights order by raising less urgent (socioeconomic) claims. This objection is telling only if one accepts the implausible stipulation that the important interests of persons can be narrowly confined to barely adequate domestic justice only. But it is profoundly counter-intuitive to assume that parties should take no interest at all in the well-being or standard of living of persons, 'beyond the minimum necessary for [minimally] just institutions'.[28]

[26] Rawls, 'Law of Peoples', 43.

[27] There is a historical story to be told which impugns the convergence claim too; for this, see H. Arendt, *The Origins of Totalitarianism* (New York: Harcourt Brace & Company, 1973), 290–302. She writes that after the French Revolution, humankind 'was conceived in the image of a family of nations, [and] it gradually became self-evident that the people, and not the individual, was the image of man. The full implication of this identification of the rights of man with the rights of peoples [was "severe"]', especially for marginalised (not to mention stateless) individuals and minorities (*LP* 291–3). Rawls' vision would avoid many but arguably not all of these adverse consequences.

[28] This point has been developed eloquently by several theorists of economic justice who criticise Rawls' refusal to extend the difference principle to global distributive justice (my focus lies elsewhere). The quotation is from T. Pogge,

Rawls himself acknowledged that a just regime cannot be a final and circumscribed end in itself, rather it is 'something we ought to realise for the sake of individual human persons, who are the ultimate units of moral concern . . . Their well-being is the point of social institutions'.[29]

Of course, some interests are more important than others, and it might be thought that a thin statism secures the most important interests of all persons, in world peace and respect for minimal human rights. But this begs the question: it cannot be assumed that thin states best secure persons' important interests; *if* states do so, *then* that is something that will count for parties representing individual persons, thus parties *will* endorse thin states (as the basic institutions of global justice). There is the greatest difference between a liberal constructivism which takes thin states as a possible outcome of the procedure, on the one hand, and thin statism—which assumes states as foundational to global justice—on the other. The former leaves two possibilities open: (1) thin states may not *best* secure those important interests; and (2) there may be an alternative which secures those interests *and more*, such as added security and increased well-being. (I offer such an alternative in Sections 3 and 4, below; here I have simply established that these are live issues.) In sum, because of its potentially suboptimal results for persons, any initial demarcation of groups must be justified. Rawls' first main argument—that persons' fundamental interests would be addressed already by peoples since peoples take members' interests into account—fails to justify his basic assumption of thin statism.

2. Toleration: The Universal Scope of Global Justice

We have seen that the law of peoples may represent the fair terms of cooperation for peoples, but it certainly does not necessarily represent the fair terms of cooperation for all the persons of the world; this is a serious concern for the liberal. But Rawls' most powerful and explicit argument might be thought to provide reasons to *override* this concern, since it stresses the overwhelming importance of recognising—by starting with the idea of peoples—the value of

'An Egalitarian Law of Peoples', *Philosophy and Public Affairs*, Vol. 23, No. 3 (1994*a*), 195–224, at 209–10. Also see B. Ackerman, 'Political Liberalisms', *Journal of Philosophy*, Vol. 91, No. 7 (1994), 364–86, esp. 381–2; C. Beitz, 'Cosmopolitan Ideals and National Sentiment', *Journal of Philosophy*, Vol. 80, No. 10 (1983), 591–600, esp. 594.

[29] Rawls, *Theory*, 115.

national–cultural affiliation:

Leaving aside the deep question of whether some forms of culture and ways of life are good in themselves (as I believe they are), it is surely, *ceteris paribus*, a good for individuals and associations to be attached to their particular culture and to take part in its common public and civic life. In this way political society is expressed and fulfilled. This is no small thing. It argues for preserving significant room for the idea of a people's self-determination and for some kind of loose or confederative form of a Society of Peoples (*LP* 61).

The common sympathies arising out of a shared history and tradition are profoundly valuable to individuals, and an adequate theory of global justice must recognise and respect that fact—rather than insensitively and destructively ignoring it. I am in full agreement with Rawls that it would be foolish and wrong not to recognise the value of culture to individual persons; but the question is not *whether* to tolerate cultures, rather it is *how* to do so. In this section I argue—from politically liberal premises—that the Rawls of *LP* seeks toleration *of the wrong kind*. Only an original position that includes all the persons of the world as free and equal persons can express toleration in the right way.

Rawls' argument for toleration of decent non-liberal peoples seeks to establish that this kind of toleration is required because of features internal to liberal justice theory. His argument proceeds by analogy to domestic justice:

If all societies were required to be liberal, then the idea of political liberalism would fail to express due toleration for other acceptable ways (if such there are, as I assume) of ordering society. We recognise that a liberal society is to respect its citizens' comprehensive doctrines—religious, philosophical, and moral—provided that these doctrines are pursued in ways compatible with a reasonable political conception of justice and its public reason. Similarly, we say that, provided a nonliberal society's basic institutions meet certain specified conditions of political right and justice and lead its people to honor a reasonable and just law for the Society of Peoples, a liberal people is to tolerate and accept that society (*LP* 59–60).

A law of peoples, then, embodies 'principles of the *foreign policy*' of a liberal people, where the requirement of toleration of other societies' comprehensive doctrines is met by ensuring that such policy norms could also be acceptable 'from a decent non-liberal point of view. The need for such an assurance is a feature inherent in the liberal conception' (*LP* 10).

This argument is unconvincing because it trades on a partial analogy between peoples and persons—organising their respective 'lives' around reasonable comprehensive doctrines—that Rawlsian constructivism cannot sustain and liberals should not endorse. States, even thin states, institutionalise political coercion, and any coercive institution raises questions about its legitimacy. Rawls recognises this element of disanalogy and tries to deal with it by stipulating that each people simply is legitimate, in virtue of having decent institutional features. To tolerate decent societies is, then, to tolerate what is sufficiently tolerant of persons already, all with a view to achieving broad agreement on common principles of justice. But here Rawls is mistaken.

'Sufficient tolerance' is not simply a pale approximation of full liberal tolerance; rather the two are deeply contradictory. *Liberal* tolerance expresses *ethical* neutrality, by remaining impartial between particular moral conceptions of the good; for this very reason, liberalism must reject any *political* neutrality, that is, neutrality in respect of justifications for coercion: 'a commitment to ethical neutrality necessarily entails a commitment to a particular type of political arrangement, one which, for one, allows for the pursuit of different private conceptions of the good'.[30]

As Thomas Pogge put it, while a society or world can contain numerous associations and conceptions of the good, its basic political structure 'can be structured or organised in only one way . . . There is no room for accommodation here' since it is precisely the characteristic of a fundamental law backed by coercive force that it must apply to and be justifiable to all.[31]

The idea of tolerance in *LP* is, then, fundamentally different from and opposed to—and not simply a less demanding version of—the idea of a liberal regulatory framework presented in *Political Liberalism*. There Rawls argues repeatedly that it would be intolerant, oppressive, and unjust for a state to be organised around any one comprehensive doctrine—precisely because such endorsement fails to respect other such doctrines, and the persons that hold them.[32] And there he is correct. It is the essence of a politically liberal regulatory framework that it expresses toleration by *not* incorporating any comprehensive doctrine in the principles of justice; to fail to do so is not to extend but rather to eliminate liberal tolerance. In *LP*, on the other hand, he is mistaken. Decent peoples are not ethically neutral, nor is a Law of Peoples which recognises their comprehensive doctrine ethically

---

[30] Kok-Chor Tan makes this point in respect of Rawls' earlier 'Law of Peoples' article, in 'Liberal Toleration in Rawls's Law of Peoples', *Ethics*, Vol. 108, No. 2 (1998), 276–95, at 283.

[31] Pogge, 'An Egalitarian Law', 217.

[32] Rawls, *Political Liberalism*, 10, 37, 60, 137, and 154. It is especially evident from 190–200 that politically liberal toleration is of an ethically neutral sort.

neutral; thus at neither stage is there any basis for saying that what is being expressed counts as liberal toleration.[33]

One can imagine Rawls making the following reply: 'The idea of ethical toleration in a liberal society is all very well, but it is much too stringent for global toleration. For one thing, it is simplistic to regard decent peoples as ethically intolerant; they are better characterised as ethically "not intolerant" [my term, though Rawlsian in spirit]. Unlike outlaw states, decent peoples show significant respect for persons not only by honouring basic human rights but also by allowing associations in civil society that hold a range of comprehensive moral doctrines. Further, the political structure of a decent society, although organised around a comprehensive common good conception of justice, does not entirely reject citizens' comprehensive doctrines. One condition stipulated for a decent people is, as we saw, that citizens' interests must be taken into account; but for this to be the case, "the basic structure of the society must include a family of representative bodies whose role in the hierarchy is to take part in an established procedure of consultation and to look after what the people's common good idea of justice regards as the important interests of all members of society" (*LP* 71). This is a strong demand for what might be called a "decent consultation hierarchy" (*LP* 71–8). It cannot be said that where peoples have these features, there is no bona fide system of law: extensive consultation ensures an "institutional basis for protecting the rights and duties of the members of the people", thus persons have their interests taken into account and can be morally motivated to obey the law (*LP* 71). These protective, expressive, and deliberative features "deserve respect, even if their institutions as a whole are not sufficiently reasonable from the point of view of political liberalism" (*LP* 84). Ethical toleration is not an on–off affair: a decent people is structured around one comprehensive doctrine only in a very limited way and does pass an adequate threshold of respect for persons; we must, in turn, respect the basic institutions of such a people.'

This argument appears to be appealing in that it seems to take cultural pluralism seriously, but—I now want to argue—it does so by *not* taking seriously the reasonable pluralism of individual persons. Consider, for one thing, some profoundly anti-liberal implications of

---

[33] Which is why, contra Rawls' assertion in *LP* at 82–3, we can know that decent regimes are unacceptable from a liberal point of view. Respect for persons' comprehensive conceptions of the good precisely does not translate into respect for comprehensive regimes.

'toleration' as specified in *LP*:

> The fact is that none of Rawls's 'well-ordered' hierarchies will be free of natives who are themselves inspired by liberal ideas of liberty and equality. There is no Islamic nation without a woman who insists on equal rights; no Confucian society without a man who denies the need for deference. Sometimes these liberals will be in a minority in their native lands; but given the way Rawls defines a 'well-ordered' hierarchy, it is even possible that they might be a majority . . . [Why] should we choose to betray our own principles and side with the oppressors rather than the oppressed?[34]

When a liberal regulatory framework recognises a decent hierarchical regime as sufficiently just, it participates in the denial of freedom and equality to such individuals. Dissenting individuals with liberal views would surely, it seems, dispute the idea that accommodation of reasonable pluralism requires that their individual moral claims be taken less seriously. But then one could not really know what they would think, since their views could well be sealed off from view by the decent consultation hierarchy.

To take only one significant instance, a regime with a decent consultation hierarchy does not allow free speech: persons may only dissent as members of associations, and only with reference to the common good conception of justice (*LP* 72–5). It follows that citizens must argue within the conceptual terms of the regime, and only through representatives of a group; this closes off large domains and numerous types of discussion. The most serious exclusion is that it prevents proper critical discussion of how the rules of discussion might be altered—the latter are determined by some interpretation of the dominant cultural tradition only (though it must make some room for the survival of others). A claim that this represents 'freedom' of speech but 'not equal' freedom of speech is thus farcical, as is Rawls' claim that barring persons of certain religions from occupying public offices represents 'liberty of conscience, but not equal liberty' (*LP* 65, n. 2).

These so-called inequalities are in fact serious restrictions on liberty which would rightly horrify a liberal at home, and it is not apparent that they should be any less rightly horrifying when perpetrated against people that are not part of one's liberal society. This would certainly be apparent to parties in a single global original position who, when the veil lifts, might find themselves dissenters in a non-liberal society. Rawls might say that other societies do not share and cannot be expected to share our conception of the person as free and

---

[34] Ackerman, 'Political Liberalisms', 382–3.

equal, and so no such original position can be constructed, but this misses the point. From a liberal perspective—for reasons Rawls himself has done most to elaborate—the geographical location and group membership-status of a woman born into an inegalitarian Islamic state, or indeed anyone else, is morally arbitrary. She does not suddenly come to be a free and equal person *for us* when she crosses the border into a liberal society. On the contrary, as Charles Beitz points out, 'Although the basis of the [liberal] conception of the person may be parochial, the conception itself . . . is not . . . One might say that we are compelled to take a global view in matters of social justice by features internal to our conception of moral personality, however parochial it may be.'[35]

It is this most basic internal feature—the respect for persons captured by the idea of ethical toleration—that must be the cornerstone of a consistent liberal global regulatory framework. Decent hierarchical peoples could not agree with it, but that is precisely the ethical problem with them, and not grounds to seek their agreement on some lesser mixture of respect in some parts and disrespect in others. As Rawls argues on the second page of *A Theory of Justice*, 'Being first virtues of human activities, truth and justice are uncompromising.'[36]

The foregoing points are no less true of non-metaphysical liberalism than they are of a metaphysical liberalism. Political liberalism starts from ideas implicit in a liberal democratic culture, but *none* of the major intellectual figures who are taken to be progenitors of that culture—Locke, Rousseau, Kant, Mill, to name but a few—does not *begin* with some idea of all persons as free and equal. Each thinker *then* goes on to *justify* the state or something like it, on the very grounds that such an institutional formation is in some way rational to will for persons thus construed.[37] Indeed, even such a vociferous opponent of liberalism as Carl Schmitt is clear that liberal community rests on the idea of a 'democracy of mankind'—which, though maybe not practically achievable, is philosophically universalist at its core: 'Every adult person should *eo ipso* be politically equal to every other

---

[35] Beitz, 'Cosmopolitan Ideals', 596.

[36] Rawls, *Theory*, 4.

[37] The assumption that persons are free and equal is more complex and varied than this makes it sound; and there are of course notorious blind spots, such as Mill's refusal of political equality to those in a 'primitive' cultural state. But leaving aside such badly justified and unjustifiable exceptions, the broad idea can be found alike in Locke, Rousseau, and Mill—and also comes out clearly, it seems to me, in Immanuel Kant, 'Theory and Practice' and 'Groundwork of the Metaphysics of Morals', in *Practical Philosophy*, M. Gregor, ed. and trans. (Cambridge: Cambridge University Press, 1996).

person'.[38] To the extent that the moral claims of states have any normative force in liberalism, that force is derivative—states must be justified. In political liberalism, we do not close off the possibility that parties representing free and equal persons in a global original position would decide in favour of thin states, or even in favour of an inferior position for that woman within a particular state (though I doubt they would); rather we say that thin states, and her occupying this position, must be justified.[39]

What then about the good of community? It would be a mistake to interpret my cosmopolitan position as a form of abstract individualism. A global original position does not rule out people banding together in communities with special bonds of sentiment and obligation between them; all it demands is that such a form of organisation— as Rawls himself once wrote—cannot be assumed as foundational or not subject to justification: 'we want to account for the social values, for the intrinsic good of institutional, community and associative activities, by a conception of justice that in its theoretical basis is individualistic'.[40]

If loyalties and sentiments of affiliation to particular cultural and national groups have value for the members of those communities (and I believe they do), then 'on a cosmopolitan point of view, this fact should matter for practical reasoning. The important question is not whether it should matter but how'.[41] This is the question that—I have argued—*LP* does not properly consider. The fact that community and solidarity enrich and partly constitute a valuable human life should *not* block consideration of the implications of such arrangements for

---

[38] C. Schmitt, *The Crisis of Parliamentary Democracy* (Cambridge, MA: MIT Press, 1986), 11. See also C. Schmitt, *The Concept of the Political* (Chicago and London: Chicago University Press, 1996).

[39] There is some question as to the nature of the cooperative activity which gives rise to the global original position. Brian Barry and Charles Beitz initially disagreed over whether international society 'constitutes a scheme of cooperation in Rawls' sense'; Onora O'Neill and Beitz now both think that in any case, since 'human beings possess these essential [moral] powers regardless of whether, at present, they belong to a common cooperative scheme', there is no need to 'depend on any claim about the existence or intensity of international social cooperation' (Beitz, 'Cosmopolitan Ideals', 595; and O'Neill, *Towards Justice*, 91–121). I will not discuss this debate here; my arguments concerning political liberalism's universalism strongly endorse Beitz and O'Neill's position.

[40] Rawls, *Theory*, 264.

[41] C. Beitz, 'Cosmopolitan Liberalism and the State System', in C. Brown, ed., *Political Restructuring in Europe: Ethical Perspectives* (London: Routledge, 1994), at 129.

non-members and dissenters. A liberal background culture implies universalist justification. That is to say, the importance of cultural differences does not obviate the requirement to refer in the last instance to individual lives and not to a social formation as 'an organic whole with a life of its own distinct from and superior to that of all its members in their relation to one another'.[42] These are Rawls' words. To say that a social milieu or institutional formation is not *automatically* sealed away from critical scrutiny—by minimal gestures towards human rights and consultation—is not to abstract from real individuals; rather it is to treat their claims to moral consideration, including their cultural claims, entirely seriously.

3. Cohesion: Towards Non-statist Principles of Global Justice

Rawls might be taken to impugn my conclusions above, in one fell swoop, with his third argument, as follows: On the second page of *A Theory of Justice*, another statement can be found: 'an injustice is tolerable only when it is necessary to avoid an even greater injustice'.[43] Now, although 'the social world of liberal and decent peoples is not one that, by liberal principles, is fully just', there are 'strong reasons' for 'permitting this injustice' (*LP* 62). One primary reason is that a world state—which Rawls might also think is the outcome of a global original position—would have even greater drawbacks (i.e. cause even more injustice) than a law-governed Society of Peoples:

These principles . . . will not affirm a world-state. Here I follow Kant's lead in *Perpetual Peace* (1795) in thinking that a world government—by which

---

[42] Rawls, *Theory*, 264. It is not the case that the cosmopolitan position necessarily assumes a self that is not embedded or that is prior to its ends, as is claimed by Michael Sandel, in *Liberalism and the Limits of Justice* (Cambridge: Cambridge University Press, 1982), and several so-called communitarian thinkers. Rather, the cosmopolitan position demands that a 'critical moment' be possible for persons living in different societies, that the value of social practices and a way of life for persons should not be fixed and determined. Just because culture is significant, in that it provides us with a context for becoming who we are, does not mean that it necessarily has normative significance in determining what it is about people that we respect. No political community has a priori legitimacy. Yet it seems quite evident that for there to be a critical moment, persons must have the freedoms that allow for such reflection and debate—*that* is what communitarian positions often ignore and wrongly sign away, in their enthusiasm to have culture respected. There is no need to pay such a heavy price.

[43] Rawls, *Theory*, 4.

I mean a unified political regime with the legal powers normally exercised by central governments—would either be a global despotism or else would rule over a fragile empire torn by frequent civil strife as various regions and peoples tried to gain their political freedom and autonomy (*LP* 36).

He also approvingly cites Kant's dictum that 'laws always lose in vigour what government gains in extent'.[44]

Rawls seems then be making one or both of the following psychological claims: persons as they are would not, on an ongoing basis, morally affirm a world state; and the centralisation and cumulation of power in a world state would encourage extreme administrative abuse, laxity, or ineffectuality. It follows that although a confederation of peoples may have some illiberal consequences, these are far less severe—given persons as they are—than the consequences of concentrating power excessively in a world state.

But, leaving aside whether this is a plausible view of moral psychology (and of institutions), we must ask: are these the only two options? We need not debate the relative merits of two illiberal conceptions of the outcomes of the global original position if there is another alternative that does not fail to be liberal. In this section I present an alternative, albeit a modest sketch. As is appropriate at this phase of Rawlsian theory, my conception is an ideal; its relevance and feasibility in non-ideal conditions for justice are considered at length in the next section.

We want principles of justice to regulate a global institutional scheme, principles which are not statist in their assumptions. It will be a cosmopolitan conception because it requires institutions to meet three criteria: taking individual human persons as the ultimate units of concern (individualism); attaching that status to every human being equally (universality); and regarding persons as the ultimate unit of concern for everyone (generality).[45] It will be a Rawlsian conception in that it uses the original position as a device to represent conditions for agreeing on fair terms of cooperation for all. But 'all' will not be defined as a closed community, involved in a scheme for mutual advantage, that needs to agree on rules of engagement with other peoples. Rather, the 'parochial' assumptions of liberalism require that parties in the original position act *as if* they represent all human persons who share this world and affect one another. These parties will be far more concerned with individuals' abilities to pursue their reasonable

---

[44]   I. Kant, 'Perpetual Peace' (Ak: VIII:367), quoted in *LP*, at 36, n. 40.

[45]   T. Pogge, 'Cosmopolitanism and Sovereignty', in C. Brown, ed., *Political Restructuring in Europe: Ethical Perspectives* (London: Routledge, 1994*b*), at 89.

conceptions of the good, and with individuals' capabilities and well-being, than would be delegates of peoples (thin states). It is not possible in this limited space to consider the many issues on which parties would decide, therefore I concentrate on only one central issue: the nature and limits of sovereignty—its appropriate moral bases and political extent.

In constructing a Law of Persons to address the question of sovereignty, I begin by recalling what the original position does: it embodies constraints on substantive argument for principles of justice; it tells us what kinds of reasons cannot count. By making some substantive points about why the notion of a people cannot be assumed to ground even thin state sovereignty, I want to show *what reasons cannot count* for parties in a global original position. Thereafter, I argue, by considering what kinds of non-arbitrary reasons are *left*—as legitimate bases for principles of global justice—we can get a surprisingly long way toward an outline of just cosmopolitan institutions.

The first thing to note is that there is a veritable catalogue of empirical difficulties in identifying any people that is not deeply contested in practice or that clearly coincides with a particular political boundary.[46] Each difficulty can be seen to underpin a reason why the idea of a people cannot justify legitimate divisions between sovereign political entities.[47] Now, it might be thought that such a catalogue, while

---

[46] The catalogue includes: (1) real persons are often unsure about their (political) identity or have multiple such identities (they may 'belong' with no people or many); (2) persons 'may find those whom they live with in a particular society are not identical with those whom they regard as of their own culture or people (O'Neill, 'Political Liberalism', 16); (3) there is no clear cut distinction between peoples, cultures, and other kinds of groupings (Pogge, 'Cosmopolitanism', 197); (4) virtually no national territory contains only the members of a single people (ibid.); (5) official borders do not coincide with 'the main characteristics that are normally held to identify a people . . . such as a common ethnicity, language, culture, history, tradition' (ibid.); (6) 'whether some group does or does not constitute a people would seem . . . to be a matter of more-or-less rather than either-or' (ibid.); (7) appeals to 'a mythical past' or a 'desired future' as constituting a people beg the question of why that particular conception of national identity ought to be constructed (O. O'Neill, 'Justice and Boundaries', in C. Brown, ed., *Political Restructuring*, at 76); and (8) 'national and community identity is always framed in terms of' concepts that have no 'sharp boundaries, and hence cannot provide a basis for sharp demarcations such as political boundaries between states' (ibid.). This list is hardly exhaustive.

[47] For defences of the nation-state premised on the 'rights' of peoples to self-determination, see: D. Miller, 'The Nation-State: A Modest Defence', in C. Brown, ed., *Political Restructuring in Europe: Ethical Perspectives* (London: Routledge, 1994); A. Margalit and J. Raz, 'National Self-Determination', *Journal*

sufficient to reject closed and organicist views of the nation, does not constitute an argument against Rawls' liberal account of peoplehood. For one thing, Rawls fully acknowledges that

if those [common] sympathies were entirely dependent upon a common language, history, and political culture, with a shared historical consciousness, this feature would rarely, if ever, be fully satisfied . . . Notwithstanding, . . . [there is a] need for common sympathies, whatever their source may be. My hope is that, if we begin in this simplified way, we can work out political principles that . . . enable us to deal with more difficult cases where all the citizens are not united (*LP* 24–5).

For another,

It does not follow from the fact that boundaries [of thin states] are historically arbitrary that their role in the Law of Peoples cannot be justified. On the contrary, to fix on their arbitrariness is to fix on the wrong thing. In the absence of a world state, there *must* be boundaries of some kind, which when viewed in isolation will seem arbitrary, and depend to some degree on historical circumstances (*LP* 39).

Such arguments do not, however, answer the empirical catalogue of critique: it may be necessary to have simplifying assumptions and historically contingent boundaries, but this does not show that *these* particular assumptions (those of Rawls in *LP*) are not bad ones. For instance, it is not apparent that bonds of sympathy need be primarily between citizens of thin states. It is true that many people have cultural allegiances, but persons have many other legitimate allegiances too, and the idealisation of a homogenous nation removes the possibility of any basic political consideration of how and to what extent claims arising from these allegiances ought to be prioritised. Those other claims are only accommodated once the basic regulatory framework has been determined, in favour of an inter*national* thin state system—to which

of *Philosophy*, Vol. 87, No. 9 (1990), 439–61; and several articles usefully collected in both W. Kymlicka, ed., *The Rights of Minority Cultures* (Oxford: Oxford University Press, 1995), and G. Balakrishnan, ed., *Mapping the Nation* (London and New York: Verso, 1996). I do not think that any of these arguments defeat all the criticisms in my catalogue above. The collections by Kymlicka and Balakrishnan also contain articles that dispute—to my mind, convincingly—the validity of notions of nation and nationalism and the normative claims that purportedly follow. Especially worthwhile is J. Waldron's 'Minority Cultures and the Cosmopolitan Alternative', in Kymlicka, ed., *Minority Cultures*. A pioneering, radical cosmopolitan argument to refute exclusivist statism—especially when the latter is based on culturalist and nationalist claims—is J. Carens, 'Aliens and Citizens: The Case for Open Borders', *Review of Politics*, Vol. 49, No. 2 (1987), 251–73.

those with other allegiances must adjust (gaining as much respect as is possible within that system). Rawls has confused the putative value of common national sympathies with their moral primacy for establishing political institutions. The effect is to give peoples or nations a veto on what identities and bonds persons may take to be of predominant political significance. Yet this cannot be assumed to be just: 'A central objective of politics may be the reconstrual of political identities, the separation or the merging of destinies rather than the working out of principles of justice to be shared within a closed society.'[48]

It is not apparent that sovereignty has to be located at one level, nor is it evident that there are not better bases for borders—bases which take different historical contingencies into account, and for good reasons. One of the most interesting attempts to reformulate the notion of sovereignty so as to encompass these complexities is that of Thomas Pogge in 'Cosmopolitanism and Sovereignty'. He proposes a multi-layered institutional scheme in which the powers of sovereignty are 'vertically dispersed' rather than concentrated almost entirely at the level of states:

What we need is both centralization and decentralization ... Thus, persons should be citizens of, and govern themselves through, a number of political units of various sizes, without any one unit being dominant and thus occupying the traditional role of the state. And their political allegiance and loyalties should be widely dispersed over these units: neighbourhood, town, county, province, state, region, and world at large. People should be politically at home in all of them, without converging upon any one of them as the lodestar of their political identity.[49]

---

[48] O'Neill, 'Political Liberalism', 16. Rawls does say that the 'psychological principle [of limits on affinity] sets limits to what can sensibly be proposed as the content of the Law of Peoples' (*LP* 112, n. 44), and that 'the moral learning of political concepts and principles works most effectively in the context of society-wide political and social institutions' (*LP* 112). But this mere assertion rests on an implausibly narrow moral psychology to which we have very little reason to subscribe. For one thing, 'society' and 'nation' come in so many sizes that stipulating numeric limits to affinity is dubious. For another, identity—and its motivational force—is not essentially unipolar. That unipolarity should even seem plausible to us is due largely to the contingent (and now changing) configuration of Europe after 1648. Those who remain in the grip of a picture which allows only a state system or a world state would do well to recall that the nation-state is such a historically recent phenomenon, and thus evidently not a necessary, eternal unit of political organisation and psychological affiliation, let alone *the* fundamental or exclusive unit. Citizenship in overlapping institutions and institutions of great scope is a central topic of Chapter 3.

[49] Pogge, 'Cosmopolitanism', 99–100.

He argues that dispersing governmental authority over such 'nested territorial units' would have significant benefits, such as reducing the stakes and hence the intensity of the 'struggle for power and wealth within and among states, thereby reducing the incidence of war, poverty, and oppression' and environmental degradation.[50]

An obvious objection to this idea is the Hobbesian claim (which makes its way into much of the later social contract literature) that there must be a final decision mechanism that uniquely resolves any dispute—thereby preventing formal, ongoing, destructive conflict—and this can only be a supreme agency of last resort. As Pogge points out, though, the history of the last two hundred years—particularly the success of division of powers within states—attests to the possibility of law-governed coexistence even when ultimate conflicts between legitimate powers are theoretically possible. The three traditional branches of government within states rarely engage in all-out power struggles, and when more minor constitutional crises do arise they tend to be rapidly resolved.[51] Similarly, the vertical division of sovereignty in federal regimes—in ways that leave open some conflict over constitutional allocation of powers and hence no authoritative path of resolution—has proved a remarkably effective underpinning of robust and enduring institutions in many cases (including the United States, the United Kingdom, Switzerland, Germany; the list is long . . .). It therefore seems mistaken rigidly to insist that sovereignty must be located in one place in the last instance.

Dispersed sovereignty of some kind may well be effective and highly beneficial—though I have not yet said which kind, if any, is most promising (see Chapter 3). For now, note simply that Rawls thinks we must rid ourselves of the cult of unqualified state sovereignty, but he does not see that the cult of unitary sovereignty may

[50] Pogge, 'Cosmopolitanism', 89, 102–5.

[51] Ibid., 100–1. Contra Weber, it is not the case that a *monopoly* on the legitimate use of force is foundational to sovereignty, as numerous empirical examples attest: who has a monopoly on legitimate violence over Bavaria—the State itself? Germany? The European Union? NATO? The United Nations Security Council? Each is legally entitled to exercise force only to achieve certain ends and only under certain conditions. True, some of these powers are a function of intergovernmental and treaty arrangements that are rescindable by the German state, but others are not (e.g. there exists no entitlement to strip Bavaria of its autonomous powers). It should be added that, contra Schmitt, it is not the case that the absence of a unitary sovereign makes decisive positive action impossible. Indeed, as I shall show in subsequent chapters, quite the reverse is likely to be true: properly understood and implemented, pluralised sovereignty would improve the overall quality of political judgement and action.

similarly deserve to be consigned to the flames. In any case, Pogge's suggestion stands as at least one broad, plausible, non-statist (in its assumptions and outcomes) alternative to both a world state and a state-dominated system. Rawls cannot assume that the problem of a world state provides, by process of elimination of alternatives, a justification for representing peoples in the original position, nor for endorsing them as the primary political configurations in the principles of global justice.

However, it seems to me that even Pogge does not go far enough, in that he has imported an unjustified assumption that sovereignty can and should only be exercised over territorially defined units. It seems that we may have escaped the cults of unqualified and unitary state sovereignty only to fall prey to the lesser cult of territorial sovereignty. Why should the parties in the original position accept this arbitrary restriction on the domain of government? Why should sovereignty not be dispersed horizontally as well as vertically? Considering the numerous issues that territorial demarcations of governmental functions could not (best) resolve—for example, crime on the Internet, prosecution of violators of human rights, and environmental protection—there seems good reason to divide the tasks of governments on *functional* rather than territorial lines.[52] Some governmental functions may be best exercised within territorial demarcations, and some groups of functions may coincide at various levels of Pogge's vertical scheme; but it is unlikely that they would exhaust all governmental functions.

But how are we to understand these 'functions'? The rapid pace of globalisation and technological innovation in several areas suggests that non-territorial spaces of interaction (from web pages to financial markets) will have an increasingly significant role in human affairs. It may thus be more appropriate to think of functional sovereignty as

---

[52] Rawls cleaves to an entirely territorial ideal on the following grounds: 'Unless a definite agent is given responsibility for maintaining an asset and bears the responsibility and loss for not doing so, that asset tends to deteriorate. On my account the role of the institution of property is to prevent this deterioration from occurring. In the present case, the asset is the people's territory and its potential capacity to support them *in perpetuity*; and the agent is the people itself as politically organised' (*LP* 8). Not only does Rawls here beg the question as to why peoples should necessarily be that responsible agent—as has become apparent, they should not—it also shifts spuriously from the idea of property to that of closed territories. Yet it is not the case that all property is or need be underpinned by territorial regimes, nor—as will also become evident—that the kinds of property we take to be important are best conserved by the political regimes of peoples.

legitimate power over *kinds* of human practice and resources.[53] In considering the political authorities that would best fulfil various government functions, parties to the original would position consider territory—restricted or global—a *derivative* basis for inclusion (along with syndicalism, to mention at this point only one other). What is needed, then, is a conception of political agencies that appropriately regulate different spheres of human action, and since not all spheres of action are primarily territorially based, neither need those authorities always be.[54] Persons would still band together over various functions, many of them territorially and communally based, but there would by no means be the overweening concentration of legitimate power in states or a state system.[55]

One initial model for such a world order is to be found in the literature on polyarchy, which looks to smaller, diverse metropolitan areas such as New York or Los Angeles as a guide to a more cosmopolitan vision:

These megalopolises comprise numerous municipal and special-purpose jurisdictions, many of which overlap, but they lack a strong central government for the whole metropolitan area. The polyarchic 'global city' could exhibit an analogous structure ... [T]ransnational institutions, with memberships and spans of control congruent with the interdependent relationships, could be accorded with responsibility for co-ordination, rule making, and even rule enforcement.[56]

---

[53] The deeper aspiration here is to have a universalist account of global justice which avoids assuming territorial boundaries, while still taking the particularity of human practices into account. (On the apparent differences between particularists and universalists more generally, and why these differences are widely misunderstood and largely bridgeable, see O'Neill, *Towards Justice*.) I cannot provide an account of this kind here. What has been provided is a range of illustrations of this line of thought. Most notably, my discussion of how to expand membership in the United Nations General Assembly (in Chapter 4) proposes some ways to individuate relevant practices and actors in that context.

[54] For example, a global or regional environmental agency for preserving wildlife habitats, wherever they may be, might better achieve that end than nation-states—or certainly nation-states on their own. Chapters 3 and 4 provide extensive examples and analysis of such non-state agencies and their place in a pluralised global order.

[55] My argument that this kind of dispersal would be beneficial is even stronger if Carl Schmitt is at all correct that bounded territoriality necessarily leads to conflict (Schmitt, *Crisis*, 53 and 69–71). In the system I propose, authorities to which sovereignty is dispersed are not individuated solely on the basis of their capacity to exercise legitimate violence; rather, in Chapters 3 and 4, I bring out the relevance and legitimacy of other forms of effective, circumscribed, and identifiable compulsion.

[56] S. Brown, 'The World Polity and the Nation-State System', in R. Little and M. Smith, eds., *Perspectives on World Politics* (London: Routledge, 1991), 263–72,

In such a world order, the dispersal of jurisdictional authority over a plurality of agencies would of course be limited, on functional grounds, by a need for effective coordination. Each will operate 'on the lowest possible level', but there will generally be advantages to assigning jurisdiction over several functions to each agency, and benefits to creating agency-clusters—not least that it is then possible (as I have shown in Chapters 3 and 4) to exercise greater democratic control over governance. Grounds of this kind for allocating authority are already recognised in Article 5 of the Treaty Establishing the European Community, which endorses both a Principle of Democracy and a Principle of Subsidiarity (this is the principle that powers and tasks should be vested in subunits, 'as close as possible to citizens', unless a more encompassing unit can better achieve the specified goals).[57]

The Treaty that enshrines these principles is a pioneering practical document for organising non-unitary sovereignty; as is well known, however, it retains a bias in favour of allocating powers, including powers to shape decision rules, to states. Both subsidiarity and democracy are understood as *delegative* principles: the authority of localities, regions, and Union is conferred by states (as a legal, not a merely historical matter), and the authority of states to delegate in this way is officially derived, in good part, from the purported fact that those states are internally democratic. These restrictions, which are applied to the detriment of other levels and kinds of political formations, are unlikely to find a place in a non-statist, non-territorialist order. Instead, that order would be governed by principles of *distributive* subsidiarity and democracy—principles that do not presume at the outset the (superior or original) legitimacy of states, or the transitivity of intra-state democratic mandates.[58]

There are, then, non-arbitrary reasons for drawing boundaries of sovereignty—boundaries that are historically contingent only in the sense that they take account of the best current means to reach the ends

at 271. See also S. Krasner, 'Power Politics, Institutions and Transnational Relations', in T. Risse-Kappen, ed., *Bringing Transnational Relations Back In Non-State Actors, Domestic Structures and International Institutions* (Cambridge: Cambridge University Press, 1995).

[57] Article 5 of the Consolidated Version (post-Amsterdam) of the Treaty Establishing the European Community, available at www.europa.eu.int. On one interpretation, the principle of subsidiarity aims to locate administrative power where it is most effective; on another (and this is probably closer to the letter of the text) the principle aims to locate that power 'as close as possible' to citizens—that is, to citizen control, largely through (local, etc.) elections.

[58] I shall return to and develop these distributive principles in later chapters.

of free and equal persons.[59] The result would be what I am calling
a system of functionally plural sovereignty—or 'plurarchy' for short.
This is merely to sketch the broad outlines of an alternative global
institutional configuration, one that cannot be assumed out of parties'
purview arbitrarily by stipulating peoples—thin, and often illiberal,
states—either as the represented subjects or as the necessary institutional outcomes of appropriately constrained practical reasoning.

4. Realism: Practical Application in a Non-ideal World

'But', an imagined critic might say, 'your liberal principles of global
justice will put us at odds with hierarchical regimes: they will not
accept the privileging of the individual as free and equal, and so will
not endorse the same principles, and we will surely come into conflict.
Whereas Rawls at least recognises pragmatic limitations and strategic difficulties, the cosmopolitan scheme you have provided is uncomprom-
isingly idealistic and of little help as a guide to political action. What
are you going to suggest that liberal regimes *do* to decent non-liberal
regimes? Are they to be subject to military attack, colonisation, or
intervention in their domestic affairs? Are they to be ostracised from
cooperative international schemes altogether? Rawls gives us good
reasons why liberal regimes must—by their own principles—rule out
these kinds of action. Not only that, he gives us good reasons to engage
such societies, so as at least to ensure minimal adherence to international legal rules of non-aggression and minimal respect for human
rights. And he even gives us reasons to think that non-liberal regimes
would accept engagement on these terms. In any case, setting the ideal
too high may lead to frustration and disillusionment for liberals, and
that would adversely affect progress on peace and human rights issues.
Finally, tolerance of this injustice is not as distasteful as you claim.
Liberals are still able to criticise non-liberal regimes, since acceptance
of decent peoples in international law by no means implies endorsement of their principles by liberals more generally nor does it require
that non-liberal regimes are viewed as beyond reproach. Rawls has
provided us with a "realistic utopia" (*LP* 7, 11–23); you have given us
an impracticable pipe-dream'.

This forceful critic would surely be right in one important respect:
the distance between an imagined cosmopolitan world and current

---

[59] Rawls is quite clear that these kinds of 'general facts', including economic
theory, are allowed behind the veil (*Theory*, 136–42).

grim realities 'is so great that it would be madness to use the conclusions of ideal theory as the unmediated basis for a practical application program'.[60] However, in this section I want to argue that the cosmopolitan scheme I have presented is a more useful ideal than that presented in *LP*, on two grounds: Rawls is neither sufficiently utopian nor sufficiently realistic. This may seem paradoxical, but careful consideration of the relationship between ideal and non-ideal theory reveals that Rawls has created a unitary term—'realistic utopia'—by watering down both its elements; further, a perspective which maintains the distinct role of each element is far more practical. In what follows, I discuss each element in turn.

Rawls' argument for his (in my view, limited) utopianism is in part an argument from *stability*: the situation of ideal justice must generate ongoing support and not be subject to 'assurance problems' arising out of shifts in power. It must be a sustainable ideal. But if this is to be achieved at the global level, he insists in *LP*, the standards of the reasonable need to be 'relaxed', since treating all persons as free and equal—as having the two moral powers regardless of culture or location—'makes the basis of the law of peoples too narrow'.[61] Actual peoples *do* cleave so strongly (and not unreasonably) to their 'different cultures and traditions of thought', and a liberal world order will constantly be faced with civil strife if it expects them to sacrifice what is most dear to them in order to endorse global legal rules and institutions (*LP* 11): 'Historically speaking, all principles and standards proposed for the law of peoples must, to be feasible, prove acceptable to the considered and reflective public opinion of peoples and their governments.'[62]

This is not simply a matter of actual recognition (fortunately for Rawls, since in Section 2 we saw that this argument must fail), rather it is a matter of 'speculation' on what is 'feasible and might actually exist', given that persons do in general organise themselves into peoples (*LP* 12–13). Liberals should thus adopt 'a minimum standard of realism which requires that the law of peoples not call into question the existence of the international state system', at least where that refers to a confederation of what I have called thin states.[63]

---

[60] Ackerman, 'Political Liberalisms', 377–8.

[61] This is his most succinct, explicit statement of the stability argument (Rawls, 'Law of Peoples', 55).

[62] Ibid., 43.

[63] D. Moellendorf, 'Constructing the Law of Peoples', *Pacific Philosophical Quarterly*, Vol. 77 (1996), 132–54, at 135. Moellendorf characterises Rawls' position only in order to dispute its force.

The fatal flaws in this argument are immediately apparent if we recall the meaning of stability in *Political Liberalism*: a regime is stable when 'members will tend increasingly over time to accept its principles and judgements as they come to understand the ideas of justice expressed in the law among them and appreciate its benefits'.[64] Breadth of agreement, Rawls writes there, can establish a wide modus vivendi—an agreement based on prudential considerations, which is therefore unstable—but not an *overlapping consensus*, which is the only kind of agreement that is stable. The former is a question in non-ideal theory of how assent could be won from within current societies, given that so many are organised into states that cleave to comprehensive doctrines; the latter is a question of ideal theory, and involves a *moral* affirmation by the politically relevant subjects of the social framework regulated by principles of justice.[65] *Who* those subjects are is not settled by the ease of achieving assent from peoples rather than individual persons (once the veil is dropped). Rather it is settled by (1) who is an authentic source of moral claims in this domain; and (2) whether those agents would continue to support the resultant conception of global justice, even if shifts occurred in their conceptions of the good.

Regarding (1), I have tried to show not only that peoples (thin states) are not self-authenticating sources of valid moral claims but also that their having taken each person in each territory's minimal interests (in liberty rights and peace) into account is insufficient to secure that authentic status. It is in any case deeply questionable whether an historical analysis would guide us to an acceptance of peoples as the politically relevant subjects. The horrors of nationalistic wars, xenophobia, and unnecessary starvation might motivate instead a greater focus on human individuals regardless of their geographical location, and—as Pogge argues—on lowering the stakes and incentives to abuse that attach to each level or locus of authority.[66] If history suggests anything, it is that we should scrupulously interrogate and dismiss assumptions which might be destructively 'trapping us in the buildings and boundaries' of the past or present.[67]

[64] Rawls, *Political Liberalism*, 48. See also: ibid., 133–72; Rawls, *Theory*, 336; and Moellendorf, 'Constructing the Law', 147–8.

[65] Rawls, *Political Liberalism*, 64.

[66] Indeed, Rawls has answered one set of Realists, but not all. Structural Realists insist that it is the interaction between states and not features internal to states per se that generate conflict.

[67] This felicitous constructivist phrase is from O'Neill, *Towards Justice*, 212.

The goal of any Kant-inspired utopian political theory of global relations thus cannot be to show which principles are likely to be accepted at present (by the powers that be or by persons *simpliciter*, with all our distorting prejudices). Rather, it is to specify which principles ought to be accepted by those subjects in this domain, considered in terms of the morally relevant features of their persons and situations. In this sense, the Rawls of *LP* fails to heed Kant's injunction in 'Perpetual Peace' not to end up tailoring a political morality to the concerns of those currently in power: 'I can easily conceive of a moral politician, i.e. one who so chooses political principles that they are consistent with those of morality; but I cannot conceive of a political moralist, one who forges a morality in such a way that it conforms to the statesman's advantage.'[68]

A vital task of the liberal political theorist is to subject the status quo to (sometimes speculative) critique: 'One finds no great concern to stabilise every existing order, nor should one. There is no reason to mourn the destruction of unjust social and political orders.'[69]

As for the question (2) above, as to whether the ideal presented in *LP* is sustainable, it seems quite evident that decent peoples are profoundly unstable in the modern world—and thus so too is a Law of Peoples— since they are organised around comprehensive conceptions of the good.[70] There may be demographic shifts such that a majority does not cleave to that conception, or (perhaps due to justified liberal support for those demanding greater freedom and equality within these societies) particular individuals may strenuously oppose the existing organisation of such a society, leading to civil strife. Because persons (even the majority) can reasonably claim that they should be treated equally, such fundamental strife can occur even within an ideal society where everybody acts reasonably (as we have seen, the decent consultation hierarchy does not provide any negotiating mechanisms for such

[68] Beck's 1957 translation, quoted by Moellendorf, 'Constructing the Law', 139.

[69] Moellendorf, 'Constructing the Law', 147.

[70] Again, stability in this Rawlsian sense implies not merely the survival of the society (illiberal regimes from ancient Egypt to today's China have endured for long periods) but that they obtain adequate *moral* affirmation and *hence* political legitimacy from the populace, including but not limited to powerful role-players, as conditions change over time. By 'unstable in the modern world' I do not mean primarily that so-called decent states will face overwhelming exogenous pressures from powerful liberal states; liberal and democratic notions of legitimacy (as requiring the assent of the populace) prove compelling to a significant number of dissenters whether or not other powerful states endorse this view of legitimacy or indeed pay any extensive attention whatsoever to such regimes and dissidents.

fundamental conflicts).[71] Worse still, illiberal reactions to, say, the institutionalisation of one religion might be aroused when such historically contingent shifts occur. Civil strife is hardly the basis for consistent performance of one's duties in respect of a global scheme of cooperation.[72]

Plurarchy, the functionally differentiated global scheme for which I have argued, does not face the same problems: if persons change their comprehensive doctrines, or there are shifts in demographics or power, an ethically neutral scheme of political structures is equally and always accommodating. As Ackerman points out, liberals must insistently *not* accommodate the exigencies of current power relations in ideal theory:

> Of course government officials [representing a dominant religion or comprehensive view] will not accept a fundamental critique of existing boundaries—their political power presupposes their legitimacy. Giving them a veto on the question of boundaries is like giving the rich a veto on the distribution of wealth . . . Rawls proposes a disastrous political compromise . . . [Even if illiberal regimes] satisfy these very minimal minima . . . I fail to see why it justifies anything more than a modus vivendi with oppressor states.[73]

Why is it important to keep in view the fact that this supposed ' "overlapping consensus" is really just a modus vivendi among quite different models of society'?[74] One reason is to be found in Kant: to limit a conception of global justice to a 'hybrid solution such as pragmatically conditioned right halfway between right and utility' is to 'eternalise the violation of right'.[75] A practical foreign policy is one thing, sacrificing the proper regulative ideal is quite another. It was in

---

[71] Rawls surely cannot brand politically liberal persons in comprehensive societies unreasonable. They may not agree with *this* hierarchical scheme of cooperation, but wanting benefits and burdens to be shared more equally is wrongly characterised as unreasonably uncooperative. Those persons would hold a liberally justifiable interpretation of cooperation, and it does not cease to be so because they happen to be unlucky enough to be born into a less than liberal society. To say otherwise would be to repudiate the value of even the minimally free exercise of reason, to characterise such liberal dissenters as obstructionist misfits.

[72] Here again we note the deep disanalogy between tolerating persons as opposed to regimes with comprehensive doctrines: internal strife in most individuals tends not to impact on the broader system of cooperation, whereas internal strife in hierarchical societies has the potential to impact far more adversely.

[73] Ackerman, 'Political Liberalisms', 381–3.

[74] S. Hoffman, 'Dreams of Just World', *New York Review of Books*, Vol. 42 (1995), 52–7, at 54.

[75] I. Kant, 'Perpetual Peace', in Hans Reiss, trans. and ed., *Kant's Political Writings* (Cambridge: Cambridge University Press, 1991); see 119–25.

this spirit that Rawls wrote in 'The Idea of an Overlapping Consensus' that: 'The politician looks to the next election, the statesman to the next generation, and philosophy to the indefinite future.'[76] This is what is meant when I say that the Rawls of *LP* is insufficiently utopian: his conception is neither robust nor aspirant enough.

But there is an even greater pragmatic danger than limiting our distant future—a danger of not being appropriately *realistic* at present, if we do not keep the correct ideal in view. We need, as Rawls put it in *A Theory of Justice*, 'a standard for appraising institutions and for guiding the overall direction of social change'[77]; and if we do not get the standard right, we will misjudge how to pursue justice in the present non-ideal conditions: 'Non-ideal theory is . . . more immediately relevant to practical problems, but ideal theory is more fundamental, establishing the ultimate goal of social reform and a basis for judging the relative importance of departures from the ideal.'[78]

A modus vivendi with hierarchical regimes may be the best that is achievable right now, and it will have its own special prudential rules; but let us be aware of what we are compromising, and let us be able to judge which are the least offensive such rules. It is well, then, to constantly bear in mind an injunction from Thomas Pogge, which is very much in the spirit of Kant and the early Rawls:

Realism hardly requires that the principles of justice conform themselves to the prevailing sordid realities. We don't feel justified to give up our ideals of domestic justice or personal honesty just because we despair of achieving them fully. We cannot reasonably demand of moral principles that they vindicate the status quo. All we may ask is that a conception of justice provide a criterion for assessing our global order that allows us to [identify and] choose from among the feasible . . . avenues of institutional change and thus specifies our moral task gradually to improve the justice of this order.[79]

I now want to complete this reply to my imagined critic by demonstrating that Rawls' conception in *LP* leads him to prioritise the wrong things, and that my 'relevant utopianism' serves as a better guide to political action.[80] I will focus on the omission of free speech and democracy from Rawls' list of basic human rights. Consider the

---

[76] See Pogge's discussion of this statement in 'An Egalitarian Law', 224. Rawls' two essays on the overlapping consensus are reprinted in his *Collected Papers*, 421–48 and 473–96.

[77] Rawls, *Theory*, 263.

[78] Carens, 'Citizens', 225.

[79] T. Pogge, *Realizing Rawls* (Ithaca, NY: Cornell University Press, 1989), 260.

[80] The term 'relevant utopia' was suggested to me by Stanley Hoffmann. Hoffmann's historically informed and prescient works include *Duties Beyond*

following two statements from *LP* about political strategy:

> With confidence in the ideals of constitutional liberal democratic thought, it [the Law of Peoples] respects decent peoples by allowing them to find their own way to honor those ideals (*LP* 122).
>
> The Law of Peoples considers this wider background basic structure and the merits of its political climate in encouraging reforms in a liberal direction as overriding the lack of liberal justice in a decent society (*LP* 62).

These points suggest that peoples are more likely to come round to liberal views if they are engaged as full participants and are included as members in good standing of the Society of Peoples under international law.[81] But, insofar as we can make informed judgements about these matters, is any part of this claim plausible? Why should the liberal expect that deliberative rationality—leading to a liberal outcome—is a characteristic of the decent consultation hierarchy? The most that dissent can expect to achieve, according to Rawls, is that the government 'spells out how the government thinks it can both reasonably interpret its policies in line with its common good idea of justice and impose duties and obligations on all members of society' (*LP* 78). There is no reason that constrained internal critique within a comprehensive notion should have liberal results; if anything, it is more likely to result in a spiral of doctrinal self-confirmation. So perhaps Rawls means only that engagement will encourage decent peoples to respect human rights and the laws of peace—the limited 'liberal' aims of a Law of Peoples—on an ongoing basis.

There are extremely strong empirical reasons to doubt this latter claim. The single most extensive analysis of the effects of non-democratic political structures on the rights and well-being of persons is to be found in the work of Amartya Sen. In wide-ranging diachronic and synchronic studies, Sen and his collaborators have demonstrated repeatedly that non-democratic regimes are in fact almost unfailingly detrimental to human rights and well-being.[82] The most significant

---

Borders: On the Limits and Possibilities of International Politics (Syracuse, NY: Syracuse University Press, 1981).

[81] In particular, international law ought to recognise and support peoples' domestic institutions of public reasoning, including their decent consultation hierarchies. The idea seems to be that cultures have their own modes of argument and processes of change, and where these are sufficiently deliberative we not only have grounds to believe that they will lead to more liberal principles for regulating a people's common life, but grounds to respect those modes themselves.

[82] There are numerous related and confirming studies, and there is simply no more impressive body of theory and evidence for the empirical judgements

reason for this—though there are many—is that there are insufficient political incentives for the regime to secure decent social, economic, and legal conditions for persons. Rulers owe their legitimacy to a tradition, a way of life, and not so much to their efficacy in achieving the present important interests of individual persons; states are thus insufficiently attentive and unresponsive to persons' plights:

[There are] extensive interconnections between political freedoms and the understanding and fulfilment of economic needs. The connections are not only instrumental (political freedoms can have a major role in providing incentives and information . . .), but also constructive. Our conceptualization of economic needs [as well as, Sen goes on to say, our interpretation and application of rights-claims] depends crucially on open public debates and discussions . . . Furthermore, to express publicly what we value and to [effectively] demand that attention be paid to it, we need free speech and democratic choice.[83]

The highly likely and disturbing results of not having democratic freedoms are dramatic: social disintegration, famine, and abuse of rights. This is not good for cultures or ways of life either. Sen adds that respect for a number of fundamental human freedoms and for a range of democratic ideas is by no means a function only of 'Western' values or impositions, but that elements are to be found in all major cultures and traditions, despite the claims of non-democratic rulers (who have an interest in persons thinking otherwise).[84] He also makes the crucial epistemological and eminently practical point that without

---

I discuss. The most relevant of Sen's monographs in this respect are *Development as Freedom* (New York: Alfred A. Knopf, 1999), *Inequality Re-examined* (Oxford: Oxford University Press, 1992), *Poverty and Famines: An Essay on Entitlement and Deprivation* (Oxford: Clarendon Press, 1981), and—together with J. Dreze—*Hunger and Public Action* (Oxford: Clarendon Press, 1989). Edited volumes confirming the accuracy and fecundity of this approach to development and democracy include: J. Dreze and A. Sen, eds., *The Political Economy of Hunger* (Oxford: Clarendon Press, 1995); M. C. Nussbaum and A. Sen, eds., *The Quality of Life* (Oxford: Clarendon Press, 1989); and M. C. Nussbaum and J. Glover, eds., *Women, Culture and Development: A Study of Human Capabilities* (Oxford: Clarendon Press, 1995).

[83] Sen, *Development as Freedom*, 147–8 and 154–5. I am in full agreement with Sen's arguments for democratic rights as intrinsically important too. Rawls mentions Sen's work repeatedly (see esp. *LP* 108–11), but fails to see that Sen's 'insistence on human rights' includes an insistence on democratic rights. Sen's perspective on this is borne out by other commentators on global justice, including T. M. Franck, 'The Emerging Right to Democratic Governance', *American Journal of International Law*, Vol. 86, No. 1 (1992), 46–91.

[84] Sen, *Development as Freedom*, 227–48.

democracy it is impossible to tell which interpretations of a culture are the impositions of semi-autocratic rulers, and which are widely held and justifiable.[85]

So we can accept, with Rawls, the notion that we should respect cultures, and even that 'the crucial element in how a country fares is its political culture' (*LP* 117), even while we strenuously insist that political cultures ought to become liberal and democratic. This seriously undermines Rawls' project, since he writes that, 'Should the facts of history, supported by the reasoning of social and political thought, show that hierarchical regimes are always, or nearly always, oppressive and deny human rights, the case for liberal democracy is made. The Law of Peoples assumes, however, that decent hierarchical peoples exist, or could exist . . .' (*LP* 79).

On these terms, the case for liberal democracy has been made: there are no secure minimal human rights without (a governing principle of) democracy. And it has been argued—though I shall not do so much here—that without the political incentives that liberal democratic political institutions provide, (thin) states are likely to become aggressive.[86] It is the less powerful sections of the population—and not the leaders of associations or states, unless they are subject to popular judgement—that suffer the full ravages of war; so giving every person a say is likely to be more conducive to the perpetual peace we seek. In sum, my arguments together with the best empirical evidence available establish that the notion of an ongoing scheme of cooperation that has the features of decency is unstable, unrealistic, and undesirable from the point of view of justice.

At this point, my critic throws up his or her hands: 'Fine, our liberal principles do not lead us to accept decent peoples as sufficiently just. But what do you propose to *do*?!' My answer is that decent regimes must be engaged in a global legal structure but only to a limited extent. First, the conditions for entry must require reforms in a democratic direction rather than avoiding this issue. Far from being impracticable, that is increasingly the practice of transnational bodies such as the Commonwealth (as with its suspension of Zimbabwe), the European Union (which makes democratic reforms a condition for entry), and the World Bank Group (which—whatever else it does

---

[85] Sen, *Development as Freedom*, 227–48; also A. Sen, 'Human Rights and Asian Values', *The New Republic*, 14 and 21 July 1997; and A. Sen, 'Our Culture, Their Culture', *The New Republic*, 1 April 1996.

[86] See O. Otunnu and M. Doyle, eds., *Peacemaking and Peacekeeping for the New Century* (Oxford: Rowman & Littlefield, 1998).

wrong—puts some key democratic conditions on aid and loans). Rather than being a pipe dream, this kind of perspective has won the support of, and been implemented by, numerous hardened pragmatists.

Moreover, the theory and practice of international law increasingly, and rightly, invokes such democratising imperatives. Since the initial United Nations endorsement of those imperatives in Article 19 of the 1966 'International Covenant on Civil and Political Rights', full free speech and democracy requirements have been increasingly crisply and demandingly formulated in broad African, American, and European conventions on human rights, and now are to be found in most such charters.[87] In Rawls' scheme there is, on the contrary, *no* 'political case for intervention [*of any kind*] based on the public reason of the Law of Peoples' (*LP* 84). While liberals can express their private views about the injustices in non-liberal societies, 'Rawls's international law principles do not even authorise representatives of liberal societies to publicly (i.e. in an international forum such as the United Nations) *criticise* the non-liberal practices (e.g. suppression of speech) in hierarchical societies, when such practices are consistent with hierarchical conceptions of the good.'[88]

Liberal complaints have the same political status in Rawls' idea of international law that comprehensive doctrines have in his idea of domestic society; that is, they carry no political weight whatsoever. While minimal human rights remain a national duty—with potentially more efficacious institutions than the state having only default obligations—rights such as free speech and democracy are removed from global view entirely. It seems to me deeply regrettable that Rawls has taken a step backwards from recent hard-won advances in international law,[89] and from the possibility of using global forums to

---

[87] See F. R. Teson, 'The Rawlsian Theory of International Law', *Ethics and International Affairs*, Vol. 9 (1995), 79–99, at 95.

[88] Teson, 'Rawlsian Theory', 88–9. This marks an increasingly conservative turn in Rawls, since—in debarring all but intrastatal efforts to change cultures (excepting minimal rights)—he leaves liberals wringing their hands about socially oppressed minorities beyond their current society's borders. Cultures are difficult to change and must be treated with sensitivity, but that does not imply a counsel of despair so much as a careful and inclusive (proto-democratic) approach to the process of change. For a wide-ranging survey of just how many abhorrent behaviours are cloaked and defended with the exculpatory phrase 'in our culture', see Roger Sandall's *The Culture Cult: Designer Tribalism and Other Essays* (Oxford: Westview, 2002).

[89] The telling contrast between Rawls' conception of international law and current international law is illuminated in J. Tasioulas, 'From Utopia to

bring about change in a liberal democratic direction—especially since political practice has shown this compromise to be unnecessary.[90]

This leads to my second illustration of the practical application of ideals: humanitarian intervention. I simply want to point out that Rawls and my imagined critic have confused two things. It is one thing to treat illiberal regimes as outlaws—to a greater or lesser extent, depending on the extent of violation, that is, on where they fall on the decent–tyrannical continuum—but it is quite another to think that it is morally permissible to colonise or eliminate them by force. The legitimacy of a regime is only one among many reasons that preclude war and the use of force:

War [may be] excluded because it is grossly disproportionate to the goal sought. Even in cases where the regime is overtly tyrannical (such as the present Chinese regime) waging war would be wrong because of the impossibility or prohibitive cost of victory, that is, for purely prudential reasons. So humanitarian intervention (that is, wars to liberate oppressed populations) is subject to a number of moral constraints that counsel moderation . . .[91]

It is a simple and unfortunate category error to confuse illegitimate interventions, on the one hand, with judgements of regime illegitimacy, on the other.

The use of force must be reserved for cases where force is the only realistic way to encourage sustainable democracy or to prevent egregious abuses of human rights. Clearly if force will do more harm than good, then force is not to be adopted, and clearly there are other methods that should be preferred. Every effort should be made first to use moral suasion and bring diplomatic pressure to bear on illiberal regimes. It follows that there are independent grounds for rejecting heavy-handed intervention. Further, the efficacy of less drastic and morally vexing *means* than force would be increased by the existence of a global law that recognises the underlying value of the *ends* that cosmopolitans promote.[92]

Kazanistan: John Rawls and the Law of Peoples', *Oxford Journal of Legal Studies*, Vol. 22 (2002*a*), 367–96.

[90] See Chapter 4; pioneering arguments to similar effect can be found in P. Allot, *Eunomia: New Order for a New World* (Oxford: Oxford University Press, 1990) and G. Fox, 'The Right to Political Participation in International Law', *Yale Journal of International Law*, Vol. 17, No. 2 (1992), 539–607.

[91] Teson, 'Rawlsian Theory', 97.

[92] The implications of cosmopolitan theory for development practice are explored in the 'Debate on Global Poverty Relief' between Peter Singer and me. See A. Kuper, 'More Than Charity: Cosmopolitan Alternatives to the "Singer Solution"'; P. Singer, 'Poverty, Facts, and Political Philosophies: Response to

It is absolutely critical that these shifts in conceptions of sovereignty be encouraged *along with* a focus on how institutions can be made democratically responsive, otherwise we are likely to be left with either non-democratic dispersed sovereignty or a state-dominated order. I have suggested that neither sort of global basic structure is an appealing prospect. There are good reasons to develop a relevantly liberal and realistic utopian democratic alternative. As Edvard Hambro put it, when he was President of the UN General Assembly, 'We ought not to be satisfied when people tell us that politics is the art of the possible. Politics should be the art to make possible tomorrow what seems impossible today.'[93]

Commitment to such an ideal vision is entirely consistent with and even requires realism about practical obstacles, constraints, and opportunities. Our practical task—a task explored in the coming chapters—is gradually to pluralise the current global order by creating a variety of forms of democratically responsive, semi-autonomous legal authority; they could in turn develop a texture of relationships that is sufficiently complex and that meets an important range of interests, so that the entire scheme is widely accepted and stable. In the coming chapters I shall explore one scheme that could meet these requirements. It is time to end the dominance of what David Luban has called 'the romance of the nation-state'[94] and to discern principles for a more complex and more promising global institutional configuration. Those principles will take individuals to be the normative epicentre of a system of plurarchic sovereignty. In this chapter, I have critically engaged the work of John Rawls to begin constructing such a cosmopolitan Law of Persons.

"More Than Charity"'; A. Kuper, 'Facts, Theories and Hard Choices: A Reply to Peter Singer'; and P. Singer, 'Achieving the Best Outcome: Final Rejoinder'—all in *Ethics and International Affairs*, Vol. 16, No. 1 (2002), 107–128.

[93] Speech to the American Society of International Law (1971), cited in K. Suter, 'Reforming the United Nations', in R. Thakur, ed., *Past Imperfect, Future Uncertain: The United Nations at Fifty* (Basingstoke: Macmillan, 1998), at 203.

[94] D. Luban, 'The Romance of the Nation-State', in C. Beitz, M. Cohen, T. Scanlon, and J. Simmons, eds., *International Ethics* (Princeton, NJ: Princeton University Press, 1985).

2

Why Deliberation Cannot Tame Globalisation
The Impossibility of a Deliberative Democrat

But the little prince was puzzled. The planet was tiny. Over what could this king really rule?

'Sire . . .' he began, '. . . please excuse my asking you a question . . .'

'I order you to put your question to me,' the king was quick to reply.

'Sire . . . over what do you rule?'

'Over everything,' replied the king very simply.

'Over everything?'

The king made a sweeping gesture taking in his own planet, the other planets and the stars.

'Over all that?' said the little prince.

'Over all that,' replied the king.

For he was not only an absolute monarch but a universal one.

'And the stars obey?'

'Of course,' said the king. 'They obey immediately. I do not tolerate insubordination.'

The little prince marvelled at such power . . .

'I should like to see a sunset . . . Please, do me that kindness . . . order the sun to set'.

'If I were to order a general to fly from one flower to another like a butterfly, or to write a tragedy, or to change himself into a seabird, and if the general did not carry out the order, which one of us would be at fault?'

'It would be you,' said the little prince firmly.

'Exactly. One must demand of each and every one what he or she is capable of. Authority is first and foremost based on reason.

If you order your people to throw themselves into the sea, you
will have a revolution on your hands. I have the right to demand
obedience because my orders are reasonable ones.'
'What about my sunset?' the little prince reminded him, for he
never forgot a question once he had asked it.
'You shall have your sunset. I shall demand it. But, in accordance
with scientific government, I shall wait until conditions are
favourable.'
'And when will that be?' asked the little prince.
'Hum! Hum!' replied the king, consulting his big calendar. 'Hum!
Hum! It will be around ... around ... it will be this evening about
twenty minutes to eight. And you shall see how well I am obeyed.'
The little prince yawned ... and then, with a sigh, took his leave.
'I make you my ambassador,' the king called after him in haste.
He had a magnificent air of authority.

A. de Saint-Exupery, *The Little Prince*, 44–7.

1. *The Scale of Politics*

The previous chapter developed an account of moral *as well as* institutional cosmopolitanism: a pluralised political authority structure is
necessary to satisfy the universalist requirements of justice. But the
cosmopolitan theory presented thus far is seriously incomplete since it
confronts a peculiar worry: that the inclusive scope of cosmopolitan
institutions would be incompatible with democracy. The underlying
idea can be put simply and seemingly plausibly as follows: the larger
the social group among which decision and deliberation must take
place, the less the political power or autonomy of the individual. At
a certain size (which?), talk of democracy is misguided. This idea has
a long historical pedigree, and finds its apotheosis in the argument—
often attributed to Aristotle and then Rousseau—that democracy is
impossible except in small groups.[95] Indeed, the association of genuine
democracy with small groups tends to dominate our imaginations,
perhaps because of the resonant image of the Athenian forum (*agora*).

Implicit in this primal romantic vision is a certain idea of inclusion:
the more direct each person's input into a political process the better
its outcomes embody his or her wishes, interests, and/or will. This
idea gains political currency in the hands of those who favour non-
cosmopolitan institutions of government (e.g. states) on the grounds

[95] See J. J. Rousseau, *The Social Contract*, M. Cranston, trans. (London:
Penguin, 1968), Book 4, 149–87.

that such institutions are more democratic than larger ones, since each person's views and interests can count more. I wish to dispute the idea that scale undermines political representation and decreases citizen control over political decisions. I shall argue that this idea gains its force from serious deficiencies internal to the presently dominant theories of democracy. I shall try to develop a more plausible theory of democracy—one that complements and is even required by a cosmopolitan theory of global justice. On this theory of democracy, greater scale could contribute to better quality representation and citizenship.

This argument, in combination with a continuing critique of nationalist and statist conceptions of justice and democracy, defeats those objections to cosmopolitanism that appeal to the values of collective and individual 'self-determination'. If we do not succumb to pessimism about the effects of scale, it becomes clear that cosmopolitan principles and institutions are not only compatible with but can better realise both values.

My extended argument to establish and outline this possibility takes the following route: I begin with an explication and critique of deliberative democracy, largely as articulated by its most prominent exponent, Jürgen Habermas. Deliberative democracy is at present the leading normative democratic theory, and is thought by many to supply the conceptual foundations for democratisation of the global order. I show that deliberative democrats fail to take seriously the problems and opportunities of scale, and that this theory cannot provide firm foundations for deepening and globalising democracy. It is particularly important to focus on Habermas because he himself is not opposed to a strong role for large and encompassing institutions, and he does think they can be democratised.[96] However, Habermas's conceptual schema still succumbs to the mirage of the forum: he conceives of actual, real-time institutions of public reasoning as attempts to maximise direct participation in public decision-making. This creates insuperable difficulties for his theory as soon as it confronts problems of numbers, time, information, and understanding—problems that arise in any remotely large-scale and pluralistic society.

In order to rescue the theory, deliberative theorists turn to five modified conceptions of deliberation; but each fails because representation continues to be understood as an attempt to 'mirror' direct

---

[96] J. Habermas, *The Inclusion of the Other: Studies in Political Theory*, C. Cronin and P. De Grieff, trans. (Cambridge, MA: MIT Press, 1998), 126–7 and 146–51.

participation. I argue that this conception of democracy is metaphysically overblown, epistemologically deficient, psychologically overly demanding, and operationally unfeasible. Does the failure of deliberative democracy force us to revert to the 'thin' theories of democracy (Popper's Minimalism, Schumpeter's Elitism) that dominated the field before the Habermasian intervention? In Chapters 3 and 4, I argue not. By taking account of crucial metaphysical, epistemological, psychological, and operational constraints relevant to public reasoning, it is possible to develop a conception of 'representation as responsiveness'. This innovative conception, combined with the theory of cosmopolitan justice presented in Chapter 1, forms the basis for a theory of Responsive Democracy that could realistically orient the democratisation of great and global institutions.

2. Does Habermas Demand Too Much of Persons and Institutions?

Democracy 'is one (very broadly defined) form of being ruled . . . It is not, and cannot be, an alternative to being ruled'.[97] It could not be otherwise: government exists because of a shared need to make collective, binding decisions—democracy is a way of meeting, not removing, this need. Decisions will not be binding unless those subject to them can be coerced to comply; thus the question of what makes a form of government legitimate is not whether we can do without coercion (*pace* anarchism), but rather how such coercion can be justified.[98] Habermas puts this well when, following Kant, he maintains that it is a precondition of legitimate law that those subject to it are able to view it and be motivated by it under two perspectives, the factual and the normative: 'They can either consider [legal] norms merely as factual constraints on their freedom and take a strategic approach to the calculable consequences of possible rule violations, or they can comply with legal statutes in a performative attitude, indeed

[97] J. Dunn, 'Situating Democratic Political Accountability', in A. Przeworski, S. Stokes, and B. Manin, eds., *Democracy, Accountability and Representation* (Cambridge: Cambridge University Press, 1999), 342.

[98] Justification of the latter kind does not remove the fact that addressees *must* comply (whether they wish to or not). Rousseau is often, rightly or wrongly, taken to be the villain of the piece (and the peace) for obscuring the fact that justifying coercion does not eliminate it. This elision achieves particular poignancy where human judgements and interests are irreconcilably plural and often conflicting (i.e. if Isaiah Berlin is to be believed, almost everywhere and almost always).

comply out of respect for results of a common will formation that claim legitimacy'.[99]

Democracy is not the only interpretation of the last part of this statement. Almost every form of government purports to be the most suitable mechanism for forming and acting on the 'common will'; and democratic governments are hardly distinctive in claiming to 'represent' this will. From Solon to Kim Il Sung, it is difficult to find a government that does not make the normative claim that it is 'acting in the best interests of the public, in a manner responsive to them'—to cite Hannah Pitkin's memorable definition of representation.[100] So what then is distinctive about democracy, and in what special sense is its contemporary form supposed to be representative?

This question is complicated and lent an unprecedented urgency by two striking historical facts mentioned in my Introduction. First, democracy is now the most widely accepted form of legitimation for modern political rule, even while the theoretical underpinnings of purportedly democratic regimes are markedly at odds with their practices. Second, the issues and institutions that impact on the world's inhabitants increasingly transcend, bypass, and even overwhelm the state—the traditional formal locus of democracy. This is why, in our time, the pressing set of problems becomes not only *what* democracy is and ought to be but also *where* it is and ought to be.[101]

---

[99] Habermas, *Inclusion*, 255. Habermas's interpretation of the Kantian conception of legality is, however, a far cry from Kant's own conception of legality; see O. O'Neill, *Bounds of Justice* (Cambridge: Cambridge University Press, 2000), 65–80.

[100] H. Pitkin, *The Concept of Representation* (Berkeley and Los Angeles, CA: University of California Press, 1967), 210. I thank Eric Hobsbawm for pointing out a notable exception: theocratic governments do not necessarily claim to represent the collective will.

[101] This increased problematisation of the location of democratic rule seems to constitute part of a third stage in the development of democracy. A rough institutional history might be outlined as follows: In the first stage, until the eighteenth century, *laws and policies* are selected, and subject to amendment, by those governed within a *city state* (see J. Elster, 'Accountability in Athenian Politics', in A. Przeworski, S. Stokes, and B. Manin, eds., *Democracy, Accountability, and Representation* (Cambridge: Cambridge University Press, 1999) and Q. Skinner, 'The Italian City-Republics', in J. Dunn, ed., *Democracy: The Unfinished Journey, 508BC to 1993AD* (Oxford: Oxford University Press, 1992)). In the second stage, from the eighteenth to the late twentieth century, emphasis is placed on how *rulers are elected* and subject to regular re-election by the governed, within a *nation-state* (see Habermas, *Inclusion*, 105–26; C. S. Maier, 'Democracy since the French Revolution', in J. Dunn, ed., *Democracy: The Unfinished Journey, 508BC to 1993AD* (Oxford: Oxford University Press, 1992)).

Deliberative democratic theory is presented by its major exponents as a consistent answer to both sorts of problems.[102] In the next section, I argue that because of irremediable flaws in its conceptualisation of democracy, deliberative theory is a misleading and inadequate aid to identifying the proper loci of democratic rule. But in the present section I first provide a general outline of deliberative theory in what I and many others take to be its most sophisticated (Habermasian) form. Only then is it possible to offer a critique of deliberative theory that does not—as is all too popular—caricature its form and force.

Since communicative ethics in one or another form provides the historical and conceptual basis for deliberative democratic theories, we can begin by delineating its basic features. Exponents of communicative ethics share with cosmopolitan liberals the view that the moral community is universal: the ambit of moral concern includes everyone who could be capable of practical reasoning. The crucial difference is that, on the Habermasian interpretation, we cannot discern our own interests or those of others or our common interests, nor can we discover the appropriate collective action norms through which to realise those interests, unless we engage in actual public discussion oriented towards reaching mutual understanding and agreement.

In the third, presently emergent stage the idea seems to be that the governed subject public institutions and rulers to multiple 'accountability regimes' within a system of 'global governance' (see D. Held, *Democracy and the Global Order* (Cambridge: Polity Press, 1995)). Each stage might be seen as superseding the last even while incorporating some of its central components: election retains voting, but voting becomes predominantly a mechanism for selecting legislators rather than laws directly; accountability regimes retain election, but elections are treated predominantly as indirect mechanisms, for regulating institutions (e.g. political parties) through which rulers as role-players are in turn constrained. It should be obvious that these three stages are not entirely distinct from one another in practice but are analytic tools for distinguishing certain political modes as more valent than others. My purpose here is not to narrate this historical story but rather to contribute to a better conceptualisation of this third alternative, moving the discussion on from brute 'accountability' to more complex 'responsiveness'.

[102] Here I am thinking particularly about Jurgen Habermas, Thomas McCarthy, Joshua Cohen, Seyla Benhabib, James Bohman, and James Fishkin. That they have attempted to answer both sorts of problems is not a function of mere intellectual over-inclusion or ambition. Given the historical story outlined in the previous footnote, which shows democratic conceptions and practices to be closely tied to the locus of legitimate rule, it would be odd indeed if an important contemporary theory of the nature of democracy provided little guidance on the location of democracy.

The argument for this conclusion elaborates the following propositions: (1) No transcendental and universally agreed foundation for reason and morality can be discovered. (2) In order to validate our value-orientations and norms, we can only draw on unavoidable features of common practices that we already share. (3) Since persons under modern conditions of pluralism do not already have any notion of the good in common, those shared features 'shrink to the fund of formal features of the performatively shared situation of deliberation'. (4) Primary amongst the formal presuppositions of such rational discourse is that it is pragmatic in the sense that it aims at being comprehensible and convincing to all participants, motivating them to act on its results. (5) Rational discourse motivates agents not via sanctions or incentives to behave in one way or another, but rather via 'the illocutionary binding/bonding effect (*Bindungseffekt*)' of speech acts that constitute 'offers' of intersubjective recognition of validity claims.[103] (6) Therefore, where normative statements could prove acceptable to every participant in rational discourse, they can be presumed to be valid (comprehensible, convincing, and motivating) action norms. Hence the *Discourse Principle*: 'Only those norms can claim validity that could meet with the acceptance of all concerned in practical discourse.'[104]

The discourse principle explicates the point of view from which norms for action can be impartially grounded. But it is not clear yet why 'the justification of norms and commands requires that a *real discourse* be carried out and thus cannot occur in a strictly monological form, that is, in the form of a hypothetical process of argumentation occurring in the individual'.[105] Habermas offers two connected reasons. First, other people—even ideally motivated others—tend to have a distorted conception of one's wants and interests, the best remedy to which is one's actual participation in articulating those interests. Second, at the same time, the terms in which each person perceives and asserts their wants and interests within such a discourse must be open to actual criticism, since wants and interests are always understood against real, intersubjective background practices that an individual

---

[103] Actors make three kinds of claims to validity: to truth (about states of affairs in the 'objective' world); to rightness (about intersubjective relations in the 'social' world); and to truthfulness (about an individual's 'subjective' world of experience to which he or she has privileged access). I will not discuss Habermas's views on language, motivation, and social integration at any length here. See J. Habermas, *Discourse Ethics: Moral Consciousness and Communicative Action*, C. Lenhardt and S. W. Nicholsen, trans. (Cambridge, MA: MIT Press, 1990), esp. 58–68.

[104] Habermas, *Inclusion*, 39–46.

[105] Habermas, *Discourse Ethics*, 68 (my italics).

cannot interpret and revise on his or her own.[106] In short, since I as well as others can be 'mistaken' about my wants and interests, it is an error to privilege either first-person or third-person discernment and description. Instead of 'subject-centred notions of practical insight,' reliance is to be placed on 'the rules of discourse and forms of argumentation that borrow their normative content from the validity basis of action oriented to reaching understanding. In the final analysis, this normative content arises from the structure of linguistic communication and the communicative mode of sociation'.[107]

We might of course be concerned that the actual acceptance of norms is sometimes the result of misinformation, confusion, incapacity, inequalities of power, or some other circumstance of vulnerability. Habermas attempts to address this concern by positing the idea of an ideal speech situation, in which every participant in the discourse is willing and able to act in certain ways: to offer reasons for claims as well as to express his or her 'attitudes, desires, and needs'; to consider the reasons offered by others for their claims; to modify claims solely on the basis of the better argument; to seek an agreed decision; and to comply with the results.[108] It is a condition of this discourse that participants are free from constraints both external (e.g. the threat of force) and internal (e.g. debilitating neuroses), such that 'there is a symmetrical distribution of chances to select and employ speech acts . . . an effective equality of opportunity for the assumption of dialogue roles'.[109] Habermas is *not* suggesting—as some critics have supposed—that this situation is ever achieved in reality.[110] Rather, the ideal speech situation functions at once as the unavoidable supposition of discourse and as an

---

[106] Ibid., 67–8. 'From the very start, communicative acts are located within the horizon of shared, unproblematic beliefs . . . The constant upset of disappointment and contradiction, contingency and critique in everyday life crashes against a sprawling, deeply set, and unshakable rock of background assumptions, loyalties, and skills' (see, for this marvellously mixed metaphor about the relation between discourse and lifeworld, J. Habermas, *Between Facts and Norms: Contributions to a Discourse Theory of Law and Democracy*, W. Rehg, trans. (Cambridge: Polity Press, 1996), 22).

[107] The first quotation is from W. Rehg, *Insight and Solidarity: The Discourse Ethics of Jurgen Habermas* (Berkeley, CA: University of California Press, 1994), 15; the second is from Habermas, *Facts and Norms*, 296–7.

[108] Habermas, *Discourse Ethics*, 89.

[109] T. McCarthy, *The Critical Theory of Jürgen Habermas* (Cambridge, MA: MIT Press, 1978), 306.

[110] These critics are not entirely to blame, however: they have been misled in part by Habermas's promiscuous use of the term 'deliberation' to refer both to this epistemic level and to actual public reasoning in a real-world democracy.

epistemic device: all actual modes of discourse aimed at justifying norms must presume and be judged against this *counterfactual* ideal.[111]

Deliberative democracy is only one way in which this ideal is to be 'operationalised'; in this case, so that it can orient 'the deliberations of political legislators'. The distinction is crucial. The discourse principle can and must be 'interpreted' and 'applied' in different ways depending on the subject matter (e.g. law versus morality).[112] Communicative ethics, then, offers a general answer to the question 'how is any norm validated?' whereas deliberative democracy, although guided by that answer, responds to a more specific question: 'how can the people make the law?' The task of the deliberative theorist is to elucidate the ideals as well as the communication procedures and institutions that could best approximate the ideal speech situation in actual conditions where the aim is to derive 'valid' legal and policy norms.[113]

Deliberative theorists evoke three ideals that seem to best approximate the ideal speech situation—'rational legislation, participatory politics, and civic self-governance'[114]—each of which can be understood more particularly as follows. First, each citizen must be prepared to give publicly accessible reasons for favouring certain political outcomes, they must be open to revising these views in the light of

---

[111] The idealisation is supposed to serve as a 'methodological fiction in order to obtain a foil against which the substratum of *unavoidable* social complexity becomes visible' (Habermas, *Facts and Norms*, 323). The question, of course, is whether Habermas can make good the claim that a tension between ideal discourse, on the one hand, and a requirement for actual dialogue, on the other, is revealing rather than destabilising when it comes to public reasoning.

[112] The Discourse Principle is 'operationalised' with respect to the particular subject matter of *morality* via the Principle of Universalisation: '(U) A norm is valid when the foreseeable consequences and side effects of its general observance for the interests and value-orientations of each individual could be jointly accepted by all concerned without coercion' (Habermas, *Inclusion*, 45–6). The latter principle has been emphasised increasingly by Habermas in his later work, in part to avoid the problems and misunderstandings that beset the ideal speech situation (discussed below). But (U) is not directly applicable to *political* or *legal* norms. Indeed, the latter are supposed to compensate for 'the cognitive indeterminacy, motivational insecurity and the limited coordinating power of moral norms and informal norms of action in general' (Habermas, cited in J. Bohman, *Public Deliberation: Pluralism, Complexity, and Democracy* (Cambridge, MA: MIT Press, 1996), 13).

[113] Habermas insists that this is 'just *one* action system among others', such as the economic system; the political system is neither 'the peak nor the center, nor even . . . the structuring model of society' (Habermas, *Inclusion*, 251).

[114] J. Bohman and W. Rehg, eds., *Deliberative Democracy: Essays on Reason and Politics* (Cambridge, MA: MIT Press, 1997), ix.

reasons and criticisms offered by others, they must attempt to offer reasons persuasive to all and thereby to arrive at a consensus, and—failing that—they must be prepared to forgo the application of their convictions unless and until a majority concurs.[115] Second, citizens must be substantively equal in an extensive sense:

Everyone with the deliberative capacities has equal standing at each stage of the deliberative process. Each can put issues on the agenda, propose solutions, and offer reasons in support of or in criticism of the proposals. And ... the existing distribution of power and resources does not shape their chances to contribute to deliberation, nor does that distribution play an authoritative role in their deliberation.[116]

Third and finally, citizens regard themselves as bound only by the results and conditions of this process of exchanging reasons. Since citizens already accept the preconditions of the actual attempt to come to an understanding, and its implications, and since citizens are able to put forward any validity claims and subject any validity claims to critique, there is adequate reason for contributing to and acting on the norms that are produced and confirmed by this deliberative process. Thus motivated and constrained, members of an ongoing, pluralistic association are thought to be able to freely and collectively generate norms that are also—precisely for that reason—authoritative. Deliberative theorists take it that in this way they have revealed a necessary 'internal relation' between sovereignty (understood as the making of authoritative legal norms) and democratic will formation.[117]

Some deliberative theorists, and some of their critics, have understood the three ideals above as unmediated bases for political action; again, this is to caricature deliberative theory. We must distinguish the three ideals—which constitute an interpretation of the discourse principle so that it applies to the political system—from the actual communicative processes and institutions through which the three ideals are operationalised in any particular social context. (Habermas is

---

[115] Habermas speaks of a 'conditional consensus' and cites Frobel: 'Certainly one does not require that the minority, by resigning their will, declare their opinion to be incorrect; indeed, one does not even require that they abandon their aims, but rather ... that they forego the practical application of their convictions until they succeed in better establishing their reasons and procuring the necessary number of affirmative votes' (J. Habermas, 'Popular Sovereignty as Procedure', in Bohman and Rehg, eds., *Deliberative Democracy*, 47).

[116] J. Cohen, 'Deliberation and Democratic Legitimacy', in Bohman and Rehg, eds., *Deliberative Democracy: Essays on Reason and Politics* (Cambridge, MA: MIT Press, 1997), 74.

[117] Habermas, *Inclusion*, 253–64.

particularly critical of Rousseau for conflating 'the introduction of a new principle of legitimacy' with 'proposals for institutionalising just rule'.)[118] These actual mechanisms operate in two domains: 'informal networks of the public sphere' and 'institutionalised deliberation in parliamentary bodies'. A brief characterisation of these domains brings us directly to the problems I want to consider.

Habermas has lamented the disintegration and deformation of the public sphere, and pursued its reinvigoration as the central political task, ever since his *Habilitationsschrift*. Here he shares with many champions of 'civil society' the aim of characterising and 'mobilising' a domain of interaction that voids or avoids especially the unequal power relations of 'state' (legal) and 'market' (exchange) 'action-systems', and that operates as a regulative and countervailing force to those systems. In its most recent formulation: 'The public sphere can best be described as a network for [freely] communicating information and points of view (i.e. opinions expressing affirmative or negative attitudes); the streams of communication are, in the process, filtered and synthesized in such a way that they coalesce into bundles of topically specified *public* opinions'.[119]

It is not, then, an 'institution' or an 'organisation' or even a 'framework of norms with differentiated competences and roles'; nor is it reducible to 'forums, stages, arenas . . . concrete locales where an audience is physically gathered'. The public sphere is in fact only constituted to the extent that information and points of view 'are uncoupled from the thick contexts of simple interactions' so as to 'extend to the virtual presence of scattered readers, listeners, or viewers linked by public media'. In this 'abstract' public sphere, and in more 'episodic' and 'occasional' interactions—from 'coffee houses' to 'rock concerts'— information and arguments can then be 'worked into focused opinions' about how we should live together: 'What makes such "bundled" opinions into *public opinion* is both the controversial way it comes about and the amount of approval that "carries" it . . . [but] only if . . . [that approval is] preceded by a focused public debate and a corresponding opinion-formation'.[120]

---

[118] J. Habermas, *Communication and the Evolution of Society* (Boston: Beacon, 1979), 186.

[119] Habermas, *Facts and Norms*, 360. On the early history of Habermas's conception of the public sphere, see McCarthy, *Habermas*, esp. 381–3.

[120] Habermas, *Facts and Norms*, 361–2 and 373–4. The public sphere plays two major roles: (1) 'the [joint] detection, identification, and interpretation of problems affecting society as a whole', and (2) the generation of what Habermas calls *ethical* self-understanding, by discerning and clarifying the interests and

All this seems very far from a description of current societies, but we might begin to be suspicious that it is not even a plausible description of and prescription for *any possible* large-scale and pluralistic society, confronted with a need for decisions. For one thing, under conditions of cultural and social pluralism, as Habermas acknowledges, 'a common will is produced . . . not just [via] ethical self-clarification but also [via] the balancing of interests and compromise, the purposive choice of means, moral justification, and legal consistency-testing'.[121] Habermas assures us that there is nothing to worry about: there is a place in his account for 'representative' legislative and judicial institutions that generate actionable and enforceable decisions.

These institutions enable more contained and constrained forms of public reasoning, by a smaller number of agents, structured in a more hierarchical fashion—in a situation where some ethical 'interests and value-orientations . . . conflict with one another within the same polity without any prospect of consensual resolution'.[122] It is merely that the resulting decisions are legitimate because such reasoning 'incorporates', 'proceeds from', and 'lead[s] back to' the reasoning of citizens in the public sphere.[123] Notice that this is not a mere requirement that decision-making *procedures* and *actors* are to be selected by citizens (although it is that too); the requirement is far, far stronger. Citizens must endorse the substantive ends and means chosen: 'The enlightenment of political will can become effective only within the communication of citizens. For the articulation of needs in accordance with technical knowledge can be ratified exclusively *in the consciousness of the political actors themselves*. Experts cannot delegate to themselves this act.'[124]

---

value-orientations of participants as members of shared forms of life—'a particular nation, . . . a community or a state, . . . a region, etc., which traditions they wish to cultivate, how they should treat each other, minorities, and marginal groups, in what sort of society they want to live' (Habermas, *Inclusion*, 240–5).

[121] Habermas, *Inclusion*, 244–5.

[122] The paradigm case of such intransigent disagreement for Habermas, as for Rawls, is religious conviction. It is not at all clear that the use of religion as the prime exemplar serves us well, since religious action tends to (indeed, is often designed to) conflate the notions of practice, culture, tradition, and institution. A much better—more differentiated and revealing—case here may be that of architecture; see Z. Emmerich, 'Architecture as a Social Contract', *Scroope: Cambridge Architectural Journal*, Vol. 11 (1999), 32–9.

[123] See McCarthy, *Habermas*, 15.

[124] Habermas, 'The Scientization of Politics and Public Opinion', *Towards a Rational Society* (Boston: Heinemann Educational, 1971), 75 (italics in original).

It is at this point, with this strong participatory requirement, that deliberative theorists run into the problems of scale. Any attempt to identify actual procedures and institutions that enable ideal deliberation faces constraints on numbers, time, and distance; these become pressing practical problems in any remotely large-scale and pluralistic society. A quick calculation from Robert Dahl makes the deliberative ideal seem grievously optimistic even in a tiny state: 'if an association were to make one decision a day allow ten hours a day for discussion, and permit each member just ten minutes—rather extreme assumptions . . . —then the association could not have more than sixty members.'[125]

Athenian democracy has perhaps come closest to satisfying such extreme assumptions; but it is not necessary here to rehearse its many failures, its unrepeatability, and its inappropriateness as a model for vast and pluralist modern societies.[126]

What 'representative' institutions and procedures bridge the gap between public sphere and legislative decision? For instance, in what way does the communicative action and situation in legislative institutions 'correspond to'—to use another elusive Habermasian phrase— that of citizens in the public sphere? Here deliberative democrats have to respond with a plausible *institutional* account that meets the demanding criteria of being both workable and structured by the three ideals of rational legislation, participatory politics, and civic self-governance. It is of course true that the relevant institutions will differ depending on the social–historical context; but we need to know whether such institutions *could ever exist* in pluralistic societies of any scale.

A popular move by deliberative democrats, when confronted with dangers of impracticability, is to try to head off this line of inquiry entirely by saying something along the following lines: 'But Habermas acknowledges that the formal, administrative sphere is necessarily characterised by hierarchical relations, which make government role allocation and decision possible. He is simply saying that "the definitive institution of democracy" is the public sphere, while "rights, representation, voting, and balances of power . . . are important . . . primarily as

---

[125] R. Dahl, *After the Revolution?* (New Haven, CT: Yale University Press, 1970), 67–8.

[126] Most notably, slavery and the subordination of women were necessary conditions for the propertied men to be at the forum, deliberating. (On the severe limitations of Athenian democracy see J. Dunn, 'Conclusion' and J. Elster, 'Athenian Politics', both in J. Dunn, ed., *Democracy*. Habermas himself is critical of Republican ideas that presume that the whole people in a modern society could be assembled together (Habermas, *Inclusion*, 239–52)).

means of enabling public spheres".[127] And what is implausible about the argument that all individuals can and should participate in that informal sphere? Many of us already do participate actively in something like it.'

This defensive theorist might continue: 'As for the exact representative institutions and procedures, Habermas presents what seems a familiar institutional picture: "Informal opinion-formation result[s] in institutionalised election decisions and legislative decrees through which communicatively generated power is transformed into administratively utilizable power."[128] An extensive system of rights, a separation of powers including judicial review, support for various aspects of civil society, and a deep attachment to constitutionalism and constitutional courts (all explicated at great length by Habermas in his tome *Between Facts and Norms*) will enable this process in contemporary conditions.'[129] Joshua Cohen put the point as follows: Do not all normative theories of democracy face the same issue, namely how to understand and design electoral procedures and representative structures that convert citizens' informal judgements at elections and between elections into authoritative formal decisions?[130]

I think the answer here is a resounding 'no'. Many of the terms used in the last quotation from Habermas no longer mean what we normally take them to mean—they are much more demanding. 'Opinion', for instance, now means not any views we come to hold but the set of views that arises and survives after a stringent process of interactive reasoning in which there is potentially 'universal' participation. And, as we have seen, the 'decrees' issuing from legislative institutions can only derive their justification by first incorporating and expressing the 'validating' communicative rationality of the public sphere. That is precisely what is unique about deliberative conceptions of democracy, in contrast to liberal conceptions—as Habermas is at great pains to point out.

On liberal conceptions, according to Habermas, the 'focus is not so much [on] the input of a rational political will-formation but [on] the output of successful administrative accomplishments'.[131]

---

[127] M. Warren, 'The Self in Discursive Democracy', in S. White, ed., *The Cambridge Companion to Habermas* (Cambridge: Cambridge University Press, 1995), 171.

[128] Ibid., 249–51. This institutional picture will seem remarkably familiar to theorists and observers of German social democracy; and, ironically, much less familiar to theorists of radical democracy.

[129] Habermas, *Facts and Norms*, esp. chapters 7 and 8, 287–387.

[130] I thank Josh Cohen for pressing me on this (paraphrased) point.

[131] Habermas, *Inclusion*, 247. For Habermas, the liberal conception involves the input of whatever individuals happen to *prefer*. In the next chapter, I show

Representatives identify and pursue what they take to be citizens' interests, and citizens decide—generally in retrospect—whether the basic judgements and overall efforts of representatives were adequate, and whether they are likely to remain so. On deliberative conceptions, in contrast, the interests that are pursued and the judgements that are made by representatives must be recognisably those that citizens have themselves *already* discovered, interpreted, and confirmed. In order for this demanding interpretation of sovereign popular decision to be achieved, it is necessary to show that citizens could in fact give their assent to legislative and policy norms in some way.[132] Otherwise, the three ideals that purportedly interpret the Discourse Principle (so that it is applicable in the domain of politics) run the risk of being lovely but misleading fantasies.

The next section concentrates on five basic strategies adopted by proponents who wish to rescue deliberative democracy as a realistic ideal to be instituted in contemporary conditions. All these strategies are aimed at enabling citizens' deliberations and decisions to be incorporated into public decisions by actors in representative institutions. If all of these strategies fail, as I argue they do, then we must find another regulative ideal—one that, I shall show, includes a thicker conception of representation and a different conception of knowledge about interests—in order to avoid misdirecting efforts at global democratisation. While deliberative democratic theory contains some useful insights, the theory as a whole must be abandoned if it cannot avoid making the purportedly 'best' the enemy of the right.

3. The Deliberative Hall of Mirrors

> O, that deceit should dwell in such a gorgeous palace!
>
> *Romeo and Juliet*, III. ii.

Can the deliberative idea of a highly active role for citizens in generating and validating public decision be redeemed in practice? The last section

---

that this understanding of liberal democratic representation is caricatural, and I attempt to present a plausible liberal alternative.

[132] Shifting modality from 'could' to 'would' does not solve the problem. For instance, Thomas McCarthy writes: 'The point is, rather, to find in each set of concrete circumstances institutional arrangements that justify the presumption that basic political decisions would meet with the agreement of all those affected by them if they were able to participate without restriction in discursive will-formation.' (McCarthy, *Habermas*, 332). It must be shown that this last clause is not nonsense (e.g. the clause must not require agents who are not at all like human beings).

made it clear that attempts to fob off the criticism of institutional impracticability will not do. If deliberative theorists are as unconcerned as they claim, why are they—as will become evident—spilling so much ink on trying to develop mechanisms that satisfy a requirement of practicability? The answer is that if it could *never* make any sense at all to talk of a public decision to which all in a large society could actually assent in the ways deliberative theorists suppose, then there is no prospect of the fully shared identification and interpretation of interests that deliberative democracy posits. For deliberative theorists would then be claiming what is in effect a contradiction: that validation takes place through a potentially fully inclusive process but in which not all citizens could ever actually be included. Either citizens play the primary generative role of identifying and interpreting norms for the purposes of action, or they do not; it cannot be both ways. If inclusion does not have the strong sense suggested here, then deliberative theorists are saying virtually nothing different from liberal democrats.[133] Deliberative theorists cannot, therefore, avoid the need to redeem a claim of practical possibility. They must supply an account of mechanisms by which inclusive deliberation can be achieved, not just in the public sphere but by having citizens' decisions there worked up through representative institutions and procedures into public decisions.

In this section, I begin by identifying five strategies for rescuing deliberative democracy as a relevant ideal. Here I follow the fivefold classification of Robert Goodin, himself a deliberative democrat.[134] I then show how each strategy fails in turn. Each failure provides us with a lesson as to the constraints on participation, and as to how these constraints form broad parameters for a more adequate account of representation.

The first two strategies aim to reduce the number of people deliberating together. Strategy one is *serial deliberation*: Have citizens

---

[133] They would of course be saying the same things as liberals in different terms. This leads to implausible formulations at times, such as 'expert legislative subcommittees are merely a part of the conversation'.

[134] Goodin offers a friendly criticism of four strategies, designed to make room for his fifth alternative to supplement them. I am indebted in this section to his excellent analysis. However, I try to show not only that his alternative strategy fails to rescue deliberative democracy, but that a critique of the four other strategies can cut much deeper than he thinks, undermining the idea of deliberative democracy as a regulative ideal altogether. My labels for each kind of deliberation also diverge from Goodin's, in the interests of what I hope is clarity. See R. Goodin, 'Democratic Deliberation Within', *Philosophy and Public Affairs*, Vol. 29, No. 1 (2000), 81–109.

deliberate directly—as Aristotle suggests—'not all in one body, but by turns', thereby reducing the number of citizens with whom each citizen has to engage at any one time.[135] Each small, partial, and over-lapping group or association makes separate judgements that then serve as inputs both into other similar groups' deliberations and into a decisive 'meta-deliberation'.[136] The outcome of that meta-deliberation is purportedly representative.

Strategy two is *substitute deliberation*: As J. S. Mill suggests, replace deliberation between all citizens with that between a subset of partic-ipants that accurately reflects the demography and range of views of all.[137] The decision of this 'microcosm'—for instance, of a citizens' jury—is thought to be binding because it identifies what decision everybody would have made if fully inclusive deliberation had been feasible.[138] Since the deliberators are a fair sample of the citizenry, the decisional outcomes are purportedly representative.

The third and fourth strategies aim to reduce not the number of synchronic deliberators but rather how much they communicate. Strategy three is *restrictive deliberation*: Place limits on what infor-mation is admissible, thereby reducing the range of issues to be dis-cussed and the considerations relevant to each issue. This strategy

---

[135] Aristotle, *The Politics*, Carnes Lord, trans. (Chicago and London: University of Chicago Press, 1984), Book 4, 122–8.

[136] For versions of serial deliberation, see J. Cohen and C. Sabel, 'Directly-Deliberative Polyarchy', *European Law Journal*, Vol. 3, No. 4 (1997), 313–42; I. M. Young, 'Together in Difference: Transforming the Logic of Group Political Conflict', in W. Kymlicka, ed., *The Rights of Minority Cultures* (Oxford: Oxford University Press, 1995); J. Dryzek, 'Political Inclusion and the Dynamics of Democratisation', *American Political Science Review*, Vol. 90 (1996), 475–87; J. Cohen and J. Rogers, *Associations and Democracy*, E. O. Wright, ed. (London: Verso, 1995).

[137] J. S. Mill, *Considerations on Representative Government* (New York: Prometheus, 1991).

[138] Here the most prominent institutional mechanisms are legislatures or rep-resentative assemblies, but recent theory and practice have revivified citizens' juries and deliberative polling. See J. Fishkin, *Democracy and Deliberation: New Directions for Democratic Reform* (New Haven, CT: Yale University Press, 1991) and *The Voice of the People: Public Opinion and Democracy* (New Haven, CT: Yale University Press, 1995). For a positive assessment of citizens' juries, see A. Coote and J. Lenaghan, *Citizens' Juries: Theory into Practice* (London: Institute for Public Policy Research, 1997). For a highly critical evaluation, which concludes that 'juries promote not so much a critically detached view as a particular evaluative framework suited to the bureaucratic idiom of social wel-fare maximisation', see D. Price, 'Choices Without Reasons: Citizens' Juries and Policy Evaluation', *Journal of Medical Ethics*, Vol. 26 (2000), 272–6.

typically involves quantitative criteria (e.g. restrictions on the length and number of speeches) and qualitative criteria (e.g. rules of germaneness), combined with more or less independent application of these criteria by intermediaries.[139]

Strategy four is *selective deliberation*: Create an intermediary forum (such as a journal or Internet site) where people can post notices and reply to one another's notices. There will then be 'selective uptake' by participants, with those issues and arguments that are most salient percolating to the top. The outcomes from this strategy, as for strategy three, are purportedly representative in that participants have considered the restricted class of relevant information and arguments.

The final strategy is *internalised deliberation*: Enable each deliberator to undertake separately 'empathetic imagining' of potential interlocutors' points of view, which serves as a supplement or substitute for actual engagement with others.[140] Practical approaches include educating citizens' sensibilities—for example, through public subsidies for the arts, and by encouraging people to read great works of fiction. Much deliberation can then supposedly be processed in the 'forum' of a mind sensitive to competing reasons and not in the public domain itself. The claim is that this eases both the informational and the numerical burdens of deliberation; and, since participants consider each other's reasons fully, the results of voting include consideration of everybody and are 'representative'.

We have, then, five purported solutions before us: serial deliberation (in turns), substitute deliberation (by a microcosm), restrictive deliberation (limiting information), selective deliberation (limiting uptake), and internalised deliberation (empathetic imagining of interaction). Many of these ideas and mechanisms must play crucial roles in large-scale democracies, but they face insuperable difficulties *as mechanisms and models of inclusive, rational deliberation* of any scope. I now want to elaborate these difficulties by tracing them to a common source: a failure to take seriously the nature of and constraints on actual communication.

There is a bad way to approach this topic. Many writers about politics have gone seriously wrong by arguing that real conversation is a good model for discursive procedures that aim to generate political

---

[139] Intermediaries such as international negotiators and parliamentary speakers might filter out everything from insults to exaggerated demands in order to facilitate productive discussion and perhaps bring parties to an agreement; see O. R. Young, *The Intermediaries: Third Parties in International Crises* (Princeton, NJ: Princeton University Press, 1967).

[140] The purpose of Goodin, 'Deliberation Within', is to develop this strategy.

decisions. In several ways, it is not. Conversation tends to have some kind of expressive or aesthetic function—to edify, to entertain, to console, to show social recognition, and so forth—which is not intrinsic to the objectives of a public political institution.[141] Conversely, conversation lacks the fundamental objective that is the generative source of public institutions: no coercive, collective decision has to be made. This to some extent explains the structure of conversations: they tend to range unsystematically over a wide range of issues, often without seeking or finding any resolution for differences in viewpoint. Conversation involves more allusive 'loose talk', aimed at describing, illuminating, rehearsing, etc., rather than necessarily at bringing about assent to the truth of propositions.[142] Public reasoning is often, and always ought to be, more strictly continuous and consistent: coercion raises questions of justification, to which only some kind of systematic and presumptively conclusive reason-giving is adequate.[143]

All that said, conversation and public reasoning do share important features and constraints that imperil the inflationary deliberative account of democracy. Talk can never be rid entirely of its looseness: even a deductive argument has to be 'completed' or 'made sense of' by the listener or reader, who must interpret the 'implicatures' contained in the speaker's utterances.[144] (Where the listener or reader cannot do so, confusion results: consider Alice's befuddlement in Wonderland.) Yet in order to do so, the listener must assume that the utterances of

---

[141] There is of course an important sense in which a social ethos of conformity or fearful silence does reduce public participation; but there is strong empirical evidence that—even in the absence of a hostile environment of this kind—discussions amongst friends and family and the like are driven by concerns and modes of interaction that are very different from the kinds of considerations and argument even vaguely appropriate to legislative decision. See D. A. Scheufele, 'Deliberation or Dispute? An Exploratory Study Examining Dimensions of Public Opinion Expression', *International Journal of Public Opinion Research*, Vol. 11, No. 1 (1999), 25–58; also R. O. Wyatt, J. Kim, and E. Katz, 'How Feeling Free to Talk Affects Ordinary Political Conversation, Purposeful Argumentation, and Civic Participation', *Journalism and Mass Communication Quarterly*, Vol. 77, No. 1 (2000), 99–114.

[142] The term 'loose talk' is from D. Sperber and D. Wilson, 'Loose Talk', *Proceedings of the Aristotelian Society*, Vol. 86 (1986), 153–71. On differences in the structure and purposes of speech acts, see J. L. Austin, *How to Do Things with Words* (Oxford: Clarendon Press, 1962).

[143] Rawls, 'Idea', 576–7.

[144] See P. Grice, *Studies in the Way of Words* (Cambridge, MA: Harvard University Press, 1989), 22–40, 138–44, 269–82; and D. Lewis, 'Scorekeeping in a Language Game', *Journal of Philosophical Logic*, Vol. 8 (1979), 339–59. For further discussion, see Goodin, 'Deliberation Within', 93–4.

the speaker or writer proceed from a more or less coherent nesting of background propositions; she must further supply the outlines of this unexpressed background, either by simulating what it is like to be 'inside' the other's mind or by adopting a folk psychological theory of some of its contents.[145] Such interpretative action is required whether or not those others are understood in terms of 'generalised' roles or 'particular' viewpoints.[146] In the context of large-scale linguistic inter-action, this need for a construal of other minds becomes extremely— and worryingly—demanding. Habermas, for instance, insists that it is a precondition of moral and political justification that

everyone is required to take the perspective of everyone else, and thus project herself into the understandings of self and world of all others ... from this interlocking of perspectives there emerges an ideally extended 'we-perspective' from which all can test in common whether they wish to make a controver-sial norm the basis of their shared practice; and this should include mutual criticism of the appropriateness of the languages in terms of which situations and needs are interpreted.[147]

How feasible is such deep and inclusive intersubjective justification at any sort of scale? It seems beyond improbable that any person, let alone all persons, could construct the divergent sets of background assumptions necessary in order to make each and every other inter-locutor intelligible. Clearly a person could not understand a thou-sand, never mind a million or a billion, people's utterances pretty much simultaneously under conditions of pluralism. The main prob-lem is that if such deliberators *could not* even begin to understand one another, how could they possibly *integrate* all divergent views into the shared 'ideally extended "we" perspective' that Habermas claims is necessary to generate valid normative political decisions? But— assuming we do not want to be anarchists, a position profoundly anti-thetical to the Habermasian project—perhaps one or all of the five strategies above can help the deliberative account along.

Reducing the size of the group seems a promising way to ease the cognitive burdens, until we notice what is lost in serial and substitute deliberation. Goodin points out one serious problem: 'Given the path dependency of conversational dynamics, and the sheer creativity of

---

[145] See D. Davidson, *Inquiries into Truth and Interpretation* (Oxford: Clarendon Press, 1984).

[146] The distinction between generalised and particular others is that of S. Benhabib, 'Liberal Dialogue vs. a Critical Model of Discursive Legitimacy', in her *Situating the Self* (New York: Routledge, 1992).

[147] Habermas, *Inclusion*, 58.

conversing agents, it beggars belief that any one group would come to exactly the same conclusions by exactly the same route as any other.'[148]

But the most serious problem has to do with a divergence not of routes and destinations but of starting points: one of the major claims made in favour of deliberative democracy is that it is necessarily 'reflexive' and always keeps open the possibility of 'transcending' the initial terms of the question.[149] Indeed, it will often be the mark of successful deliberation that a change in the question occurs. Yet conversations can contingently proceed in any number of directions, and this has several crucial consequences. In the case of serial deliberation, reflexivity and contingency together imply that *the conclusions reached by each group in turn will be answers to different questions*. It is, further, difficult to see how answers to all these somewhat different questions could be combined, unless the meta-deliberation involves considering which formulation of the question to accept. Yet even in that case, *whichever* formulation or synthesis is accepted, it will not be the question upon which almost all the initial groups decided and judged.[150]

One might argue that the problem can be solved by careful 'agenda setting', but this raises questions of who sets the agenda.[151] Any reply must of necessity vindicate a large degree of discretion for some person or group to decide upon a fairly firm question. If there is to be no *reductio ad absurdum*, the formulation of that firm question cannot itself be subjected to popular deliberation. The needs for discretion and agenda setting (subject to only limited contestation) exist quite apart from the difficulties of dividing people into groups, making those groups typical, and ensuring that everybody gets a say. This in turn eliminates much of the distinctiveness—for example, the 'openness' and 'non-hierarchical character'[152]—claimed for the deliberative account.

---

[148] Goodin, 'Deliberation Within', 89.

[149] The central purpose of Benhabib, 'Other', is to establish this claim. For a critical analysis of these kinds of 'transcendence' and 'emancipation' claims, see R. Geuss, *The Idea of a Critical Theory: Habermas and the Frankfurt School* (Cambridge: Cambridge University Press, 1981).

[150] Arguments about which meta-deliberative mechanism is best, although important, risk distracting us from this deeper problem.

[151] D. Protess and M. McCombs, eds., *Agenda Setting* (London: Lawrence Erlbaum, 1991). The issue at this point would change dramatically; it would become 'who is entitled to constrain the reflexive capacities of the demos and on what grounds?'

[152] See, for example, Benhabib, 'Other', and the 'Introduction' in S. Benhabib, ed., *Democracy and Difference* (Princeton, NJ: Princeton University Press, 1996).

It is necessary for us to constrain to a significant extent the reflexivity *allowed* to us as the demos when it comes to *public* reasoning when it comes to any one decision. It is not enough to say 'nobody will be involved everywhere, but everyone will be involved somewhere': a much stronger demand for practical possibility has to be—and is not—cashed by deliberative democrats.

In the case of substitute deliberation, things are no better. The reflexive conclusions of a microcosm are *different answers to different questions* from those that the demos as a whole would ultimately have pronounced upon. For one thing, there is no such thing as what the demos as a whole would have decided; we have seen that deliberation at this scale is impossible for human beings. Limited as we are, we are not attempting to resolve the problems of democracy for a society of gods. For another, even assuming that the notion of 'mirroring' a vast deliberation is intelligible, this purported 'accurate reflection' would quickly dissipate. Debate is a dynamic process: 'The question is whether people who started out being representative . . . are also representative of that wider community in the ways in which they *change* over the course of the deliberation.'[153]

There is no way to ensure such dynamic direct representation. Consider the two kinds of representational device that could be adopted—numerical and non-numerical. In the former, each person in the microcosm is taken to represent a specified group of people throughout the discussion. But this would effectively preclude members of the wider community who wish to change or merge their group identifications from being represented—unless they changed in conjunction with the initial group as a whole. They cannot in this model change group identification as a result of individually persuasive argument. Yet in reality, partly because actual people construe the background of utterances differently, not everybody will be convinced by the same arguments. It is not just that this restriction risks essentialising group identities, but that this kind of model is profoundly antidemocratic insofar as it rules out free thought and free association. However, on any form of non-numerical representation, the majority achieved in a microcosm might well be a minority in the demos. Yet we have seen that it is a precondition of deliberative justification that decisions not be endorsed unless and until a majority of those affected concurs or would concur. It follows that a proportionate representation

---

[153] Goodin, 'Deliberation Within', 88. See also E. Scarry, 'The Difficulty of Imagining Other People', in M. C. Nussbaum and Respondents, *For Love of Country*, J. Cohen, ed. (Boston: Beacon Press, 1995).

of initial (pre- or proto-dialogic) attitudes is just that, and nothing more: even if a microcosm does allow for articulation of initial views, it is not a strictly representative way of *coming to* or *making* decisions.[154] Ironically, this deliberative conception is in an important sense anti-proceduralist.

But perhaps—says the foundering deliberative theorist—all these disjunctions between the demos and the microcosm should not bother us; surely the questions and answers agreed upon by a microcosm are at least those that the demos *could* have settled on? I believe that it should bother us immensely. In shifting modality, from actual to hypothetical to possible agreement, we are no longer talking about anything that can be recognisably called democracy. We are entitled to ask: The populace could imaginably agree to many things, but would or do they?![155]

Since limiting the *number* of deliberators will not work, perhaps it will help to limit the *amount* that they communicate; so let us turn to strategies three and four. There are several reasons to think that these strategies are bizarre and misguided in cutting down how much information may be supplied, in the interests of making a decision more democratically legitimate. Goodin argues, correctly, that restrictive deliberation—limiting informational inputs—would at times exclude informational inputs that are relevant to decision-making, leaving our cognitive capacities 'undernourished', and governance at risk of becoming a 'democracy of sound bites'.[156] It seems to me that if we cleave to the deliberative ideal, this is not a risk but a certainty. At scale, and where time is limited, it turns out to be impossible for any except a very tiny portion of the population to utilise their opportunity to speak, internalise, and respond to reasons at any statistically significant length. This is the case regardless of how little information is fed into the system. My optimistic calculation is that—even in one of the smaller of present states, and with only one in 50,000 people expressing views—there would be less than 1.5 seconds for each response.[157] Such extreme

---

[154] For a different argument to similar effect, see Pitkin, *Representation*, 60–91.

[155] It is a serious mistake to confuse Kantian moral justification (could) with democratic political legitimacy (do). Whether or not the problems of liberal constitutionalism can be solved using devices of hypothetical consent (e.g. Rawls, *Theory*, *Political Liberalism*) or possible consent (e.g. O'Neill, *Constructions*, *Towards Justice*), these devices are generally out of place when it comes to political decision in a large-scale representative democracy.

[156] Goodin, 'Deliberation Within', 90.

[157] Let us make some outrageously optimistic assumptions: assume each person could make intelligible and retain the views of sixty others; assume that finding

limits on both the number and the length of contributions makes a mockery of the ideas of inclusive and rational deliberation—especially where issues are complicated. Indeed, I may have a better chance of winning the lottery under such conditions than of meeting the popular participation requirement on public deliberation.

Selective deliberation—limiting the amount of uptake—fares no better as a strategy to rescue the ideal of rational and inclusive deliberation. For one thing, 'posting notices for all to read' is very different from the give and take of reasons involved in actually 'talking to one another' (just think about college notice boards!).[158] For another, even if selective uptake were adequate for informal discussion, it would not be a good source for making nor route to making authoritative decisions. In formal public reasoning, the quality of reasons plays some role in their being taken into account (reasons must at least be put through a structured process of exchange) rather than their being taken into account primarily because they are interesting to discuss. Proponents of this fourth strategy therefore fall into the trap of modelling public reasoning on conversation. This is quite apart from the fact that strong limits on interchange between decision-makers are likely to undermine the quality of public reasoning, and with it the normative ground of coercive authority.

Finally, there is Goodin's suggestion that public reasoning could be modelled by retreating into the inner citadel of the imaginative, empathic mind. This seems to me to be the least promising of the lot. If it is difficult to elaborate a structured external procedure to combine multitudinous, plural reasons, it seems even more difficult to conceive of a mind capable of judicious combination of this kind. The cognitive burdens would be immense; indeed, it seems contradictory to talk of a *human* being who develops and holds such an encompassing

---

agreement after that is unproblematic; assume that these exhaust the range of viewpoints. Now assume that each person is a member of only four groups, and there is no overlapping membership of groups, and there is no problem of changing questions and answers between groups; and assume that every person is able to work at 'taking the perspective of everybody else' for 10 hours a day. In two days of deliberation, agreement could be achieved between 12,600,000 people (this is on the small side for a state). But *only* if every person has only 5 minutes to put his or her point, internalise, and reply to everybody else! Let us continue to assume, wildly, that only one in fifty thousand others' opinions are forthcoming and are opinions to which other citizens wish to respond. With 5 minutes to respond to around 250 opinions, each interlocutor has about 1.2 seconds to discuss rationally each other interlocutor's views.

[158] Goodin, 'Deliberation Within', 91.

'we-perspective'. At the very least, the human mind is not as structured as the forum in giving equal sway to competing considerations: if 'public' reasons were largely processed internally, they would be under-articulated and half-formed on the whole, dismissed before they could be properly developed and evaluated. I seriously doubt, for instance, that the internal dialogues of George W. Bush, Ziang Zemin, and Atal Vajpayee (respectively, the rulers of the USA, China, and India in 2002) could ever be at all similar. It is not at all plausible to think that they or any of us can justifiably assume the authority to internally represent most or all others. An inner dialogue, even if it is imaginative, highlights issues and treats them idiosyncratically, depending among other things on their resonance with each one's own life history and social roles; it is very far from public deliberation.

Further, while sensitivity to others' perspectives is something devoutly to be wished in a populace, it is by no means clear that litera-ture and the arts are going to do the job. It is a commonplace that Hitler was freely elected, in the country of Goethe and Mann, by a compara-tively well-read populace. Literature and the arts may improve us, but are we sure they make us more moral? (Consider, as the extreme and disturbing case of quite the contrary, Martin Heidegger.) In fact, as Habermas himself points out, there is more reason to think that the effectiveness of some kind of public engagement conduces to sensitiv-ity to other perspectives than that the causal story operates the other way round.[159] But even if the two are mutually supportive, this sensit-ivity must ultimately take the form of an external articulation of reasons if it is to serve as an input into authoritative decision. The constraints on numbers and time discussed above are still extreme, and the many problems with the external deliberative ideal remain.

4. Representation Contra Deliberation

The failure of all of the five strategies above renders deliberative democracy highly impracticable. No institutional account can redeem the requirements that flow from the conceptual structure and ideals of deliberative theory. Its flaws can be summarised now across four dimensions that together show the impossibility of any such agent as a deliberative democrat. Each criticism along the four dimensions applies to most or all of the five versions above.

---

[159] J. Habermas, *Legitimation Crisis* (Boston: Beacon, 1975), 108; see also Warren, 'Self'.

Metaphysically, the idea of a we-perspective postulates agents who are capable of simultaneously understanding and integrating the views of huge numbers of interlocutors. These agents would have to be gods, or at least very far from human in their capacities and limitations; but we are not attempting to solve the problem of democracy for gods.

Epistemologically, there is no such thing, and no way to get at any such thing, as what the public in a large and pluralistic society would actually choose. As Madison puts it,

> if the opinions of the people were to be our guide, it would be difficult to say what course we ought to take. No member of the convention could say what the opinions of his constituents were at this time; much less could he say what they would think if possessed of the information and lights possessed by the members here; and still less what would be their way of thinking six or twelve months hence.[160]

This is no mere technical or technological failure, but a function of the disjunction between the knowledge (of ends and means) required for making public decisions, on the one hand, and deliberative demands that such knowledge be derived from an all-inclusive inter-subjective process, on the other. The deliberative requirement that interests, and ways to pursue those interests, must be discerned through citizens' interaction thus has no chance of being met; but if it is not met, all legitimate legislating becomes, on a deliberative account, strictly impossible.

Psychologically, the idea of participative validation demands a clarity of imagination and of unexpressed reasoning—whereby the views of 'everyone else [are made] "imaginatively present"'—that is attained perhaps by a few great thinkers but is unattainable for all others (and is perhaps undesirable, on the grounds that the contemplative life is not the only good one).[161] Note that even such thinkers do not meet the criteria for being deliberative democrats: a reasoner who cannot engage the rest of the population on equal terms such that they come to share his or her 'we-perspective' is no Habermasian deliberator.

---

[160] Cited in Pitkin, *Representation*, 197.

[161] This requirement also seems to place onerous demands on the time and efforts of citizens—creating an 'overload of obligation' which would scupper many of their other important life-projects and even their capacity to engage in basic economic activity. On the notion of an overload of obligation, see B. Williams, 'Consequentialism and Integrity', in S. Scheffler, ed., *Consequentialism and Its Critics* (Oxford: Oxford University Press, 1988).

Operationally, deliberative theory either (1) presumes that people who initially hold similar viewpoints will be convinced by the same arguments thereafter, and thus change perspective and association only when all other members of the group do; or (2) avoids such a failure to model free thought and free association by modelling deliberation in a way that allows a minority to be determinate over a majority for no good reason. Hence, to the extent that deliberation is 'operationalised', it is anti-democratic.

There is a remarkable irony in all this: from Chaucer to Tolstoy to Nabokov, a dominant theme in great literature has been how mental reflexivity—the fount of freedom—is closely linked to our limitations in understanding and to our 'relationship to time'.[162] Yet those who claim to emphasise reflexivity in politics the most are least careful to keep these fundamental constraints in view. We must seek a more realistic ideal. And here there are important lessons to be learned from the failure of the five strategies—lessons that set broad parameters for any adequate account of representation.

Briefly, and as a prelude to arguments in the next chapter: From the failure of serial deliberation, we learn that public reasoning, since it has to lead to administrative decision, requires firm and discretionary agenda setting by a group or groups of agents much smaller than the demos as a whole. From the failure of substitute deliberation, we learn that there is no process of simulation that directly mirrors the actual deliberations of citizens; what is 'in the best interests' of citizens on each issue will have to be determined by reference to citizens' judgements but will in large part have to be judged by the smaller group of agents. (At this point we have gone some way to characterising the role of liberal representatives.) From the failure of restrictive deliberation, we learn that since that group is smaller, it can be empowered better to make informed decisions on the basis of cumulated knowledge and extended discussion. From the failure of selective deliberation, we learn that that group must communicate in a way that is properly constrained so as to ensure that the group tends to concentrate on publicly relevant reasons; at the same time it must not be too constrained when it comes to access to information and time to consider arguments. From the failure of internalised deliberation, we learn that that reasoning must be made explicit and publicly scrutinisable. (At this point

---

[162] The quotation is from L. Tolstoy, *War and Peace* (Oxford: Oxford Paperbacks, 1998), 976; see also G. Chaucer, 'The Nun's Priest's Tale', *The Canterbury Tales* (London: Penguin, 1992) and V. Nabokov, *Speak, Memory* (London: Penguin, 2000), esp. 18–19.

we have gone some way to characterising the features of a representative assembly.)

From these lessons flow some large and familiar questions: What kinds and degrees of discretion should representatives have? How is the group of representatives to be appointed, empowered, and constrained in order that they make 'good' judgements as to the interests of citizens and the means to realising those interests, and act 'responsibly' on those judgements? If representatives fail to discharge their obligations or perform their tasks well, how are they to be sanctioned and/or removed from office? How are citizens' active judgements to be elicited and taken into account, such that they exercise adequate control over representatives and political decisions? What sorts of publicity should be required? I now turn to these related questions. We have seen that a thicker conception of representation is a necessary part of an adequate democratic theory; the difficulty now lies in developing the positive and specific conception that can play that pivotal role. I shall argue that existing conceptions of representation are inadequate in several respects, and I shall attempt to present a more coherent and practicable alternative.

3

Representation as Responsiveness

In framing a government to be administered by men over men, the great difficulty lies in this: you must first enable the government to control the governed; and in the next place oblige it to control itself.

Madison et al., *Federalist*, No. 51.

1. Representation by Whom or What?

Representation is a normatively laden and rhetorically resonant term, and for this reason is much used and abused. People have disagreed, sometimes violently, about whether and by whom they are represented; theorists as dissimilar as Burke and Mill, supreme courts as different as the Frankfurter and the Rehnquist courts (to name but one constitutional tradition), have contradicted and tied themselves into knots in the search for a core, univocal meaning.[163] Yet it is profoundly unlikely that a term used for a range of purposes and in varied contexts should have a single meaning. It is hard enough to specify a determinate, limited, and consistent set of meanings relevant to a definite purpose.

My aim in this chapter is to develop a plausible conception of political representation appropriate to a practicable theory of democracy for societies of great and even global scope. As such, several more particular purposes, contexts, and uses must first be considered. I defend and elaborate a new conception of what Hannah Pitkin calls 'substantive' representation, that is, 'acting in the best interests of the public, in

[163] R. Rogowski, 'Representation in Political Theory and Law', *Ethics*, No. 91, No. 3. (1981), 395–430.

a manner responsive to them'.[164] Much of the chapter is devoted to characterising these terms and how they could fit together. I emphasise the institutional conditions necessary for good judgements about interests to be made, by adequately informed and capable agents, who are empowered and constrained to act on such judgements responsibly.

I argue that elections, competitive party politics, the classical tripartite separation of powers, media, and 'civil society'—in their various incarnations and combinations—are insufficient social and institutional mechanisms for securing this conception of representation. I propose an alternative institutional configuration. It includes these limited mechanisms for achieving representation, but supplements and transforms them by adding several new types of mechanisms as well as introducing new fruitful relations between mechanisms. I show that this institutional configuration could be stable and could significantly *reduce* adverse bureaucracy from current levels.

The chapter ends with a lengthy discussion of the basic roles and relations of citizens within this configuration. I show that, on my account of representation, most citizens could exercise more and more appropriate control in a plurarchic global order than they could exercise in a state and under a system of states. My account of the meaning and mechanisms of (potentially global) representation is thus coupled with my cosmopolitan account of global justice, and both are rounded out by a preliminary account of feasible global citizenship. I call the theory as a whole Responsive Democracy. In the next chapter, I illustrate the implications of this theory for reforming specific global institutions.

Before setting out a substantive conception of representation, one can ask: who or what does the representing? Three broad answers can be suggested. (1) Liberal theories of democracy usually take representation to be an *individual agency* concept; thus Pitkin writes that the 'representative must act independently [on behalf of the represented]; his action must involve discretion and judgement; he must be the one who acts'.[165] In conventional liberal democratic theories, representatives of the public are agents—on the whole natural persons, but sometimes artificial, legal persons—who make the law and are elected by citizens. (2) For deliberative theorists, as I pointed out, that is *not* the core meaning of 'representative'. They apply the term to laws and policies generated by citizens through an inclusive discursive process; and they confine so-called representatives to doing what citizens would do, or to guiding, refining, and implementing citizens' decisions.

---

[164] Pitkin, *Representation*, 209–40.
[165] Ibid., 197.

Deliberative theory can allow for elected representatives, but their agency role is dramatically reduced and even supplanted by *processes* in which there is apparently a far more active legislative role for citizens. (3) It is also common to talk of *systems* of representative government—emphasising the way in which political institutions function so as to consistently produce outcomes that take into account the interests and/or views of the public. A political system can reflect some views and realise some interests of citizens without those outcomes being intended by representatives or chosen during citizens' deliberations.

It matters immensely which of these three senses we focus on. The last chapter brought out significant differences between (1) and (2), and argued for the priority of (1). It would of course be mistaken to think that there is an entirely zero-sum trade-off between liberal representation and public participation: public discourse between citizens can help elected representatives to discern the interests of the public better. Nevertheless, there is something of a trade-off if interests can *only* be discovered and validated in public discourse: representatives may provide input into—or even lead—public discussion; but they do not have the discretion necessary to make decisive judgements about interests independently of or prior to public discourse, and that discourse is not validating unless it is potentially fully inclusive.

I argued that deliberative theorists are unable to deliver on their own participation requirements, which demand an impossible degree and type of participation. The main problem is not representatives' level of activity, but rather their lack of discretion to judge and act on the interests of the public where the public has no will (as yet or ever) or has a different will; the need for rulers with a wider sort of discretion cannot be avoided. On the debate between (1) and (2), then, we can acknowledge that there are potential benefits to some public participation—of a less exhaustive kind than envisioned by deliberative theorists—while coming down firmly on the side of the liberals.

The choice between (1) and (3), between an agent-centric conception of representation and a system-centric conception, is not so stark and often not necessary. Any democratic *system* will require *agents* who act as representatives, and must resolve some crucial questions: who appoints representatives, on what basis, what powers do they have, who judges whether they have attempted to use those powers in the interests of and with appropriate attention to views of the public, by what process, and how can rulers be sanctioned and/or removed?

However, for the purposes of an *overall* judgment of the extent to which citizens are represented by their political order and its outcomes, the agent-centric view is insufficient. Governments are typically highly internally differentiated, and are always constituted and led by human beings. Just as constituents lack certain information and capacities in the face of a complex and vast set of considerations and numerous other agents, so too do representatives. Just as constituents operate against a background of rules and institutions, and are subject to a complex division of political labour and to time constraints, so too are representatives (despite their different position). The system-centric view of representation thus incorporates a wider set of questions: what are the indirect and unintended effects of representatives' efforts, of relations between representatives themselves, and of interactions between representatives and the rest of the institutional framework?

As we shall see, the latter questions can pull us in a very different direction from agent-centric questions. For instance, adopting an agent-centric view, we may regard the inclusion of certain actors (e.g. some NGOs) in governance as unwarranted, because such 'representatives' could not be appointed by citizens. But, adopting a system-centric view, we may discover that the inclusion of these actors increases the responsiveness of other representatives and of the political system overall to the views and best interests of the public. Moreover, other representatives may in turn constrain the unelected actors in important ways, reducing the scope of those actors themselves for unresponsiveness. In this and similar cases, while the agent-centric view is indispensable, we can have good reasons to give priority to system-centric representation: we may care more about the overall control over and outcomes of government than about any particular agent's status.

2. The Role of the Represented

It is crucial to see the question of representation from the side of citizens too: a political system will not be representative unless they too can exercise political agency.[166] When we ask whether a government is representative, we are not asking whether it has the power to bind persons to its decisions. Any effective regime could have such de facto

---

[166] There is a closely related sense of representation as trusteeship for those of certain kinds of agency. Deliberative theorists have great difficulty explaining how the interests of such impaired or non-agents could be discerned: if a person cannot enter the discursive process, how are his or her claims to be validated? The account below does not suffer from this deficiency, insofar as it does not require deliberation to discern interests. Trusteeship raises quite discrete issues that I shall not address here.

power while consistently using it against the interests of the public. Nor is it sufficient to ask whether constituents approve of the government. A despot could successfully brainwash his or her subjects, and then not act in their interests, or act only on the basis of the putative interests that he or she has inculcated in them with propaganda or pills. Such delusions need not be intentionally orchestrated by an evil-doer either: consider fairly spontaneous mob celebrations (popular after victory in war and soccer). Nor are we asking simply whether the conditions for constituents are good or improving. A government might be acting in the best interests of the public, but under difficult or worsening conditions; or if conditions are improving, that might be due to factors other than the government's policies. Finally, we are not even asking simply if the government's policies promote what an informed and uncoerced public take to be in their interests. A non-representative government may contingently act in the interests of the public, but this benefit can and may be suspended or destroyed at any time at the whim of the rulers.

What is missing entirely even from this last conception of acceptable rule is any consideration of citizens as *agents with a degree of active control* over rulers and policies rather than as merely passive recipients, beneficiaries, or victims of rulers' actions.[167] For government to be representative, the public need not cause or generate every decision, but they must be able to have an impact on government—and thereby on policies that impact on them—through their own judgements and actions. It is not enough for that impact to be accidental, transitory, and insignificant: it must be regularised, unavoidable, ongoing, and significant. Of course, where government is representative, the public need not actually exercise this power in most instances, but they must have some kind of systematic control over authoritative decision rather than being mere objects of their rulers' exercise of power. To which extent, and through which mechanisms, the public must exercise such control are questions that remain to be answered.

For now, we can note three broad requirements for representation: (1) the representative has the discretion and capabilities to judge and act—or a representative system is structured so as to operate—in the best interests of the public; (2) he, she, or it is impelled to do so because of institutional empowerment and constraints rather than whim, luck, or other caprice; (3) he, she, or it does so in a way that elicits and takes into account the active exercise of judgement by the public in a way that justifies the attribution of systematic control to the public.

[167] Pitkin, *Representation*, 232–3.

These requirements are difficult to square with one another because, as we have seen, rulers are employed to perform the tasks that citizens cannot. Rulers are required to make detailed judgements of law and policy in advance and to orchestrate action on those judgements. This sets the first constraint on access to and the exercise of discretionary power: 'the represented have no will on most issues, and the duty of the representatives is to do what is best for them, not what they latently want'.[168] Pitkin's statement here rightly denies as nonsense the deliberative epistemic view that people's interests can be discerned solely by asking them in advance—in a purportedly inclusive debate—what those interests are, or by simulating what they would say if they were asked.

An equally implausible epistemic view, familiar from vanguardist Marxism, is that there is no need to consult people about their actual opinions. To presume that rulers or revolutionaries are epistemically privileged agents, whose views on others' interests are unrebuttable, is to court disaster. The truth surely lies somewhere between these two implausible accounts—one of which (as we saw in Chapter 2) assigns almost all power to judge to the public, resulting in almost complete inertia, while the other (as we saw in the previous century) assigns almost all power to judge to the rulers (or proto-ruler revolutionaries), resulting in near certain subjection. Neither captures the dynamic interplay between the ruled as agents and rulers as agents that is fundamental to representation. Is it possible to find, between these two extremes, a more plausible epistemology for construing the interplay between judgements by rulers and judgements by citizens? I shall argue that it is.

3. Judging the Best Interests of the Public

3.1. An Epistemology for Judging Interests

Every major contemporary regime—except the radically theocratic—seeks to legitimate itself by claiming to act in 'the best interests of the public'. This notion will remain a site of struggle in political theory and practice because any set of criteria for its interpretation and application will draw attention to some claims and persons while deflecting attention from others.[169] Many disputes over interests can be resolved only

---

[168] Pitkin, *Representation*, 163.

[169] This in part explains why political theorists have not succeeded in developing an account of judging interests that is widely regarded as normatively compelling, empirically and analytically tractable, and intuitively appealing.

in political practice, rather than prior to or in abstraction from politics. Nevertheless, the identification of interests cannot be left to politics alone: many interests are suppressed and ignored in politics. One important test of the plausibility of a general account of interests is whether and in what ways it allows a normative point of view from which judgement of the adequacy of an institutional regime and politics can be made.

The concept of an interest has its home in objective theories of value, which have traditionally contrasted an individual's (true) interests with his or her (subjective) choices or preferences. The concept of the interests of the public correspondingly contrasts the (true) interests of the public with public choices or preferences, as indicated—for example—by electoral processes. In this chapter I shall bracket claims about true or real interests, and about the metaphysics of value, in favour of certain epistemological and institutional constraints on preferences and choice. I choose to limit my argument in this way because it is notoriously difficult to deliver a plausible and full account of human nature and flourishing on which stronger claims about true interests depend. Accordingly I shall rely on a notion of informed and constrained judgements of (best) interests, while leaving it open that stronger conceptions of (true) interest might be supported by a realist theory of moral value. I begin by articulating that epistemological constraint.

Many liberals—and they are not alone—maintain that interests are best judged by considering what individuals themselves (1) do choose or (2) would choose if they were choosing under 'ideal conditions'.[170] I shall begin by showing these two subjectivist views to be false, before developing what I take to be a more plausible view.

1. Interests cannot be derived from actual choices because one's immediate preferences can reflect false views of one's own advantage. Preferences are adaptive even to the grimmest realities: the most deprived people often acquiesce in their lot, accepting that small mercies are all they deserve, and viewing those who have a direct hand in their deprivation as benevolent father-figures.[171] Hence the happy

---

[170] The former kind of analysis, popularised by rational choice theory, forms the basis for most neoclassical economic theory for incisive critique, see A. Hirschman in *The Passions and the Interests* (Princeton, NJ: Princeton University Press, 1977). The latter (counterfactual) kind of analysis of choice was clearly articulated without reference to notions foreign to liberalism by S. Benn, 'Interests in Politics', *Proceedings of the Aristotelian Society*, Vol. 60 (1960), 123–40 and developed by W. E. Connolly in 'On "Interests" in Politics', *Politics and Society*, Vol. 2, No. 4 (1972), 459–77.

[171] O. O'Neill, 'Justice, Capabilities, and Vulnerabilities', in M. C. Nussbaum and J. Glover, eds., *Women, Culture, and Development: A Study of Human Capabilities* (Oxford: Clarendon Press, 1995), esp. 142–3.

slave, and the millions of poor women who underestimate their own health problems—with severe consequences of (otherwise avoidable) morbidity and death. Can we really call a system 'just' if it satisfies only the few preferences that deprived people dare to articulate and act upon, while securing immense wealth and power for the already wealthy and powerful, who had no hesitation in conspicuously wanting more? In constructing a theory of justice, it may be analytically simplest to look at what people say or do ('real' or 'revealed' preferences), but this does little more than systematically incorporate information that is corrupted by the very circumstances that give rise to concerns about justice in the first place.[172] The notion of interests is valuable partly because it allows us to recognise that people may be acting systematically in ways that are not good for them. Straightforwardly subjectivist approaches lack serious critical purchase.

2. Nor can judgements of interests be derived from imagining what would be chosen under ideal conditions. This is evident when we consider the two basic approaches to judging interests in this counterfactual way: a 'perfect knowledge' approach and an 'optimal conditions' approach.[173] The first approach begins from the thought that if a person knew more than she did when she made a choice that was not in her interests, she might have been able to identify her interests better. The second approach begins from the thought that an agent's conception of her interests can be misguided because it was formed under adverse circumstances—say, the person who has been subjected to extreme abuse and thus believes that her needs are of little or no importance. But the grain of truth in these thoughts tends to be quickly ground to dust by overly strong formulations.

Perfect knowledge implies the knowing of all relevant facts and theories provided by the most refined sciences possible as well as the right kind of self-knowledge (and perhaps of knowledge of others) provided by the right psychology.[174] It is not, then, an attainable or comprehensible ideal for human beings. On the other hand, the idea that in order to identify our interests we need to know what we would choose under *optimal* conditions—of non-coercion, appropriate motivation, and all relevant information—runs into two problems. One, 'all relevant information' tends to be a mere rhetorical mask for

---

[172] Revealed preference theory, so popular in economic analysis, has the particularly pernicious consequence that 'the compliant actions of the intimidated and vulnerable will be interpreted as showing that they prefer to comply, so suggesting that they are getting what they prefer' (Ibid.).

[173] This distinction is owed to Geuss, *Critical Theory*, 45–54.

[174] Ibid.

the perfect knowledge approach. Two, it may be important to conceive of our interests under optimal conditions—assuming this notion to be intelligible—and thereby to help ourselves to aim at a better state of affairs, *but* our interests under optimal conditions do not replace our present interests. For instance, saying that in optimal conditions a talented child would have an interest in tertiary education should not blind us to the thought that *as things are* in hard times she may have an interest in starting to earn a living.[175] It may be deeply misguided—count seriously against one's interests—to attempt to approximate as closely as possible what one would choose if one were in optimal conditions.[176]

These difficulties in deriving judgements of interests from agents' own actual or hypothetical choices seem to me to be insurmountable. We are not in optimal conditions nor do we have perfect knowledge (and each requires the other); but we need not entirely despair: 'although we do not live in that utopia, we may be free enough to recognise how we might act to abolish some of the coercion from which we suffer and move closer to 'optimal conditions' of freedom and knowledge'.[177]

This is an important acknowledgement of our limited capacities for self-emancipation. The thought needs extending, however, because the 'we' here could be understood (and is understood by deliberative theorists) to imply that each agent herself or himself does or could recognise the relevant coercive constraints and potential remedial actions.

This subjectivist view is false: A person can have an interest in a piece of legislation whether or not the proposals *could ever* be put to her as a competent assessor. For example, the enacting of some complicated financial or pensions legislation may be in my interests, even if my innate numerical abilities are far too limited for me ever to grasp the content of such legislation. This suggests that there are reasons that

---

[175] Geuss put this point for a *society* as follows: 'To be sure, if the conditions of existence for the Ik [which are horrific, leading them to act ruthlessly towards one another] were radically different from what they are, the Ik would have a very different set of interests—they themselves realise that—but from that it in no way follows that the interests they would have had in some totally different situation are their present . . . interests' (Ibid., 52–3).

[176] Envisioning a more ideal situation may shed light on what I ought to do now, adding to the judgement of my present interests, but it cannot replace that judgement. It is for this reason that, in Chapter 1, I spoke of ideals as 'orienteering mechanisms' and warned against the use of ideals as unmediated bases for action. Chapter 4 and the Conclusion continue this discussion.

[177] Geuss, *Critical Theory*, 54.

apply to me—that I can have certain interests—regardless of whether I can ever understand and deliberate on their content directly.

In most cases, our limitations in judging our own interests are not this stark. Often we could understand the relevant proposals, although it would require so much time and effort that there are strong reasons to have someone else acquire the necessary skills and make the necessary judgements. This is obvious in cases of expertise: surgeons are better judges of what operating techniques to use on me than I am. In such cases, it is sensible to acknowledge limitations in my potential abilities to judge some of the reasons that are relevant for me and yet recognise others as competent judges of those reasons. I am then warranted in accepting—indeed, I ought to accept—the view of *the most informed and capable agents* about the reasons that apply to me.[178]

That expert may of course be wrong—a new and better economic or medical theory, or a true theory of human flourishing, might even prove every such expert to have been mistaken—so it would be too strong to call her judgement 'objective'. But we should have little problem in terming her judgements 'good' or 'excellent', since we have strong reasons to regard her as possessing greater *knowledge* relevant to judging our interests in this respect than the rest of us. Moreover, she is operating in better *conditions* than the rest of us, in a special sense: she is more likely to be appropriately motivated, uncoerced, informed, etc., because she is judging and acting against a background of rules of accreditation, professional regulatory bodies, legal protections, peer scrutiny, and many other social and institutional mechanisms of empowerment and constraint.

Our *belief* that it is reasonable to place trust in certain others to act as good judges of our interests on an ongoing basis is warranted if and when they have been adequately selected, empowered, and constrained. While these precautions and powers are lacking, others may act ignorantly, selfishly, or irresponsibly, mistaking our interests, or

---

[178] I take this point to be a development of Joseph Raz's argument concerning exclusionary reasons. Raz maintains that some reasons are typically independent of their content; thus, for instance, one typically obeys authoritative commands or fulfils promises because they are commands and promises and not because they contain reasons that apply to one directly. The reasons provided by commands and promises in this sense pre-empt and exclude weighing up of other reasons for or against the course of action. Similarly, on a wider interpretation of Raz's argument, one may recognise—independently of any prior binding agreement—that others are better judges of a matter, and this leads one to accept and act upon their judgements, excluding one's own direct judgements. See J. Raz, *The Morality of Freedom* (Oxford: Oxford University Press, 1986), esp. 53.

pretending to mistake our interests when that is to their advantage. At each point at which expertise is relevant, 'we' 'recognise' the appropriate course of action only in the sense that, and to the extent that, the social system functioned so as to identify, empower, and constrain competent agents—who thereby became the most informed and capable agents—to make the judgements on our behalf.

Is there any analogy with the judgements that we need rulers to make on our behalf? It would be wrong to treat rulers as experts for three main reasons: (1) There is no demarcated and established body of knowledge in which they can demonstrate mastery—such a body of knowledge would probably have to be a comprehensible synthesis of almost all others; (2) Political judgements often depend on non-technical judgements (some of them 'value choices') where there may be nothing that counts as expertise; (3) Rulers are required not merely to judge one kind of interest of each agent taken singly and in turn but to judge simultaneously the interests of many agents with many (intra- and inter-personally conflicting) interests.[179]

Nevertheless, there are important similarities between our position vis-à-vis experts and our position vis-à-vis rulers. In large-scale societies, where complex divisions of labour are essential, we need professional agents of both kinds, devoted full-time to identifying and addressing problems and opportunities in their respective domains. With rulers, as with experts, we have no option but to trust, but our trust can be better or worse placed[180]—depending, in large part, not so much on the personal characteristics of the rulers, or on their knowledge, as on the quality of background mechanisms of appointment, empowerment, and constraint.

Much can go wrong here. We may fail to identify the best candidates to do the judging, expecting or hoping that they have competences which they turn out not to possess. They may, when in power, act irresponsibly or selfishly, pretending that something is in our interests when they know it is not. We can obtain no full guarantees. But it is possible to institutionalise better procedures for appointment (e.g. open rather than secretive), better means of empowerment (e.g. making available high quality information relevant to their decisions), better systems for discovering and penalising wrongdoing (e.g. financial audits and serious penalties). Political systems can be crafted and adjusted

---

[179] I shall return to all these points, repeatedly.

[180] On trust, see O. O'Neill, *A Question of Trust: The BBC Reith Lectures 2002* (Cambridge: Cambridge University Press, 2002*b*). O'Neill argues compellingly that quality and quantity of regulation are often at odds.

to enable and constrain rulers to judge our interests less selfishly and more responsibly.

Each successful adjustment constitutes an improvement in conditions that is likely to improve the *quality* of political judgements of—and actions in—our interests.[181] Equally importantly, each adjustment may increase the *control* exercised by members of the public, since they may be able to acquire more or more effective access to mechanisms (e.g. elections, judicial review) for appointing, empowering, and constraining rulers. 'We' need not depend predominantly on the intrinsic competences of rulers, nor need we rely on what citizens would do, or could choose as the standard for judgement of interests. Social and institutional constraints can inform, develop, and discipline the cognitive processes of rulers, positioning them to make judgements that are likely to be more knowledgeable and 'uncoerced' than citizens' judgements—while reducing the propensity of rulers to judge and act in ways that take advantage of those improved positions, and providing remedies if and when they do. Processes of this kind do not guarantee that our true interests (whatever those are) will be discerned but, were they in place, they would allow us to get as close as possible—epistemically and practically—to identifying and pursuing the interests of the public.

It must be stressed that, in locating the source of judgements of best interests in judgements by institutionally constrained and empowered agents, one is *not endorsing any form of 'normative elitism'*—the notion that those more capable and knowledgeable agents are more virtuous. From the fact that some agents are better equipped and positioned institutionally to make judgements of certain kinds, it does not follow that they have fine characters and/or will behave better. Knowledge and power create temptations to take advantage of others' vulnerabilities, and it is difficult and rare to remain uncorrupted. Scepticism about normative elitism is one of the bases for effective institutional design: it will

[181] Mechanisms of appointment, empowerment, and constraint can also play an important role in minimising—though not eliminating—the problems associated with the three important disanalogies between rulers and experts (outlined above). As we shall see, certain mechanisms might weed out candidates for appointment whose competences have in the past proven to be poor or irrelevant aids to judgement, or hone the skills of those whose competences have tended to prove more relevant; mechanisms might inform and clarify value judgements; and mechanisms might reduce interpersonal conflicts of judgement by offering fairer and more consistent processes of resolution. It is tempting to say that, after that, the public will have to 'decide for themselves' in elections or referenda but—as I shall show in the next section—that would be a mistakenly blanket statement.

seldom be reasonable or prudent to expect rulers to represent citizens well simply because of their intrinsic character and competence. On the contrary, we find it prudent to select and empower them only to the extent that the institutional structures by which they are selected and empowered provide strong reasons for them to attend to citizens' interests and views. Here it is often not possible to make them do the right thing for the right reasons (e.g. because it is right); frequently, we will have to find institutions that incline them to do the right thing for the 'wrong' reasons (e.g. because they are greedy, fear disgrace, or are preoccupied with the fickle applause that comes with holding office).

Nor does this account of judgement of interests commit one to 'institutional elitism'. From the general fact that some set of offices is constructed to make office-holders the most informed and capable with respect to a decision, it does not follow that any specific person or party or arm of government is or could be the sole and sufficient occupier of that position, or indeed that there is any one such privileged position from which good judgements issue. Typically, there are many interests that ombudsmen, judges, parts of the media, opposition legislators, citizens—and so on—can be better positioned and constrained to judge and pursue than is a government of the day. The problem, of course, is determining how to appoint, empower, constrain, and dismiss those agents: what kinds of institutions and communicative interchange are helpful and required? In the rest of this chapter, I shall argue that a specific plurality of decision-makers, selected and situated via certain processes, interacting in specified ways, is optimal for taking into account the views and judging the best interests of the public.

3.2. The Public, Vulnerabilities, and Capabilities

One of the important disanalogies between experts and rulers to which I pointed above is that political judgement concerns many interests of many agents. When a large group of people have to make a coordinated decision, the interests at stake are those of a complex, internally differentiated group of agents, the membership of which changes across time. Before turning to some mechanisms for securing representation, then, my account of judging interests in politics must be supplemented by a practicable conception of 'the public'. To whom does this term refer?

There are at least five common uses of 'the interests of the public':

1. *The common good*—as in, 'this amalgam of shared purposes and standards has priority over individual interests because it is fundamental to the way of life of a group'.

2. *Good for all*—as in, 'these benefits are shared or shareable by all constituents; *ceteris paribus*, a better health-care service is in the interests of the public'.
3. *Good for the scheme of social cooperation*—as in, 'this society has always been able to accommodate conflicting interests of plural groups, and it remains in the interests of the public that labour and capital resolve their dispute'.
4. *The aggregate of subjective individual goods*—as in, 'this policy is in the interests of the public because it produces the most preference-satisfaction overall, regardless of the distribution of satisfaction'.
5. *Good for a majority of individuals*—as in, 'this policy is in the interests of the public because it benefits the poor and/or the middle class, who are a numerical majority'.

I do not propose to discuss these extensively explored notions in any depth. It suffices to say that there are good reasons, presented in Chapter 1, to be suspicious of (1) as a basis for political decision, since it generally presupposes and can only be relevant to a fairly homogenous society. Further, most of the vexed decisions of politics cannot be resolved by reference to the sort of Pareto-optimality articulated in (2) or (3): many political decisions do not benefit everyone and are not resolved by reference to whether they promote wider social cooperation.[182] The problems with (4), utilitarianism and its subjectivist adjuncts, are familiar and irremediable. And (5) runs into the many problems under the rubric of 'the tyranny of the majority'. Nevertheless, I initially articulate a conception of representation by adopting usage (5).

My reasons for starting with (5) are fairly simple: The priority accorded to justice—including obligations and rights—in the cosmopolitan theory presented in Chapter 1 places significant constitutional constraints on the powers of the majority, preventing tyranny in any strict sense, though not all milder forms of domination. The remaining and important problems of majority domination arise where there are permanent minorities due to settled social stratifications. Yet if my account of representation cannot work in conditions that are *not* so stratified, then it has little chance of being applicable where social cleavages are acute and enduring.[183] Therefore, I begin by

---

[182] See J. Dunn, *The Cunning of Unreason: Making Sense of Politics* (London: HarperCollins, 2000).

[183] While in some cases the ideal case and the messier non-ideal case of a phenomenon cannot be usefully brought together, I try to show that the two do come together in respect of representation as responsiveness.

taking 'the public' to mean 'fluid majorities'; by this I mean that the majority always trumps, but its internal constitution shifts over time, and each person is just as likely as every other to be within any particular absolute majority. On this assumption, the best interests of the public are those interests that would be chosen for the majority, of shifting composition, by the most informed and capable agents. Yet fluid majorities are obviously not present in many areas of politics; thus, in the three concluding sections of the chapter, I focus on what can be done to conceptualise and achieve representation in paradigmatic functional domains where social conditions are not so fluid, and where the boundaries of societies are disputed.

Even with this simplifying assumption about the public in place, it is unclear what exactly rulers are trying to judge when making judgements of the public's interests. There is a limited amount that can be said here without delving into theories of true interests or real needs, but my arguments thus far do suggest a useful initial orientation: Our interests in an ideal world are not our present interests. In considering how to act in concrete non-ideal circumstances we have to try to begin with 'an empirically realistic view of the capacities and capabilities [actual] agents have, of ways in which they are vulnerable to others'.[184] Who knows what? Who has the power to do what? In any social system, there will be inequalities in possession of information and—partly for that reason—power. It is this situation of *relative* vulnerability that must concern us: 'Agents become victims not just because they are poor, ignorant, unskilled or physically weak or emotionally fragile, but because they are confronted by others who are richer, more knowledgeable, more skilful or physically or emotionally stronger, and prepared to exploit these advantages'.[185]

Which descriptions should be used is of course a vexed, and not entirely empirical, issue. But these thoughts about vulnerability do suggest that the 'capabilities approach' to identifying relevant interests (pioneered by Sen) is likely to be more plausible on the whole than the 'primary goods' approach to identifying relevant interests (pioneered by Rawls). The capabilities approach rightly emphasises two points: First, goods 'convert' into well-being and freedoms at differential rates

---

[184] O'Neill, *Bounds*, 7.

[185] Ibid., 95. This emphasis on vulnerability rather than absolute position could also be justified on analogous grounds to Thomas Scanlon's grounds for maintaining, in moral philosophy, that it is more plausible to begin with 'wrongness' rather than 'rightness'. See T. Scanlon, *What We Owe to Each Other* (Cambridge, MA: Belknap Press of Harvard University Press, 1999).

for different people. For example, pregnant women will starve if they obtain only the amount of food sufficient to keep most other people adequately nourished. Equal possession of primary goods is therefore not sufficient to remove the vulnerability of many people. Second, relative inequalities in social position can be an important source of vulnerability, and the goods necessary to reduce such vulnerability depend heavily on the local context. For example, possessing a shirt is necessary for a poor person to avoid further social and economic exclusion in some contexts, but not in others. Similarly, the primary good of income of some kind may be useful for obtaining prescription medicines in a market economy but not very useful in a planned economy such as North Korea, where political contacts may be the necessary means to obtain those medicines. A list of 'universally necessary means' to pursuing 'all reasonable conceptions of the good' is therefore unlikely to be exhaustive of the goods necessary in any—let alone every—context.[186]

As for supplying a specific list and priority ordering of capabilities, it seems to me that this area is so contested that a profitable strategy for identifying interests is to ask first which agents are or could be best positioned to make which judgements of interests. At any rate, that is the strategy I shall pursue.

4. The Limits of Elections: Accountability, Reliability, Receptivity

What institutional mechanisms can be used to best identify, empower, and constrain the most informed and capable agents to judge the interests of the public? How can those institutional mechanisms also compel political rulers and political systems to 'elicit' and 'take into account' the active judgements of the public about their own interests in a way that justifies attributing systematic control to the public? If these two questions do not seem to demand that we square the circle, that is because we are so used to presuming that elections constitute

---

[186] See esp. Sen, *Development as Freedom*, chapter 3, and *Inequality Reexamined*, chapter 5. It seems to me that these criticisms of the primary goods approach still apply both when the analysis moves beyond more 'basic' capabilities and when there is highly limited information on relative positions and conversion rates (as in some developing countries, war zones, etc.). But I shall not debate the points here; see Sen and Nussbaum, eds., *Quality of Life*, and Nussbaum and Glover, eds., *Women, Culture, and Development*.

the basic answer to both questions. But does popular voting in a public competition for political offices get us as close as is possible to achieving representation? I shall argue that elections are nowhere near sufficient *nor do they have primacy* of impact in democracy, when it comes to compelling rulers and the political system to act in the best interests, and attend to the views, of the public.

Elections displace the problem of identifying interests into politics, but they do so only by making implicit commitments to a hybrid conception of the types and times of judgements appropriate to identifying interests. I begin by outlining the three ways in which elections are thought to achieve representation—accountability, reliability, and receptivity.[187] I then show that elections understood in these three ways—whether taken alone or in combination—constitute an inadequate route to representation. However, it is possible to conceive and establish further institutions that can play the primary role in mediating between judgements by citizens and by rulers, and between divergent judgements by a range of rulers themselves.

Reliability: A government is reliable if it seeks to implement the undertakings or manifesto on the basis of which it was appointed, and thereby lives up to its purported promises. The principals (the public) indicate to their agents (rulers) what basic courses of action should be taken, by choosing certain agents and not others.

Accountability: A government is accountable if the prospect of future assessment—leading to reappointment or to dismissal—leads that government to seek to judge and act in the best interests of a majority.[188] Sanctions and rewards are supplied retrospectively, through assessment by principals (the public) who evaluate their agents (rulers) as responsible for past actions, and reappoint or dismiss those agents.

Receptivity: A government is receptive if, in the inter-electoral period, it adopts policies that a majority of citizens 'signal' that they favour. Receptivity too works prospectively, because it depends on the prior articulation of the 'signals' from the principals (the public) through non-electoral mechanisms such as opinion polls or direct action. On a reductionist view, however, such non-electoral signals derive their force only from the prospect of reappointment or dismissal of rulers (agents) in future elections.

---

[187] In distinguishing these three elements, I have found invaluable A. Przeworski, S. Stokes, and B. Manin, 'Introduction', Manin, Przeworski and Stokes 'Elections and Representation', in Przeworski et al., eds., *Accountability*.

[188] Unfortunately, most definitions of accountability in the political science literature link the concept to preference satisfaction and not to (best) interests.

Clearly, these three ways of attempting to achieve representation through election can be combined in various fashions. The question is whether any or all of them can succeed.

A purely prospective reliability model is the least promising of the three ways to achieve representation, because it fails to recognise the *raison d'être* of political rule. We need rulers in order to deal with changing circumstances; taking these circumstances into account is an essential part of what it is for them to act in our best interests. Yet it is impossible to predict how circumstances will change over the coming years between elections. If we wish our best interests to be pursued throughout a term of office, then elections should not be understood as establishing a firm and specific mandate that rulers must implement in the ensuing years, come what may. It would be bizarre if rulers were unable to learn from and be persuaded by one another, or if they were prevented more generally from adjusting their decisions in the light of new information and arguments—derived from constituents, NGOs, corporations, experts, citizens, and others. Certainly, such restrictions would not contribute to realising the public's best interests: 'we expect governments to do all that is possible under the circumstances to improve our welfare [as well as capabilities], rather than fulfil contracts'.[189]

Electoral pledges come with *ceteris paribus* clauses, and the situation never stays the same; democratic governments must govern and not simply implement their electoral pledges. This explains, in part, why *no* existing democratic system legally obliges its politicians to be faithful to the platforms on which they were elected.[190] Of course, politicians who deviate from mandates often have some explaining to do, but explain they may.[191] So we still need an account of when and how to assess such explanations and performance; understood purely in terms of reliability, elections cannot achieve representation.

[189] Przeworski et al., 'Introduction', 12. This is one of the reasons that promises of a binding 'Contract with America' and the like are misleading political ploys.

[190] Manin et al., 'Elections', 38–9. There are legally binding referenda in three countries in the world—Switzerland, Italy, and Argentina—but these concern single issues rather than platforms, and are subject to several restrictions. No proposals put forward in elections are binding in these countries either. Indeed, citizens' suits against governments, for betraying campaign promises, have been rejected by the courts in several countries (ibid.).

[191] 'The representative ... must not be found persistently at odds with the wishes of the represented without good reason in terms of their interest, without a good explanation of why their wishes are not in accord with their interest' (Pitkin, *Representation*, 210).

A purely retrospective accountability model, on which 'elections establish the calendar for when the accounts are to be taken',[192] fares only a little better. This model seems to allow citizens to take account of how well a government has dealt with changing circumstances, and to consider the extent to which rulers deviated appropriately from their initial pledges. The idea is that—in between elections—rulers anticipate such judgement, and pursue the best interests of the electorate so as to retain their positions as rulers. The first problem is this: where politicians are not ideally motivated—where they are prepared to prioritise their own interests where those conflict with the interests of the public—a 'trade-off' is set up between losing office, on the one hand, and self-regarding 'rent seeking', on the other. Yet an accountability model cannot prevent the latter, since rulers can extract 'rents' all the way up until the point where doing so threatens their occupancy of office, with the result that there is likely to be highly suboptimal pursuit of citizens' interests.[193] Insofar as citizens unavoidably have less information and capacities than rulers to identify rulers' opportunities and means for rent seeking, rulers will have that immense leeway. Fixed term limits create further problems: rulers are compelled to leave office anyway, so the threat of not being re-elected has less weight.[194]

These problems would not be so severe under idealised conditions of complete publicity and information where citizens would know of rent seeking behaviour and punish rulers for it. However, 'complete publicity and information' is a phrase that hides large issues (as the foregoing discussion evinced), despite its pivotal place in many democratic mythologies. Rulers have interests of their own, and these prove extremely difficult to find out about. Further, 'representatives become different from their constituents by the mere fact of being representatives'.[195] Rulers can devote their full-time attention to discerning

---

[192] Manin et al., 'Elections', 39.

[193] Ibid., 40–4. Moreover, rent seeking can over time—as exemplified by Mugabe in Zimbabwe—lead to accumulation of excessive power between elections and eventually to election rigging.

[194] Even rulers coming to the end of a fixed term can be constrained to some extent: they are typically concerned with their reputations after they leave office, and have social and institutional links (e.g. through political parties) to those who could stand for election in future. A stark example is the US presidential election of 2000, where the option to choose George W. Bush was linked to judgements of his father's legacy and the option to choose Al Gore was strongly linked to judgements of Bill Clinton's legacy. Candidate and previous office holder were in a powerful alliance in both cases. But note that none of this stopped extensive rent seeking, through pardons, at the end of the Clinton administration . . .

[195] Ibid., 32.

problems and opportunities, deliberating, and acting in light of that information and insight. They have knowledge and can undertake actions that citizens cannot monitor or can only monitor at a prohibitive cost at any time. Even the retrospective judgements of citizens are made, therefore, on the basis of incomplete and asymmetric information. Elections, understood as retrospective scrutiny of rulers by the public, must to that significant extent fall short of achieving representation.

There is some evidence that a mixed model—where elections are understood as both a prospective and a retrospective form of institutionalised judgement—provides a better basis for representation than pure models, as well as being more true to life. People use the vote both to sanction previous governments and to select new ones, and this seems entirely rational.[196] On the one hand, we wish to make credible threats to throw out rulers if they do not act in our best interests; on the other, the past is past, and we wish to select the best rulers now to grapple with whatever problems and opportunities arise in future. At the moment of election, we aim both to show any potential ruler that past failure to act in the best interests of the public will generally be sanctioned *and* to select the best rulers to act in the interests of the public for the coming period.

We aim, then, to entrench the rules as well as to play successfully within the game. These aims do not always converge, simply because they have different (temporal) objects in view. The relative importance of these aims has to be decided upon by voters, as well as by makers and interpreters of constitutions. The American founding fathers displayed the virtue at least of explicitly prioritising one way or another; they gave precedence to the prior selection of competent leaders over retrospective holding of rulers to account: 'The aim of every political constitution is, or ought to be, *first* to obtain for rulers men who possess most wisdom to discern, and most virtue to pursue, the common good of the society; and, *in the next place*, to take the most effectual precautions for keeping them virtuous whilst they continue to hold the public trust.'[197]

But even on this mixed model, elections are never sufficient to secure representation: the vote can only be one instrument with at

---

[196] J. D. Fearon, 'Electoral Accountability and the Control of Politicians: Selecting Good Types versus Sanctioning Poor Performance', in Przeworski et al., eds., *Accountability*, 76–81.

[197] J. Madison, A. Hamilton, and J. Jay, *The Federalist*, W. R. Brock, ed. (London: Phoenix Press, 2000), Federalist 57 (my italics).

least two purposes, and asymmetric and incomplete information make it a blunt instrument at that.

Are there ways to make government receptive to non-electoral signals, then, so as to come much closer to achieving representation? A pure receptivity model is exemplified by Rawls' notion of a 'decent consultation hierarchy', where there is no vote to appoint office-holders but there is some attention to the views of persons (qua members of associations) at important junctures of decision. I criticised this model as illiberal and anti-democratic in Chapter 1: where rulers' legitimacy depends largely or entirely on a tradition or the like, a common consequence is that they become unreceptive even to the most dire and obvious needs of citizens (such as avoiding famines, rights violations, and political instability).

Perhaps the solution is to combine receptivity with electoral accountability and reliability as ways to achieve representation. The distinct advantage of adding measures to improve receptivity is that it allows for various signals to be sent, making for a less singular and blunt instrument than the vote on its own. But even a combined model, thus understood, is far from sufficient to achieve representation. I cannot discuss here the many ways in which 'civil society' sends signals, and the different respects in which signals often prove ineffective (even in conjunction with the vote) or clash with electoral mandates and retrospective evaluation in elections. Instead, I shall concentrate briefly on three generic difficulties that remain even where receptivity forms part of a mixed approach.

First, it is a commonplace in the literature on leadership that ruling in the best interests of the people at times requires the courage *not* to be receptive to shifts in public opinion, which can be fickle, reactive, short-sighted, and misinformed. Consider the groundswell of aggressively retributive opinion against criminal suspects of certain kinds—where the public may show little care for norms of fair treatment of prisoners and fair trial procedure (from the presumption of innocence to consistency in sentencing). Second, the problems of asymmetric and incomplete information tend to be even more severe when trying to achieve receptivity than when trying to achieve reliability and accountability. The build-up to elections is typically long and sustained, providing time for rulers to clarify platforms somewhat, as well as time for citizens to access more information and develop some considered convictions on platforms, potential rulers, and the performance of government in the previous inter-election period. Yet—as demonstrated in Chapter 2—informal mechanisms for expression of public opinion (e.g. deliberative opinion polls) cannot in general offer even this mild possibility for accurately eliciting and taking into account the judgements of the public.[198] Third, those interest groups which tend to be most effective between elections in making rulers receptive to their judgements often pursue sectional interests that do not coincide with the interests of a majority, or even with the majority's judgements of their own interests. We cannot simply 'leave it to civil society' in the inter-electoral period to make up the deficiencies of elections in empowering and constraining rulers to act attentively in the best interests of the public.

But if electoral mechanisms for producing accountability and reliability—even in conjunction with receptivity to inter-electoral signals from citizens—do not come close to achieving representation, must the pursuit of representation (as anything except perhaps a useful myth) be abandoned? 'Minimalist' theorists argue that it must. I shall disagree.

5. The Democratic Doubters: Schumpeter, Popper, Przeworski

If elections are insufficient to achieve anything close to representation, then there are two conceptual paths a democratic theorist might take. One path is to accept that it is impossible to get rulers to act attentively towards the best interests and views of the public; this leaves open the possibility that democracy can still be justified on grounds other than achieving genuine representation. Another path is to specify further procedures and mechanisms in addition to election that could render rulers and a political system far more representative. The strongest formulations of the first path are found in the works of Joseph Schumpeter, Karl Popper, and Adam Przeworski.[199] On this kind of

---

[198] It would be revealing to consider why governments are generally expected to take mandates from elections more seriously than inter-election signals—i.e. as more informed, less reactive, and so forth—and why the two sometimes clash. I cannot pursue an analysis of that kind here; see S. Stokes, 'What Do Policy Switches Tell Us about Democracy?' and J. Ferejohn, 'Accountability and Authority: Toward a Theory of Political Accountability', both in Przeworski et al., eds., *Accountability*.

[199] See mainly J. A. Schumpeter, *Capitalism, Socialism and Democracy*, third edn. (London: Allen and Unwin, 1950); K. Popper, *The Open Society and Its Enemies* (London: Routledge, 1945); A. Przeworski, 'Minimalist Conception of Democracy: A Defense', in I. Shapiro and C. Hacker-Cordon, eds., *Democracy's Value* (Cambridge: Cambridge University Press, 1999). All three theorists sometimes

Minimalist account, as Przeworski states quite explicitly, there are rulers but no representatives.[200] I want to show that the Minimalist account is not simply deflationist; rather, it is unnecessarily defeatist. In considering and rejecting this account, it is possible to begin to identify procedures and mechanisms by which to salvage representation.

For Minimalist theorists, the aim of the best political system is to prevent internecine strife, bloodshed, and violent death. They differ most fundamentally from Hobbes not in their analysis of the problem of politics, then, but in the system they propose as a solution.[201] That system is what they call democracy: competitive election to offices of coercive authority. Broadly, ballots are and should be, in the words of Engels (but without his disdain), 'paper stones' by which conflict is mediated, institutionalised, and pacified. For instance, a majority voting-rule is thought of as institutionalising a 'flexing [of] muscles' which indicates the 'chances [of victory] in the eventual war'.[202] Under conditions of publicity, it becomes rational for citizens to skip straight past the nasty process of war and to adopt the outcomes supported by the likely victors. Przeworski further insists that Minimalists are distinguished by the fact that they make no claim for the *quality* of the outcomes: elections have 'no causal consequences for anything else' other than peaceful decision one way or another.[203] That peaceful decision concerns, in the first instance, who should rule, but 'the very prospect that governments may change can result in

claim that they are defending democracy, *even if* this extremely limited form of government is all democracy is, rather than *even though* this is all democracy is. Pure Minimalists deny that further justifications for democracy are possible.

[200] Przeworski, 'Minimalist', 43–4.

[201] Schumpeter does not merely define democracy as a system of rule, he *recommends* it; that is, despite his claims to provide a descriptive or empirical account, he appeals to normative intuitions too. See Q. Skinner, 'The Empirical Theorists of Democracy and Their Critics: A Plague on Both Their Houses', *Political Theory*, Vol. 1, No. 1 (1973), 287–306, at 299–300.

[202] Przeworski, 'Minimalist', 48–50. The weapon of the ballot must be held universally because, apparently, majority rule accurately indicates who is likely to be victorious in violent conflict. Meanwhile, powerful elites must be allowed to contest elections because, by institutionalising the competition for power, it is possible to get elites to 'accept defeat in return for peace and the possibility of victory in the future' (I. Shapiro and C. Hacker-Cordon, 'Introduction' to Shapiro and Hacker-Cordon, eds., *Value*, 4). It does not appear that these views can be reconciled with the fact that (modern) violent conflicts tend to be won or lost on the basis of superior technology and organisation, not numbers.

[203] Ibid., 24.

peaceful regulation of [other] conflicts' too, such as those within the ruling elites over policy.[204] Against Condorcet and Rousseau, democratic processes do not uniquely or necessarily contribute to an increase in any social welfare maximum—or indeed to any specific outcome other than the avoidance of violent death—and they cannot be justified on that instrumental basis. Democracy is 'conflict without killing'—worthwhile, but not a *summum bonum* of collective life.[205]

Minimalists altogether reject the idea that rulers can be made to act in the best interests of the public. Admittedly, Schumpeter can be read differently, as establishing that the most able rulers win electoral contests, by being most effective at 'selling' policies for votes.[206] However, in Schumpeter's account, rulers are judged 'able' because they win votes and not because they have governed or will govern well, let alone in the best interests of the public. Rulers sell—and are 'trained' in political competitions to sell—the most popular combination of policies, which does not necessarily overlap with the best interests of the majority of citizens. For example, on this view rulers may 'sell' policies to small but powerful special interest groups, in return for backing—policies that impose small or even large unnecessary burdens on the majority. Nothing in theory, let alone practice, prevents a competitive elitist system, especially one modelled on consumer pricing theory, from being subject to such distortions. Minimalists accept this—on their view, to hope for anything more is to hope in vain—and so accept that it is impossible to achieve representation in any thick sense.

How accurate is this brutal 'realism'? It may describe some practices in some putative democracies, but can it serve as a normative theory of democracy? The first thing to note is that this conception of democracy is unstable on its own terms. Can we plausibly claim 'Hitler was elected, which fortunately prevented more warlike and deadly competition'? It is simply not the case that winners and losers of elections always have more to gain by retaining the democratic system; nor is it the case that outcomes that are initially pacific will remain so. Both the durability of a democracy and its benefits to the public must depend on how firmly—and in what ways—rulers' use of power is constrained. But if that is the case, then democracy requires far more than elections.

---

[204] Przeworski, 'Minimalist', 45.
[205] Ibid., 25–6 and 49–50.
[206] Schumpeter, *Capitalism*, 250–83.

Once Minimalists accept this point, however, they find themselves committed to a much richer conception of democracy—including a system of checks and balances that keeps a specific *kind* of peace.[207] That peace is preferred to other kinds on the basis not only that it enables future democratic contests but also that it is more in the interests of the public. (Strictly speaking, on the Minimalist account, only one interest of the public—pacific order—has total priority, and this priority comes at the expense of all other interests.) Rousseau, quoting Palatine, put this point in its most extreme form as follows: 'Better freedom with danger than peace with slavery.'[208] Not every government, not even every elected government, is preferable to conflict—or even to war. What allows, indeed requires, us to make this judgement is a broad conception of government as geared towards something more than order—as justified on the basis of its pursuit of interests that go beyond mere (and sometimes reprehensible) peace.

The second thing to note is that there is no reason to couch the choice between different normative models of democracy as a stark one between naively promising perfect representation, on the one hand, and insisting that there is no such thing, on the other. As pointed out in my account of judgements of interests, representation is surely a matter of degree.[209] The problem with elections is not that they are imperfect, but that they are suboptimal and potential sources of instability on their own. There are—as I now hope to show—institutional mechanisms of appointment, empowerment, and constraint that can play the primary role in making political office-holders act and political institutions operate in a highly representative fashion. These mechanisms could achieve specific kinds of *responsiveness*—horizontal

---

[207] Przeworski admits that separation of powers might help sustain democracy, but does not pursue the suggestion, and indeed disparages it as 'less than persuasive' as a solution ('Minimalist', 44, n. 23).

[208] Rousseau, *Social Contract*, 114.

[209] Like Robert Dahl I believe that no actual democracy can be perfectly in line with an ideal model (this is in part why the early Dahl speaks of polyarchy rather than democracy), and yet that some systems do get closer than others to the ideal. See R. Dahl, *Polyarchy: Participation and Opposition* (New Haven, CT: Yale University Press, 1971). One crucial test of an ideal conception is how close we could get to it in practice. Another crucial test is whether getting as close to the ideal conception as possible leaves us in a 'second best' position, or whether a quite different destination and route should be proposed. Both tests frame Chapter 4 and my Conclusion.

responsiveness (between judgements by different representatives) as well as vertical responsiveness (between judgements of citizens and representatives). Such dual responsiveness would constitute highly representative governance.

6. The Plurality of Powers

We need an account of how the most informed and capable agents can be appointed, empowered, and constrained as representatives, and how the public's judgements of their interests can be responsibly elicited, scrutinised, and taken into account by those representatives. This account must not rely entirely on the public to do all the work of judging themselves (most demandingly) or (still too demandingly) to identify, empower, and constrain all the appropriate agents themselves in elections and between elections. At the same time, the account must show how it is still possible to attribute systematic control to the public. The account will be *institutional* in the sense that it proposes specific institutions through which information—including information about citizens' judgements—and power can be made available to and be used responsibly by rulers.

6.1 Generalising the Separation of Powers

We can take a cue from the framers of the American Constitution, who acknowledged that elections are insufficient to achieve representation and then offered some institutional approaches to dealing with this problem:

A dependence on the people is, no doubt, the primary control on the government; but experience has taught mankind the necessity of auxiliary precautions. This policy of supplying, by opposite and rival interests, the defect of better motives . . . [is] particularly displayed in all the subordinate distributions of power, where the constant aim is to divide and arrange the several offices in such a manner as that each may be a check on the other.[210]

Separation of powers can address asymmetries of both power and information between citizens and rulers by inducing institutions, and rulers who are office holders in institutions, to—in the now immortal phrase—check and balance one another. The basic idea is to assign

---

[210] Madison et al., *Federalist*, no. 51. I shall not discuss here the intellectual history of this sort of approach to government, developed by, among others, Locke, Sieyes, and Montesquieu.

authorities well-defined powers over distinct and potentially conflicting governmental functions, and yet make all those authorities dependent upon one another in significant respects if they are to fulfil their respective functions. They are then faced with strong reasons to agree to a common set of laws and policies, and this need for consensus or compromise has at least two effects. Where their preferred ends or means for fulfilling their functions come into conflict, authorities tend to attempt to harness the capacities of citizens and other authorities as resources of power against one another. Authorities also tend to attempt to monitor and constrain one another in their daily operation so as to ensure that no authority or subset of authorities comes to dominate. This much is widely accepted in the literature, but there is disagreement over how separation of powers brings about effects of this kind, and what kinds of separation of powers produce the best such effects. In any context, there is a need to consider how many and what kinds of separate authorities are best, and how those authorities can be compelled to relate to one another and to citizens to the best effect.

Our understanding of how the separation of powers works and should work to induce representation has been advanced significantly by a recent study (albeit in the language of formal macroeconomics) by Persson, Roland, and Tabellini.[211] They model the vexed situation in which a 'legislature' and 'executive' have to agree to a budget, where one policy-maker has agenda-setting power over the size of the budget and the other over its composition. Their most important finding is that the separation of powers dramatically reduces the scope for abuse of power *even where authorities are unequal in power and the public are less informed than rulers*: 'We also show that separation of powers enables the voters to elicit the private information held by the elected political officials and hence to remove any informational rents . . . We find that it is the body with the weaker bargaining power which reveals the information'.[212]

In several cases, the weaker body uses the 'voters' as a resource to increase its power, while the voters use it as a resource for information that—in turn—increases their power. In other cases, the mere prospect

[211] T. Persson, G. Roland, and G. Tabellini, 'Separation of Powers and Accountability: Towards a Formal Approach to Comparative Politics', Discussion Paper No. 1475 (London: Centre for Economic Policy Research, 1996).

[212] Ibid., vii. I will not rehearse the formal model and the assumptions it makes here. The model is a revealing place to start, but further—less etiolated— arguments will be needed to show that this general principle provides a plausible orientation for institutional design in the messier real world of democracy.

of exposure leads authorities to curtail rent-seeking behaviour, so that there is no need to actually reveal 'privileged' information in the end—a credible threat is sufficient. Separation of powers may support responsible and responsive behaviour in the pursuit of citizens' best interests—even where significant informational and power asymmetries between rulers and citizens remain.

The general principle of separation of powers can be instantiated in many forms other than the traditional Montesquieuan tripartite combination of legislature, executive, and judiciary. Persson et al. indicate that the principle could also be instantiated in competition between political parties in some areas (e.g. judging the appropriate mix of content for programs by the public broadcaster), where agreement between government and opposition could be required and have beneficial results.[213] This is to suggest that the separation of powers is not necessarily an idea limited to the usual intra-state relations but can be understood as an organising principle for politics at different levels and loci of governance—the bare bones of an idea that I shall flesh out in some detail.

For now, note that similarly positive results can be shown where non-state actors, such as powerful NGOs, are in a position to operate as robust counterweights to more formal authorities, such as states. Indeed, as I shall show in Chapter 4, state and non-state actors can be made to place firm limits on each others' abilities to use their powerful positions selfishly and irresponsibly, especially where each has strong incentives to expose deceptive reports and action by the others. I shall show also that these various instantiations of the separation of powers can be mutually reinforcing in achieving better representation.

The deeper point here can be put rather simply: from the fact that we should be concerned about discrepancies between citizens and rulers, it does not follow that those discrepancies can or should be eradicated. There are good reasons why some agents (rulers, experts) should possess certain powers and knowledge that are not shareable by the public. What is objectionable is when discrepancies of this kind have an *impact* on different members of the public that is unfair, capricious, or unauthorised. The task is to prevent not the use of power, but its abuse. It turns out that, against the deliberative theorists, it is not necessary to make intense demands on citizens in order to make

---

[213] Persson et al. 'Separation', 14 and 28. An important caveat is that it may take 'several attempts [at bargaining] before a stable framework emerges'; see A. Przeworski and twenty-one collaborators, *Sustainable Democracy* (Cambridge: Cambridge University Press, 1995), quotation at 49.

it likely that their best interests will be identified and pursued by rulers. A suitable dispersal of authority, linked with the prospect of publicity and sanction—including removal from public office through elections and other mechanisms of dismissal—might together reduce the adverse *effects* of discrepancies of power and information. Deliberative theorists are wrong also when they argue that deliberation has to take place primarily between citizens: to achieve a high degree of representation, it may be sufficient—even when there are power asymmetries—to require certain kinds of communicative interaction between suitably defined, distinct governmental authorities.

We can conclude, in very general terms at this point, that plural authority structures, suitably situated vis-à-vis one another, could induce more representative rule. This practical possibility will be an important orienting idea when approaching the problem of democratising dispersed, semi-independent great and global institutions. But the difficulty lies in giving this initial idea sufficiently determinate content, so that it can serve as an evaluative framework by which to understand current global political issues better and to identify legal and institutional solutions.

I propose to reserve the term *horizontally responsive* to denote a relationship between authorities that check and balance one another in part because (despite some divergent ends and means) they need to compromise or find consensus in order to fulfil their functions, and so will be receptive to one another's claims and counterclaims. These structured positions and relations may secure the outcomes to which deliberative theorists aspire, by ensuring that policy debates take place between informed and capable agents, who together are compelled to try to identify the best interests of the public, and are willing and able to act on the outcomes of those debates. But, whereas deliberative democracy cannot deliver on this ambition in societies of any scale, a pluralised authority structure could do so without overwhelming decision-makers. That is, where there are two or even fifty professional authorities, we need not have the same concerns about scope that scuttle the possibility of deliberation between millions of citizens.[214]

But horizontal responsiveness, thus understood, would not be enough for a system to be representative. For that, authorities must be compelled to elicit and take into account the active judgements of citizens; indeed, authorities must be able to check and balance one another precisely because they draw on citizens in this way as a robust

---

[214] Other serious concerns do arise, however, and are addressed below.

resource of power. Unless authorities are thus constrained, there is likely to be a collapse into a merely technocratic system of rule.

I propose to use the term *vertically responsive* to denote a relationship between authorities and citizens where the 'reasonable contestations' of the latter are sufficient to generate a 'proper response' from the former. A proper response would involve at least an explanation for adopting a policy that citizens oppose and at most a change of policy. Clearly, not every response from rulers can count as adequate explanation; the requirement to respond would then place almost no pressure on rulers and so would be pointless. Similarly, not every comment offered by citizens can qualify as reasonable, or be regarded as having equal force, otherwise representatives would be swamped and responses would be formulaic. (Thank you for your letter about X; unfortunately, all our resources are directed towards overriding priority Y right now—Yours truly, President Unresponsive.)

I do not think there is a general answer to this problem. Some guidance as to the relevant kinds of reasons and responses is provided by the degree to which an issue is one that involves expertise of one kind or another. Further guidance on which judgements of citizens are to be treated as reasonable might be provided by the extent to which a reason is both widely shareable and taken up by other citizens across a range of current social and geographical divides. Similarly, guidance on which responses of rulers are proper might be provided by the degree to which citizens are demanding action that a wide range of separate authorities view as significantly out of kilter with the current capacities, projects, and policies of political authorities.

However, as I argued above, interminable discussions about the abstract criteria for good reasons and true interests take us a limited distance, and the remaining distance cannot be covered by invoking elections and civil society. Instead, I shall propose an additional set of institutions for eliciting and winnowing out reasonable citizen judgements and ruler responses. Although I cannot supply a general account of the threshold for reasonableness in politics (I believe no one can), I can show that a range of citizen judgements that obviously seem to qualify as reasonable would not be elicited, and/or no response would be forthcoming, unless a certain pluralistic institutional structure was in place.

6.2. Three Great Dangers

There are, it seems to me, three great dangers that arise in taking this pluralistic route to improving representation: power imbalances, adverse bureaucracy, and passive citizenry. But these problems are not as insurmountable as those that defeat deliberative democracy. I now briefly outline each danger, and then use the remaining three sections of the chapter to develop replies to each danger in turn. In so doing, I develop the idea of a plurality of powers, elaborating the institutions that together produce responsive representation.

First, power imbalances: Political power might be asymmetrically distributed in several ways that are at once difficult to counteract and highly detrimental to vertical and horizontal responsiveness. One authority might dominate others because of a peculiar advantage, such as a charismatically legitimated executive: this was the case in newly independent Zimbabwe, where such dominance was a significant source of later oppression of citizens. Or an authority might come to dominate because of weaknesses internal to other authorities: this is the case, for example, in those developing countries and new democracies where the media and judiciary are still damaged from strife and corruption during the pre-democratic period, and remain weak even under the new democratic dispensation. Or there is the intense worry that one authority might dominate because most citizens alone, or in existing groups, are not a very robust non-electoral resource of power: this is the case, for example, where 'civil society' is weak (or 'uncivil society' is strong) after authoritarianism, as in several Balkan states, or where formal political structures outstrip civic attitudes of affiliation to such structures, as in the European Union.

Second, adverse bureaucracy: Bureaucracy—in the pejorative sense—exists where (1) many authorities have to fulfil interconnected functions so as to perform a governmental task, but (2) intricate divisions of labour, rules of operation, and lines of communication lead to a fragmentation of obligations, such that (3) each authority can fulfil its allocated function even while abjuring responsibility for the task as a whole, and thus (4) official sanctions and rewards come to derive exclusively from fulfilling narrow formal obligations, not from producing worthwhile outcomes or taking worthwhile risks; yet (5) authorities generally have more scope for action than their narrow formal obligations anticipate, and so (6) many of the powers authorities do in fact possess go unregulated and undirected, and can be used to obtain other rewards—including additional leisure time—resulting in (7) systematic underuse, misuse, and abuse of authorities' actual powers.[215] Large organisational structures, in which there are multiple

---

[215] In this characterisation of bureaucracy in the pejorative sense, I have in mind Max Weber's characterisation of modern bureaucracy in the more neutral

role-players, combined with vast but potentially poor communication systems, run a particular risk of such fragmented and anaemic responsibility.

Third, passive citizenry: In vast, complex organisational structures, it may be impossible for ordinary citizens to have much effect through their judgements and actions. For instance, where there are many public offices, it may prove overwhelmingly complicated and time consuming to vote for each occupant of every office. It may prove very difficult for citizens to discover to whom they should articulate concerns and from whom they should expect responses. Or the institutions may prove to be so removed from citizens' own immediate context and experience that citizens feel little attachment to the offices and office-holders, and see little reason to support those institutions on an ongoing basis. In each case, citizens would not exercise the control necessary for government to be representative.

Whether and in what ways these three dangers can be avoided or alleviated are questions that involve complex issues of institutional design as well as political theory.

7. Accountability and Advocacy Agencies: Reducing Power Imbalances

Entrenched and detrimental asymmetric power is an especially severe problem given the inadequacies of elections as a discipline on governance. The Persson model suggests some guidance for transforming and designing institutions that subject rulers to further, non-electoral disciplines on government: Authorities must be structured so that they are required to agree or compromise on policies at specific stages. They must be able to access support from citizens fairly

---

sense: 'I. There is the principle of official *jurisdictional areas*, which are generally ordered by rules, that is, by laws or administrative regulations . . . II. The principles of *office hierarchy* and of channels of appeal (*Instanzenzug*) stipulate a clearly established system of super- and sub-ordination . . . III. The management of the modern office is based on written documents (the 'files') . . . IV. Office management . . . usually presupposes a thorough training in the field of specialization . . . V. [Official] . . . activity demands the *full working capacity* of the official . . . VI. The management of the office follows *general rules*, which are more or less stable, more or less exhaustive, and which can be learned'. See M. Weber, *Economy and Society: An Outline of Interpretive Sociology*, Vol. 2, G. Roth and C. Wittich, eds. (Berkeley, CA: University of California Press, 1978), 956–1005, quotation at 956–8.

regularly as a resource against domination. They must be able to present an ongoing and credible threat of exposure and sanction. And they must be able to invoke constitutional protections against encroachment on each other's functions. Further guidance for institutional transformation can be derived from the histories of relatively successful federal states, where there have been sustained attempts to carefully allocate definite powers and responsibilities, communicative competences and requirements.

However, these guiding ideas and past experiences do not make it possible to eliminate the dangers of collusion between authorities, of domination by one authority, or of civil society remaining relatively weak and easily overridden or corrupted. The only general solution would be institutions that are by their very nature and function strongly resistant to being co-opted and overridden. I want to sketch two partly new and certainly under-appreciated sets of institutions that could be developed—one set that would enhance vertical responsiveness and one set that would enhance horizontal responsiveness.

The first set of institutions, suggested by recent work in Republican political theory, might be called *advocacy agencies* or *channels of dissent*.[216] These agencies include independent public protectors, ombudsmen, legal aid bureaux, consumer watchdogs, and citizens' advice bureaux—but of a stronger and more extensive kind than those extant in most democratic states today. Their task would be partly to elicit information from governmental authorities, but above all to access concerns and complaints from the citizenry, to winnow out those that are widespread and/or well-founded, and to effectively demand a suitable response from political authorities (at the very least an explanation, at most a change in policy). In this respect, advocacy agencies would serve a similar function to Letters to Congressmen or Members of Parliament, investigative commissions, and reports; but—as I shall show—they would be less partisan, ad hoc, and susceptible to capture by special interests.

The second set of institutions—designed to improve horizontal responsiveness—might be called *accountability agencies* or *channels of scrutiny*. A few of these institutions are in existence at present in quite a few countries. Their main task is to supply citizens with somewhat more independent, assessable information about governance than is made available by representatives themselves, by interest

---

[216] See P. Pettit, *Republicanism* (Oxford: Oxford University Press, 1997) who promotes somewhat similar 'institutions of contestation'.

groups, and by the media:

Such institutions may include (1) an independent board to assure transparency of campaign contributions, with its own investigative powers; (2) an independent . . . auditor-general . . . ; (3) an independent source of statistical information about the state of the economy; and (4) [an independent board with] a privileged place for opposition political parties [and public figures who are not party partisan or come from across the political spectrum] in overseeing the publicly owned media.[217]

To this one might add (5) a Corruption Commission, with statutory authority to investigate and act to prevent corruption.

None of these types of institution is intrinsically restricted to regulation within states. For instance, while Transparency International, the most successful international anti-corruption NGO, is not itself a statutory body, its measures and recommendations have been incorporated into governmental regulatory regimes both within and beyond borders. But before considering the role of such agencies in global affairs (in Chapter 4), we need to ask more generally: what are the political and judicial functions, powers, dilemmas, and dangers of advocacy and accountability agencies? Here I will only say enough to provide a plausible outline of formal but non-electoral mechanisms that induce vertical and horizontal responsiveness.

Properly constituted, accountability and advocacy agencies are less likely to be intimidated or dominated by any authority than are citizens on their own. Aside from their constitutional or statutory entrenched powers and resource-claims, they would have a wider pool of expertise and comparative experience to draw on, in providing information, analysis, and argument on citizens' behalf, and/or in assisting citizens. It is always likely that wealthier and more powerful citizens will be highly effective in forming alliances with those who share their own interests, and will employ 'professional contesters' to serve their ends. Advocacy agencies could provide the least advantaged citizens with a counterbalancing set of professional contesters, who can press those citizens' concerns against government with similar effectiveness. Just as the answer to hate speech is more speech, in general, the answer to dangers of wealthy and powerful contesters hijacking the process is, in general, more and better formal contesters with explicit responsibilities to assist and act on behalf of the poor and marginalised.

---

[217] The term 'accountability agencies' is from D. Dunn and J. Uhr, 'Accountability and Responsibility in Modern Democratic Governments', paper presented at the annual meeting of the American Political Science Association, Washington, DC, 1993; cited in Przeworski et al., 'Elections', 50.

The plausibility of these proposals is subject to empirical tests. But a comparison with other potential routes by which citizens might pursue their claims, and scrutinise and sanction rulers, highlights some severe limitations of those other routes—in particular, the judiciary and political parties. The comparison also provides empirical grounds for thinking that such limitations could be remedied by the provision of appropriate advocacy and accountability agencies.

Take the judiciary first. The judiciary has intrinsic features that prevent it from being a sufficient source of scrutiny and sanction of rulers. In order to preserve its relative autonomy, the judiciary has to conform to a rigorous jurisprudential logic and code of conduct that keep it distant from the vicissitudes of political engagement and decision. It is not generally in the business of actively *eliciting* complaints and concerns from the public, or of *educating* the public on how to exercise their political rights in distinct areas, or of *publicising* and pressing government for vital policy changes that civil society—because of the weakness of certain groups—has not sufficiently pursued.[218] All these activities are essential to reduce the extent to which marginal groups and individuals are (and are compelled to be) self-effacing in their judgements and self-censoring in their articulation of their judgements. While courts can be more or less interventionist, and while legal theorists can differ on the extent to which courts are the unacknowledged legislators of the world, there is little doubt that the kind of scrutiny for which I have argued has a political component that extends far beyond the remit of an appropriately constrained and restrained judiciary.

Unlike courts, advocacy and accountability agencies need not adopt strategies based on legal dispute resolution; the latter can amplify litigiousness beyond all sense and tends to encourage dramatic underestimation of the felicity of non-legal and quasi-legal mechanisms for pressing claims and resolving disputes. The importance of this flexibility of means becomes immediately evident if we consider empirical studies, such as Hazel Genn's studies of how citizens in England and Scotland pursued potentially justiciable civil issues.[219] Over 90 percent

---

[218] Law commissions are a notable exception, and are precisely the kind of advocacy and accountability agency for which I wish to argue. Law commissions are revealing instances of the kind because their role and rhetoric do not primarily emphasise support for people who have already been victims. Advocacy and accountability agencies are not merely routes to remedy.

[219] Genn's are among the most extensive studies of their kind; see H. Genn, *Paths to Justice* (Oxford: Hart Publishing, 1999) and *Paths of Justice in Scotland* (Oxford: Hart Publishing, 2001).

of citizens pursued non- and quasi-legal routes to resolution, or they simply 'put up and shut up'. There was, moreover, grave asymmetry of jeopardy: some categories of people were not sufficiently poor to obtain state assistance in pursuing their claims, but were still sufficiently badly off that pursuing claims through legal channels was to risk utter ruin; at the same time, they had extremely limited access to alternative mechanisms of resolution.

Compare, next, political parties. Political parties are indispensable coordinating mechanisms, as well as channels for citizens to pursue their claims; but equally evidently, there are serious and irremediable limits to the politicians' effectiveness in regulating one another. Notably, independence of scrutiny and sanction of the executive by legislators is compromised where, as is generally the case, occupancy of legislative office is the main potential route to high executive office. Partly for this reason, and partly because politicians tend to depend so heavily on their own party for re-election, backbench revolts against party heads and whips tend to be rare. It is almost as rare to find heads of parliamentary committees who are fully prepared to take members of their own party to task. Hence supporters of legislator-led scrutiny are compelled to insist that scrutiny and sanction can be left largely to the main opposition parties and/or to members of parliament who have no reasonable hope of entering the executive as ministers.

The flaw in this view is immediately evident if we recognise that professional politicians are not immune from the tendency within professions to develop unchallenged orthodoxies. Professional imperatives of competition and rule induce modes of thinking, social ties, sympathies, and corporate agendas among politicians that are widely shared within and indeed across parties. Take one prominent problem that crosses party lines: the difficulty of passing bills that limit or regulate campaign finance, let alone passing the robust bills often needed. Those who occupy political office tend to be the most successful politicians in raising funds for their campaigns; hence those agents who are most able to introduce and pass campaign finance bills tend to have the strongest interest in not doing so. Moreover, those who are still seeking office generally require preferment from a range of incumbents, so there is a strong disincentive to challengers to push the point, even if such bills seem to them clearly in the best interests of the public. Other examples abound.[220] Political careerism together

---

[220] The campaign finance example is, however, the most worrying—especially in the United States, where the dependence of political power on economic

with party and professional allegiances must be assumed to count against sufficient independence of scrutiny and sanction.[221]

None of this is to say that advocacy and accountability agencies should repeat or replace some of the important roles of political parties and the judiciary. But it is to point to serious problems internal to the traditional separation of powers approach, problems that might be dealt with in part by introducing a greater plurality of *types* of powers.

The need for accountability and advocacy agencies is particularly evident given the problem of dominating majorities, and the considerations above indicate how the problem can begin to be addressed through institutional channels rather than solely through sociocultural reform.[222] To illustrate the nature and benefits of such institutional reform, I wish to consider a crucial and not atypical problem: the racially and ethnically inflected (but arguably in good part economically induced) inequalities, stigmas, and conflicts that are a widespread concern in the United Kingdom.

The Labour government that took office in 1997, when it attempted to think through and improve the situation, established several short-lived commissions and ad hoc enquiries and reports by different public figures on discrete issues and areas.[223] Short-lived bodies cannot develop adequate cumulated learning, institutional memory, and coordination capacities for dealing with this complex and pervasive issue.

power seems to escalate daily. An electoral commission appointed largely by the judiciary and mandated to take measures to ensure the fairness of competition would not necessarily fall prey to the same logic of collusion. Such a commission would however be difficult to appoint and insulate from political meddling (some remedies are discussed below).

[221] This is one reason why Habermas's main proposal for improving citizen power in the European Union, namely Europe-wide political parties (*Inclusion*, esp. 240–64), has serious limitations when presented as the main solution to a widely deplored 'democratic deficit'.

[222] There is what might be called a 'feasibility paradox' here: in contexts where advocacy and accountability agencies are most needed—for example, Zimbabwe under Mugabe—they are least likely to be established; whereas in contexts where they are least needed—for example, Sweden—they are more likely to be established. This paradox is to be expected: it is harder to produce almost *any* improvement in situations where governance has broken down. In less extreme cases, however, there are feasible strategies for introducing and strengthening advocacy and accountability agencies—as I shall show in Chapter 4, in respect of the United Nations General Assembly and Security Council as well as Transparency International.

[223] It must be said the same government did introduce some other, more thoroughgoing reforms—none more significant than the entrenchment of a Bill of Rights.

An ad hoc way of going about things also renders proposed solutions highly susceptible to being scuppered or advanced in the interests of short-term political imperatives.[224]

Rather than elaborate the example in this limited space, I wish only to indicate that we do not lack models or historical precedents for this kind of Commission. The new Constitution of South Africa requires that there be Commissions on Human Rights and Gender Equality, and these are already having an effect in dealing with the legacies of an extremely racially divisive (albeit very different) past.[225] But the most powerful example is surely the *absence* of a strong Chief Medical Officer, Medical Ombudsman, or other medical watchdog in South Africa, where the Medicines Control Council was too dependent on government and its mandate too weak—even acting in conjunction with related regulative bodies—to prevent President Thabo Mbeki from pursuing a demonstrably irresponsible HIV/AIDS policy for several years.[226]

Strong, ongoing, and semi-independent Commissions would not only have long-term and expert staff but also standing powers to investigate causes, propose and monitor reforms, and publicise changes and challenges. (Current commissions in the United Kingdom—such as the Ouseley Commission and the non-official Parekh Commission on Racial Equality, both of which produced lacklustre reports—are pale but prescient shadows of the kinds of Commission needed.) It would be naive to think that better, standing Commissions will resolve all outstanding difficulties. But, in conjunction with the other mechanisms I shall discuss, they have a better chance of producing incisive reports, and of resisting deflection and intimidation by political masters,

---

[224] Xenophobic anti-immigrant proposals during elections are the paradigm cases of this kind of political opportunism, which has ill effects not only on potential and actual immigrants but also on minority groups and social integration more generally.

[225] Chapter 9 of the South African Constitution (available at www.gov.za) is devoted entirely to 'State Institutions Supporting Constitutional Democracy'. On the impact of these institutions, see the website of the Constitutional Court of South Africa (www.concourt.gov.za), a court which has presided over a range of cases brought to the fore by, or centrally involving, the Commissions, the Public Protector, and various ombudsmen.

[226] After a lengthy process—during which time many people were infected with the virus—the Constitutional Court made the highly activist and specific intervention needed. See the Court's judgements in the case of '*Minister of Health and others v. Treatment Action Campaign and others*' (starting with judgement CCT9/02 of 4 April 2002), at www.concourt.gov.za. I have suggested that there is a better alternative to dragging courts into more and more interventions.

than does the current system for dissent, scrutiny, and sanction on its own.[227]

The most pressing set of questions that remains is how to guard these guardians of the guardians, in ways that keep them under democratic control and yet keep them robust and independent enough to fulfil their functions. Again, the answers require detailed attention to institutional design. But we can note that markedly similar questions have arisen in respect of the judiciary, and quite powerful techniques have been developed for keeping members of the judiciary fairly autonomous. These include professional codes of ethics, long-term appointments, measures to prevent sacking by politicians, adequate salaries, clear criteria of selection, independent commissions of appointment, agreement from legislators on all sides, review by higher courts, and so forth. These do not entirely remove the problem of maintaining judicial independence while also avoiding 'rogue' judges, but they do make a world with a largely independent judiciary better than a world without it. The situation of advocacy and accountability agencies is potentially even better: there is an additional possibility that the judiciary could oversee and perhaps even appoint some significant office-holders, and could provide firewalls against malevolent budget cuts by politicians who aim to avoid genuine scrutiny. Some of these many judicial techniques have been extended to executive political bodies, such as the European Commission, with varying degrees of appropriateness and success. The project, however, holds great promise, especially if accountability and advocacy agencies bear only part of the burden of securing representation.

8. A Charter of Obligations: Reducing Bureaucracy

No extended regime of governance can entirely avoid bureaucracy, in the pejorative sense. And there is a very serious danger that an increase in the number of authorities will intensify the failings of bureaucratic structures. But some empirical pointers should make us wary of jumping to conclusions. Bureaucracy does not always increase with the size and number of institutions—as multinational companies have

---

[227] More broadly, freedom of speech and information Acts have to be supplemented by formal agencies with definite responsibilities and relations—such that there is not merely speech but effective speech by the marginal and needy, and such that there is not merely communication between authorities but purposive and accurate public communication. Transparency and communication are central topics of Chapter 4.

long been aware, but which others have unfortunately been slower to realise.[228] The burden of proof that any institutional additions will make matters worse seems to lie rather on statists: advocates of the current state system, with its derivative and state-dominated global institutions—such as the existing United Nations—have not managed to rein in the many problems of bureaucracy. They can hardly reject others' institutional proposals on the grounds that there will be some adverse bureaucracy, since it is quite possible that the existence of more institutions could be offset by the better coordination and distribution of responsibilities that such plurality might allow.

The success of extant democracies in making rulers act in a representative fashion is in no way correlated with the size or centralisation of states. India and the United States, to name but two examples, have been—for all their manifold problems—somewhat successful democracies; yet there are over a billion citizens in the former and hundreds of millions in the latter. It is notable that both political systems not only include clear separation of powers but also are highly federalist. This provides some empirical pointers but only limited political understanding of how extensive democracies can be successful: How is it practically possible to have democracy where there is no single legislative or executive body that is elected and expected to respond to citizens' express judgements, but rather multiple, decentralised places of power?

An ill-constructed plurality of institutions would indeed result in much confusion and adverse bureaucracy, and so the idea of a greater plurality of institutions must not be used or applied loosely. I have argued for two dimensions of institutional plurality: *multiple levels and loci* of overlapping governmental authority (in Chapter 1) and *multiple types* of governmental authorities (in Chapter 3). I have also suggested how these institutional reforms might be constrained so that they do not proliferate excessively. My proposal for multiple *levels* and *loci* of governance—plurarchy—is delimited by a Principle of Distributive Subsidiarity, which aims to allocate power according to the functional capacities at each level or locus of governance, and combine functions into clusters, with a view to effective governance. My proposal for multiple *types* of institutions of governance—a plurality of powers—is constrained by a Principle of Democracy, understood

---

[228] For a theory of both 'democratisation' and efficiency within multinational companies, with reference—and relevance—to governance more generally, see C. McMahon, *Authority and Democracy: A General Theory of Government and Management* (Princeton, NJ: Princeton University Press, 1994).

now in terms of responsive representation; new authorities are to be introduced only if it can be shown that they are likely to increase the overall responsiveness of representative structures. Advocacy and accountability agencies, for instance, are to be established only where existing authorities and agents—such as courts, political parties, civil society associations, citizens—cannot or should not perform crucial functions of appointment, empowerment, and constraint that are likely to improve responsiveness.

I maintained further that institutions with well-defined and inter-locking competencies must be complemented by equally well-defined and interlocking requirements to communicate. Vague injunctions to 'consult' and 'take into account' other authorities tend to damage clear lines of responsibility and are not adequate ways of ensuring that such communication occurs. Requirements to communicate are better insti-tutionalised by ensuring that each authority has full responsibility for certain indispensable components of governance, and yet is compelled to find agreement with others in order to meet its obligations, such that those obligations cannot be discharged without cooperation and coor-dination.[229] Some office-holders may resist communication, but doing so will undermine the discharge of their own clearly defined obliga-tions, and can be publicly exposed as obstruction. Sanctions could include loss of office, whether at the hands of citizens in elections or as a result of a sufficient consensus of other relevant authorities.[230]

Institutional plurality, understood in this complex way, would induce higher levels of responsiveness. The key to understanding this practical possibility is a distinctive *epistemological* idea behind the ideal of political inclusion and action presented thus far. It is the idea that we should not assume, or vainly seek to attain, any political perspective—let alone an impartial perspective—that incorporates

---

[229] This process would not be all that unfamiliar even within states: one author-ity may be obliged to supply information about income distribution and growth in the economy (e.g. a statistical bureau, one of the accountability agencies I men-tioned); another may be obliged to develop the budget partly in light of that inform-ation (e.g. a ministry of finance, which would now be unable to base the budget on inflated predictions); that budget may then have to be debated by another authority (e.g. parliament, which is likely to have some powers to amend the budget); before being confirmed by a further authority (e.g. the prime minister or president); subsequently, the implementation of the budget may be monitored by another authority (e.g. an auditor general) and its ultimate success or failure assessed by yet another important authority (e.g. ombudsmen, citizens).

[230] For example, certain courts may—following a proper process and allowing leave for appeal—review the performance of ombudsmen, against a predefined set of criteria, and dismiss ombudsmen for obstructionism and dereliction of duty.

and locates the totality of political knowledge. This is not to deny that certain truths are knowable, but rather to insist that different authorities with different institutional purposes and logics will focus on different aspects of issues, making it possible for each to develop distinctive capacities for high quality judgement when it comes to specific areas of governance. These capacities can be harnessed and connected, producing a constellation of individual and institutional knowers—each with distinct competences and obligations—that extends beyond the tripartite separation of powers, and overcomes several deficiencies of this conventional division of political labour.

This constellation would have to be legally enshrined in good part, so as to define the responsibilities of each agent within an overall division of political labour. The charters of human rights that have proliferated since the end of Second World War have been of great value, but the proliferating language of rights has also had the unfortunate consequence of obscuring the need for more adequate specification of which institutions could bear the counterpart duties to deliver on those rights.[231] The inflationary rhetoric of rights needs to be tempered by asking and answering the question 'who has to do what, for whom, when?' in almost every political context. We should for these reasons revive the idea of a Declaration of Duties eloquently envisioned by Simone Weil prior to her untimely death in 1943.[232]

A *Declaration of Human Duties and Responsibilities* was produced under the auspices of the United Nations Economic and Social Council in 1999; but the text is unspecific and non-binding.[233] It also fails to recognise that most duties are requirements and not aspirations, and so it loses the modal structure that lends force to an approach based on duties. A binding statement of principles and obligations (duties,

---

[231] The need to ask 'whose obligations?' is pressed forcefully by O. O'Neill throughout *Bounds*, esp. 97–111 and *Autonomy and Trust in Bioethics* (Cambridge: Cambridge University Press, 2002a). Raymond Geuss similarly argues that rights-talk makes sense only relative to a mechanism for enforcement; see R. Geuss, *History and Illusion in Politics* (Cambridge: Cambridge University Press, 2001), esp. 131–52.

[232] S. Weil, *The Need for Roots: Prelude to a Declaration of Duties Towards Mankind* (London: Routledge, 1995).

[233] Moreover, in its preamble, the Declaration maintains that states 'continue to exercise the primary duty and responsibility for the promotion and enforcement of human rights and fundamental freedoms' (www.cdp-hrc.uottawa.ca/publicat/valencia/valenc1.html). As I argued in Chapter 1, this item of faith—that states are the primary agents of justice—must at the very least be established, and in fact cannot be established in current conditions.

responsibilities, as well as communicative requirements), fit to structure a global constellation of authorities, would have to recognise the current capacities and potentials of specific institutions. For this reason, it should be termed a Charter of Obligations.[234]

The Charter would have to distinguish the capabilities of authorities (what they can do) from their competences (what they may do) from their obligations (what they ought to do). It would have to clarify how the three are compatible—indicating which duties are perfect duties, which are imperfect, and which duties only come into force once conditions and institutions change in specified ways. This would leave room for articulating aspirations that cannot be met at all immediately, but would also encourage those who claim rights to pay greater attention to the conditions and reforms required to impose the corresponding duties. In all these ways, the Charter of Obligations—rather than any one knowledgeable agent or perspective—would provide a framework for better political judgement by both rulers and ruled.

I have not, then, merely argued for an increase in the number of authorities. I have also sought to specify the basis for an improved, more definite and effective, division of political labour, and in particular for the necessary acquisition of knowledge and exercise of judgement. I have tried to show that such a constellation would enable more discretion for representatives *and* enable better scrutiny and sanctioning of their actions.

There is, of course, no unique institutional configuration that instantiates this coordinating constellation for every context. But, as I show concretely in the next chapter, the idea of such a constellation does provide an evaluative standpoint for reform of institutions and political action in a range of crucial contexts. Before we can turn to the specifics of institutional design at the global level, though, we need to consider further the role that citizens could play within this (potentially global) institutional framework.

9. Responsive Global Citizenship: Reducing Passivity

My argument on representation began by laying out the requirement that I have not as yet met in full: a system or ruler may only be termed representative if citizens too are political agents, exercising systematic

---

[234] Tony Blair proposed a pale and statist 'charter of competences' for the European Union in his 'A Superpower, But Not a Superstate' speech, reprinted in the *Guardian*, 7 October 2000. Avoiding bureaucracy was only one element in his mixed motivations.

control over governance through their judgements and actions. We are now in a position to see how this requirement might be met under conditions of scale and pluralism, by a global order that I shall call Responsive Democracy.[235] What exactly can and should citizens be and do within this global order? How would their situation be any better, their political power any greater, than under a system of nation-states?

9.1. What Citizenship is Not

When Diogenes the Cynic insisted 'I am a citizen of the world', he was—taken literally—quite wrong. Citizenship is a predicate of persons under common political institutions; there were no global institutions in the ancient world. The claim to world citizenship resonates through the centuries, rather, because it announces a form of identification. The *kosmou polites* (world citizen) is a person whose primary moral and psychological allegiance is to all humanity, not to any parochial group.[236] This universalist commitment is the hallmark of moral cosmopolitans to this day.

Consider the widely cited and admired statement of cosmopolitanism offered by Martha Nussbaum in *For Love of Country*. She presents an argument that we must give 'our first allegiance to no mere form of government, no temporal power, but to the moral community made up by the humanity of all human beings'.[237] She does acknowledge that, 'we should give special attention to our own families and to our own ties of religious and national belonging . . . But the primary reason a cosmopolitan should have for this is not that the local is better per se, but rather that this is the only sensible way to do good'.[238]

Since Nussbaum is a devoted neo-Aristotelian, she also holds up a range of exemplars for us to follow: Marcus Aurelius, Emerson, Thoreau, and—shifting categories of example rather swiftly—ordinary Germans who risked their lives to shelter Jews. She asks: 'would one, in similar circumstances, have the moral courage to recognize humanity and respond to its claim, even if the powers that be denied its

---

[235] I shall use the locution 'the theory of Responsive Democracy' to mean the principles (and their justifications) instantiated in this global order.

[236] It is arguable that the Greeks used the language of citizenship to make this universalist claim to allegiance only because they did not differentiate greatly between the 'private' and the 'public' person, as we do.

[237] M. C. Nussbaum and Respondents, *For Love of Country*, J. Cohen, ed. (Boston: Beacon Press, 1995), 7.

[238] Ibid., 136.

presence? That recognition, wherever it is made, is the basic act of world citizenship'.[239]

Unfortunately, this whole argument is hardly decisive against opponents of world citizenship, from romantic communitarians to Realist statists, who insist that more parochial loyalties are the necessary or best fundamental bases for governance and politics. Most contemporary statists and communitarians are *moral* cosmopolitans but not *political* cosmopolitans. Very few deny that 'outsiders' beyond 'our' borders are persons with moral claims: perhaps the central presumption of the post-1945 international order was that all persons have moral rights and should even have legal rights, but this was combined with an assumption that states are the sole or primary political and legal agent for enforcing those rights. In short, those who favour territorially bounded politics can and do claim that giving great *political* priority to compatriots is the best way for humanity to organise and govern itself, in order to protect and advance the interests of all persons. It is primarily this latter political claim that cosmopolitans have to contest, in principle and practice, if we wish to see deep, positive changes in the presumptions and practices of the current global order.

Nussbaum's conception of world citizenship as recognition of the humanity in others is, in addition, quite misleading, because it is in a crucial sense *apolitical*. It does not take seriously the difference that can exist between attitudes in the political domain and in other domains. I can be a crotchety old misanthrope and still be a good citizen (e.g. write letters to my representative, vote, make public appeals, etc.). Or I can be a paragon of empathy for individuals and yet be a poor citizen (e.g. not see the bigger picture, care little for what I cannot impact on very directly, etc.). There may certainly be some relation between my empathy for individuals and my view of the justness of particular institutions, but it is by no means a necessary relation. How many people love society and not individuals (a character type immortalised by Dickens in the person of Mrs Jellyby)? How many people love individuals but not society? Both sorts of person can have awful blind spots. But both sorts can also make helpful contributions to society, depending on how well the scheme of cooperation for mutual advantage is structured to harness varying motivations.

True, people will tend to behave better towards one another *in politics too* if they recognise each other's humanity. Encouraging such recognition may be crucial to combating racism, xenophobia, and other prejudices that crystallise as responses to the foreign and different.

[239] Ibid., 132.

But to think that a social system can or will command allegiance, or operate fairly and effectively, only if individuals have a vivid sense of different others is to succumb to a misleadingly individualist conception of political explanation. Politics operates irremediably on a large scale: we impact on each other chiefly indirectly and in a mediated fashion, through various kinds of social rules and institutions. Questions of interpersonal friendship and understanding are *conceptually* and *psychologically* distinct from questions of political coercion and command over resources. In one sense, this disjunction between personal and political attitudes is quite fortunate: to expect our recognition of humanity in others to lead to constant remedial action would be to impose an onerous overload of obligation, since it is absurd to think that each of us could have an informed, nuanced sense of millions of others. Our imaginations and purposes are not that capacious, and our politics would founder on that limitation.

How then can individuals come to see their and others' best interests as optimally formed, revised, and pursued within common institutions over time? And if we do not and cannot have an empathic interpersonal relation to the many others who are affected by our common institutions, what kind of relation can and should we have? Let me at least indicate how a theorist of Responsive Democracy could answer these questions.

9.2. Four Key Questions

We must ask four related questions of a normative account of citizenship: (1) Citizenship of what? (2) Citizenship for whom? (3) What can and must citizens do? (4) What can and must citizens be? These broad questions tend to collapse into one another in the literatures on citizenship. Essentially, the first asks which political institutions are or should be established, such that those institutions can rightfully and effectively command allegiance from citizens. The second asks when and why persons are or should be considered members in some institutions but not others. The third asks what roles citizens must play—what capabilities they must have and what activities they must undertake—to contribute to sustaining such institutions and such institutions' work over time. The fourth asks what beliefs, dispositions, and attachments citizens must have in order to be willing to discharge the responsibilities of their roles and enjoy the benefits of such cooperation.

The argument of the chapters above in respect of these questions is clear. Chapter 1 showed that enjoying the benefits of global citizenship does not require a world state or a system of (national) states; instead, it is possible to develop multiple levels and loci of governance that together constitute a just institutional structure. I called this structure 'plurarchy'. The central reason that we *should* attempt to develop this institutional formation is that it provides a better *basis* to answer the question of 'citizenship for whom?'—since individuals are not arbitrarily and wrongly excluded at the outset from equal treatment by some governing institutions. But it is a basis only. At this point, citizens appear only in their passive aspect, as beneficiaries; and institutions appear without an account of how, why, and by whom political decisions are made within those institutions.

Chapter 2 considered theories of deliberative democracy, which seem to overcome these two problems of citizen and institutional passivity *simultaneously*. We are told that all citizens could and should actively participate in a vast dialogue—or, at least, citizens' active participation could and should be modelled and mirrored—in such a way that they together freely discern their own interests as well as potentially generating and decisively considering courses of action to be refined and executed by office-holders. But the chapter demonstrated that, in pluralist societies of great scale, citizens could never generate and validate public decisions in this implausibly demanding way; nor should they aim to do so, since the consequences are highly likely to be marginalisation for many and institutional inertia for all. Relinquishing this vain hope left us with no positive answers to the questions of what citizens must do and be, and none to the dilemma of how to improve both judgement and inclusion within political institutions. However, the chapter did provide grounds to believe that a feasible solution lies in the direction of thicker forms of representation and less demanding forms of participatory process.

The present chapter has provided an account of ways in which representatives with a high degree of discretion can judge and pursue the interests of all citizens. But this will be possible only *if* representatives are properly positioned and empowered (most notably, to assess and use information) within a well-designed institutional constellation, and only *if* representatives can be subjected to constraints that dramatically reduce their propensity to act in their own interests against those of the public. Citizens themselves do not have to do the lion's share of the work of guarding the guardians. Here, finally, was the prospect of a feasible role for citizens, within a complex division of labour. But that prospect threatened to be elusive. Elections and 'civil society', even together with competitive party politics and judicial controls, prove to be seriously insufficient mechanisms to appoint and empower representatives to judge appropriately, and insufficient disciplines to constrain representatives to act responsibly on those judgements.

To answer the question 'what can and must citizens do?' we needed a better answer to the question 'citizenship of what?'. To this end, the chapter proposed a range of institutional innovations, notably: a plurality of powers—including advocacy and accountability agencies—and a Charter of Obligations. These do not replace so much as supplement and transform existing political mechanisms and disciplines. But does the resulting institutional constellation still include and treat citizens merely as passive beneficiaries? The answer is 'no', and its dimensions become evident via comparison with the theory and practice of nation-state-centric citizenship.

9.3. Global Civil Society and Responsive Citizenship

Michael Walzer has argued that formal citizenship outside of national communities would leave us passive as individual citizens and unable to decide on fair principles of distributive justice as a group.[240] His argument begins with the thought that distributing goods involves assessing the relative importance of each good; but there appears to be no uniquely rational or impartial way to adjudicate between these goods. For example, in a culture where the idea of a career is a marginal notion and subsistence agriculture is the core livelihood activity, the concept of 'equality of opportunity' would be taken to have fundamentally different contours and plausibility. Cultural presuppositions do not just matter on this account; they are the only adequate reference point for most public decisions. That is, we require 'thick' concepts embedded in the ways of life and shared understandings of each culture to make discussions of distributive justice intelligible and productive. Unfortunately for international dialogue, according to Walzer, it can only proceed by using 'thin' concepts. These more etiolated rational notions allow for certain decisions between cultures but on a very limited range of goods, not altogether distant from the narrow range on which Rawls' Society of Peoples finds agreement.

Walzer's argument has been echoed and elaborated by many other 'communitarian' critics of cosmopolitan justice and democratisation. If he is right, then the kind of responsive global order articulated in these pages could not serve the human purposes that I have claimed it would serve. But how plausible is a fundamental distinction between 'thick' and 'thin' concepts? Is it applied correctly to national versus

---

[240] M. Walzer, *Thick and Thin: Moral Argument at Home and Abroad* (Notre Dame, IN: University of Notre Dame Press, 1994).

global citizenship? I shall argue that the distinction is mistaken and misapplied in two fundamental respects, and cannot bear the weight it is expected to bear.

First, the argument is contradicted by facts about political movements and motivations that have come increasingly to the fore in recent years with the burgeoning of what is loosely termed 'global civil society': global social movements, transnational advocacy networks, global public policy networks, international NGOs, and other civil society organisations. Across the board, global civil society is denser and more efficacious than ever before, generating a host of common platforms and garnering active and sustainable support.[241] The contributions of this movement are not invariably positive and the movement itself evidences serious internal divisions; but that does not invalidate the point. Such organisations and networks can be crucial catalysts for popular movements that help dislodge illiberal and/or ineffective rulers within countries (such as Slobodan Milosevic in the former Yugoslavia or Eduard Shevardnadze in Georgia). Moreover, successful values-driven campaigns are often led by organisations that themselves cross multiple borders, such as the Open Society and Human Rights Watch, whose staff find that a host of 'thick' democratic values are shared by dissidents and other citizens in the countries in which they work.[242] The members of any society are able to consider the relative benefits and burdens of democratic versus other kinds of government, weighing the evidence and the arguments—unless, of course, they are prevented from doing so by illiberal rulers who have prejudged the questions and forcefully imposed answers. Dissenters in such countries will snort with disbelief, disappointment, and even derision on being told that such imposition is a function of these representatives acting on agreed 'thick' concepts shared by the whole society.

Insofar as differences remain within global civil society and across borders (e.g. on the powers of the president, on the role of the army, on the place of religion, on the extent of taxation and social security provision), these differences are equally in evidence *within* pluralist societies.[243] If differences are more *destabilising* in 'other countries

---

[241] See M. Kaldor, *Global Civil Society: An Answer to War* (Cambridge: Polity, 2003).

[242] The biography of Aryeh Neier, founder of Human Rights Watch and current President of the Open Society Institute and Soros Foundations Network, is entirely convincing in this regard. See A. Neier, *Taking Liberties: Four Decades in the Struggle for Rights* (New York: PublicAffairs, 2003).

[243] For strong inter- and intra-country empirical evidence to this effect, see United Nations Development Program, *Human Development Report 2002:*

and regions', then that is because such contexts are often under-institutionalised, undemocratic, and suffer high levels of poverty-driven dissatisfaction. But this is quite another matter from 'thick' versus 'thin' shared understandings: human insecurity, powerlessness, and poverty are not popular anywhere. Moreover, 'thick' interpretations of these problems and the prospects for remedying them are often *necessarily transnational*, such as gaining access to labour markets that—in all societies in the contemporary world—are driven partly by global demand, supply, and regulation.[244] In this light, it is hardly surprising that the anti-globalisation movement (which, in its more positive incarnations, is better described as the movement against unrestrained economic globalisation) has mobilised strong support in almost every country and has proved able to sustain this popular motivation over time and across borders. Whatever one thinks of this movement, there can be little doubt that it has also impacted in important respects on the global political agenda—as evidenced by some significant rhetorical and practical responses from the powerful G8 countries. The capacities of civil society to find some common platforms and generate support for these platforms are limited by diverse needs and strongly divergent convictions; nonetheless the possibilities for and realities of united action on important fronts should not be ignored.

It is a singular virtue of cosmopolitan justice and responsive representation (both the theory and the practical pursuit thereof) that they allow for, facilitate, and indeed expand thick understanding and intensive cooperation across borders. That is, cosmopolitan legal and social standards as well as norms of democratic governance (both of which are increasingly embedded in international law and human rights instruments) provide a basis for discussion and convergence by large parts of global civil society.[245] This reality should not be overstated, in the fashion of Habermas and deliberative democrats: significant disagreements remain (as they do within states) and stand no prospect of resolution. Nonetheless, contra Walzer, there are as a matter of fact

[244] See J. D. Clark, *Worlds Apart: Civil Society and the Battle for Ethical Globalization* (Bloomfield, CT: Kumarian Press, 2003), esp. Chapter 2, 'How Globalization Affects Markets—Distortion and Extortion'.

[245] For an account of how far we have come and how far we still have to go, see D. Held, 'Globalization, Corporate Practice and Cosmopolitan Social Standards', *Contemporary Political Theory*, Vol. 1, No. 1 (2002a), 59–78.

thick agreements across borders on a range of rules, codes, and procedures concerning health (consider WHO rules to curb the spread of infectious diseases), labour (consider the standards and reach of the Fair Labour Association), the environment (consider the daily work done by the UN Environmental Program), and corporate governance (consider global accounting standards), to name only four crucial areas in which there has been recent progress. These rules, codes, and procedures are not the invention of philosophers or idealists: they are entrenched in the articles of association, terms of reference, and daily practice of international organisations and trading agencies. Meanwhile, the World Social Forum—driven by numerous global civil society actors—meets and issues important statements and action-plans that extend far beyond the minima that Walzer claims are characteristic of interactions across borders. There is still, of course, a very long way to go. But it is not accurate, and it is likely to be ever further from the truth in the future, to claim that cross-national understanding is limited to 'thin' rationalist concepts only.

The second respect in which Walzer's claims are contradicted by empirical developments is this: It is good to talk and make collective decisions, but if discussions and conclusions are to be meaningful, then the participants must have real power and be able to take real (enforceable not merely nominal) decisions. Yet, as 'nationals' of developing countries are the first to point out, this is far from the reality, and will remain the case in a system of states (and particularly states of drastically divergent sizes and strengths). Citizens of states, especially those in smaller and developing states, have little or no control over factors that impact greatly on their lives but over which their particular state has no authority or sway. This near-total lack of control for most citizens (that is, for members of most states) result, above all from the absence of formal institutions with capabilities *and* responsibilities corresponding to important interests of most persons:

1. In some cases, states are allocated responsibilities that they do not and could not have the capabilities to discharge either individually or collectively.
2. In other cases, international institutions are assigned those responsibilities but lack the necessary capabilities to discharge them.
3. In yet other cases, the need for any agent of obligation is quietly dropped or ignored—leading us back to an insufficiently political form of cosmopolitanism.

Compare this highly deficient statism with the constellation which I call Responsive Democracy. Boundaries are not drawn in terms (e.g. in nationalist or statist terms) that preclude consideration of the best institutional means to the ends of free and equal persons. Instead of immediately ignoring and compromising the capabilities of other levels and loci of governance, authoritative power is situated at whichever institutional levels and loci are most effective in achieving these human ends. Plurarchy is more complex than statism in that there are more (non-derivative) levels and loci of authority, but it is simpler and clearer in deeper senses. It is structured by a principle of distributive subsidiarity, which assigns definite obligations to specific, capable institutional agents. Plurarchy is then complemented by a plurality of powers—increasing the types of authority involved in governance, and requiring each to communicate and compromise with others, such that they together inform, scrutinise, and sanction particular aspects of one another's activities.[246]

In combination, the two kinds of institutional plurality (levels and types) produce an institutional configuration that can be circumscribed and publicly regulated by a definite Charter of Obligations. Unlike emotive creeds such as nationalism and statism the components of this charter are potentially contestable in mutually intelligible and assessable terms. So, at the very least, *there are specific institutions for citizens to approach, and there is some requirement for citizens and authorities to offer mutually assessable reasons as to why authorities can and should be held responsible for certain actions.* The political argument cannot be closed down by invocations of arbitrary birthright or by ascriptions of ethnos.

'But in this scheme', a Walzerian critic may object, 'there will still be less responsiveness than in current states: citizens' reasons and actions will have less effect in a larger, more complex institutional configuration'. Yet, as I see it, existing states come out worse in the comparison. A large number of citizens of actual states have very limited control over factors *endogenous* to their particular state too. Even when institutions have the necessary capabilities and responsibilities, office-holders may not be adequately constrained to act in citizens' best interests. This inadequacy is inevitable where there are insufficient horizontal mechanisms of scrutiny and sanction (judicial oversight and competitive party politics are not enough) as well as insufficient vertical mechanisms of scrutiny and sanction (elections and action by civil

---

[246] In the language of political science, it might be said that the 'performance legitimacy' of each institution, or at least of office-holders within such institutions, depends in part on the quality of coordination and communicative relations with others.

society between elections are not enough). It will also remain the case as long as citizens ask for one set of policy prescriptions from their state representatives even while powerful states and institutions—who are in no way accountable to the same citizens—demand and obtain (with tactics not far short of direct coercion) other policies entirely.

In contrast, cosmopolitan citizens with a well-designed constellation of checks and balances have a wider variety of means by which to contribute to public decisions *and* these means are likely to be more effective. First, citizens have (often cross-border) accountability agencies to provide crucial, limited ranges of more independent and accessible information about political actors, standards, and contexts than is provided by those actors or by non-statutory agencies such as media organisations. Second, citizens have advocacy agencies that act on their behalf as professional contesters. These agencies can elicit further information from government and others where necessary (e.g. strengthened ombudsmen), investigate public issues of great concern (e.g. statutory gender commissions), press pivotal claims on citizens' behalf (e.g. public protectors), and assist citizens in pressing other claims themselves (e.g. corruption commissions). Third, citizens have a locus of mobilisation that agglomerates and pursues their concerns and yet does not require that citizens act together with high levels of mutual awareness (the intensive participation required by the latter often proves difficult for vulnerable individuals who have little discretionary time and income). Finally, citizens have greater assurance that they will not be ignored, rebuffed, or dominated by each relevant representative, since multiple authorities can improve on the available quality of information, scrutiny, and sanction—thus making other representatives more accessible and more motivated to expose and challenge such unresponsiveness.

It is true that states could adopt many of these institutional measures. But states can only go so far in securing adequate citizenship rights: as argued in Chapter 1, what is needed to remedy the situation fully is not merely a constellation of multiple *types* of authority but also one that operates at multiple *levels* and *loci* of governance, including the global level. Authorities at these other levels must not be the creatures of states, or have only delegated powers, since that would damage their capacity to scrutinise and sanction one another's use and abuse of power, as well as the use and abuse of power by states. And such limitation to politics within borders would stand in the way of making representatives at the global level accountable, not to a narrow group of influential citizens from rich and powerful states, but to all citizens of the world.

9.4. Multiple Motivations and Identity

So we come to the one remaining question, 'what can and must citizens be?'. It would be a mistake to try to answer this question at great length here, since the answers involve a different kind of project, drawing extensively on social psychology and political sociology to provide an account of (political) motivation. I do not believe that an adequate philosophical account of motivation is available at this point in time.[247] But I do want to indicate why Responsive Democracy offers better prospects for motivating citizens to act in relevant and satisfying ways than do nationalist and/or statist orders.

On its own, the fact that people are motivated to comply with an institutional order says *nothing* about whether that order is justified: consider the obedient citizens of Orwell's *Nineteen Eighty-Four* and the awfully happy citizens of Huxley's *Brave New World*. This is one reason why Rawls is right to maintain that the question of the justification of an institutional order comes first, and the question of motivation—however important—presents only a final stability constraint on that

---

[247] Liberals in search of such a theory have frequently bought into models of utilitarianism and rational choice—but these are false friends for all versions of liberalism. As a positive attempt to bring psychology into political thought, utilitarianism can be shown to be reductionist, implausible, and insensitive to differences between individuals (see A. Sen and B. Williams, 'Introduction', in A. Sen and B. Williams, eds., *Utilitarianism and Beyond* (Cambridge: Cambridge University Press, 1982)). Rational choice theory suffers similar problems and more since, as Raymond Geuss puts it, 'the notions of rationality that play a central role in mathematical modelling, game theory, social choice theory, etc. are of great use in well-defined areas; but the most important fact about politics is that it is not a closed, well-defined area' (Q. Skinner, P. Dasgupta, R. Geuss, M. Lane, P. Laslett, O. O'Neill, W. G. Runciman, and A. Kuper, 'Political Philosophy: The View from Cambridge', *Journal of Political Philosophy*, Vol. 10, No. 1 (2001), 1–19, at 10). Communitarians have apparently done better than liberal theorists: by placing duties to kinsmen and traditions at the heart of political concern, they have tapped into a ready-made and substantive account of motivation. But the political costs are high (as demonstrated in Chapter 1 and in the previous section). They have unwittingly—or wittingly in some cases—revived a pernicious 'friend–foe' conception of politics (one that is incompatible with any version of cosmopolitan politics). By focusing on historical ties and on duties to an in-group, such theorists are compelled to regard others—especially newly encountered others and traditionally despised others—as moral as well as political outsiders. By tying motivation to particularist group solidarity, they eliminate convincing grounds on which to accept differing others as equals in significant shared projects or as members of common political institutions. Beyond the failure to ensure solidarity, as I shall now show, such theorists provide no basis for multiple allegiances in the face of a global future.

order. Thus, in an important respect, nationalist and statist accounts of motivation are of limited interest: since a system of nation-states cannot be shown to be just or democratic, it is not of central concern—from a normative perspective—whether such motivations (primordial, communitarian, emotivist, etc.) could render a state-system stable.[248] I have argued that there is at least one better, justified alternative: Responsive Democracy. And so I take nationalist and statist motivations to be relevant to my argument only if they are more effective at generating adequate motivation, within a state system, or are likely to destabilise this justified alternative global institutional order. The central question, therefore, is to what extent this alternative order would generate the widespread motivations necessary to sustain it over time: 'will [members] tend increasingly over time to accept its principles and judgements as they come to understand the ideas of justice [and democracy] expressed in the law among them and appreciate its benefits'?[249]

In comparing the motivational success of potential nationalist and cosmopolitan political orders, we might apply three broad standards for citizen motivation: civility, public-spiritedness, and patriotism.[250] I wish to make the strong claim that Responsive Democracy is likely to be superior even if we adopt the last and most demanding of these three standards. The first standard, civility, only requires that citizens have sufficient motivation to obey the law and display tolerance of one another. The second, public-spiritedness, requires that citizens show concern for the well-being of fellow citizens, constraining the maximal satisfaction of their own interests, whether out of duty or fellow feeling. The third and most ambitious standard, patriotism, requires citizens to have internalised the well-being of the collective as an integral element of their personal interests. Ever-higher levels of public activity are associated with these three standards: the mildest version of the first standard demands restraint as mere non-injury

---

[248] The question of nationalist and statist motivation would be relevant for *ideal* theory only if we were condemned to live in a Westphalian world—that is, if no other system could be justified and satisfy the stability constraint—or perhaps if nationalist regimes were massively more productive to the extent that they would improve even the situation of the least advantaged persons. I have supplied grounds to doubt both possibilities. Nationalist and statist motivations are however deeply relevant to identifying the constraints on non-ideal theory, and hence to acting prudently, in the world as we find it: there are still powerful states and powerful nationalist forces in many parts of the world.

[249] Rawls, *Political Liberalism*, 48.

[250] This distinction is neatly parsed in D. Weinstock, 'Prospects for Transnational Citizenship and Democracy', *Ethics and International Affairs*, Vol. 15, No. 2 (2002), 53–66.

while the strongest version of the third standard expects citizens to willingly lay down their lives for the defence or glory of the *patria*.

David Miller has argued, in effect, that neither the first nor the second standard is sufficiently high to ensure meaningful and responsible citizenship.[251] Where there is mere civility, the polity will be undermined by individualism; where there is public-spiritedness, the polity still will be prone to factionalism. In both cases, individuals are unwilling to decide together on principles and policies which all can share, since each person has no real reason to identify with and pursue the common good but has every reason to identify with narrower groups and act on narrower goals. Thus deliberation aimed at taking the perspective of the general will is inevitably replaced by self-interested negotiation and jockeying for power. By contrast, patriotism ensures that citizens pursue the common good, not because civic engagement is some high-flown ideal but because it is integral to the self-understanding and self-realisation of individuals.

Let us assume for argument's sake that much of this is correct. Miller goes on to maintain, famously, that the sole sufficient source of such patriotism is nationalism.[252] By enlarging the outlook of individual citizens, nationalism is supposed to produce loyalty, solidarity, and responsibility—dispositions necessary for active citizenship and crucial to the stability and flourishing of polities. Most notably, *à la* Walzer, citizens can be motivated by nationalist sentiments to consider fair principles of distributive justice within their society (state), including provision of public goods that might otherwise be chronically under-funded.[253]

Regrettably, this focus on nationalism as the basis for membership and motivation in polities has three fatal flaws: It comes at great costs to individuals and groups outside the society and to dissenters inside the society (costs that none of them can reasonably be expected to bear). It is inadequate to address contemporary political problems and power relations. And it does not generate the reliable patriotic motivations it is supposed to generate. I discussed the first two flaws— injustice and ineffectiveness in the face of globalisation—at length in Chapter 1 in my critique of nationalism and statism (in their apparently most sympathetic, Rawlsian forms) and in the previous section.

---

[251] D. Miller, 'Bounded Citizenship', in his *Citizenship and National Identity* (Cambridge: Polity, 2000).

[252] D. Miller, *On Nationality* (Oxford: Oxford University Press, 1997).

[253] My criticisms of Walzer's view, in the previous section, apply equally to this aspect of Miller's view, thus in the present section I shall concentrate on another aspect of the debate.

The third, motivational flaw becomes immediately evident if we now consider why Responsive Democracy would enable potent forms of cosmopolitan patriotism in situations where nationalism would induce only paralysis or destructive divisions.

Now, difficult political situations arise where there is a dramatic gap between the psychology and conditions of actual human beings and the ideal grounds for human assent to an institutional order (I will not characterise this gap here). In recognising this gap, we must not fall into the error that traps nationalists and statists as well as neoliberal ideologues: the idea that there must be one dominant motivation that generates allegiance (e.g. fear of violent death, historically shared bonds, maximising existing preference satisfaction). Human beings have many and varied motivations.

It is simply a *misleading question* to ask *in the abstract* 'which affect and attachment should [forever] take the place of nationalism?'. What we can say in the abstract is that, to the extent that institutions are responsive to people's interests, mediating and meeting those interests, such institutions are more likely over time to be regarded as legitimate—precisely for the array of reasons to which those interests give rise. Those interests may *include* certain nationalist interests. Responsive Democracy embeds a justified refusal to incorporate nationalism as a comprehensive political doctrine into the basic structure, but it does not prevent or revile a sense of affiliation to any group. Rather, it creates conditions for the mediating and meeting of group and other interests but sets limits to this accommodation so that other people—with different attachments and aspirations—can form, revise, and pursue different interests.

In this sense, it is nationalism, and not cosmopolitanism, that is founded on wishful thinking about patriotism: the hope that one kind of motivation, one kind of group affiliation, can enjoy perpetual primacy. Nationalism is a historical phenomenon, arising in conjunction with certain institutional configurations and interests and coexisting alongside other similar phenomena (from identity politics to universalist political attachments and movements); it is not, has never been, and will never be the only natural sort of political motivation. Here, certain liberals must be faulted too, for seeking to replace nationalism with one kind of patriotic motivation or indeed for believing (as Nussbaum does) that a sufficient alternative kind of predominant motivation will come from 'better people' who are better citizens as a result.

Not all reasons for socially beneficial action are pleasant to contemplate: often people do the right things (e.g. contribute to informed political decision) for reasons we might not see as noble (e.g. the desire to dominate others). With this in mind, recall the two Kantian requirements with which my discussion of democracy began in Chapter 2: it must be possible for citizens to be compelled by a moral conception to endorse an institutional order; but it must also be possible for them to be motivated by a merely strategic and self-interested approach. A system of nation-states, I have argued, violates the first (normative) requirement because it arbitrarily excludes and unfairly disadvantages many persons. But now we can see that a state system also violates the second (prudential) requirement: if there is a multiplicity of motivations, an order that assumes one type of motivation to be dominant is doomed to instability—not least because differently motivated persons may reasonably, rightly, and inevitably resist it. Neither requirement presents problems for Responsive Democracy, however, because the institutional order is not treated as the privileged expression of some purportedly inevitable or noble motivation. Responsive Democracy does not ignore nationalism, but sets limits to it, giving some vent to nationalism alongside other motivations rather than letting it marginalise or suppress all other affiliations and motivations.

In this sense, Responsive Democracy constitutes a fundamental break from the neo-Hobbesian paradigm that still dominates both liberal and communitarian theories of citizenship and patriotism. Citizenship is no longer treated as a unitary phenomenon that resolves all motivational complexity and conflicts of allegiance by reference to an ultimate moment of primary attachment to one state or community. There is no barrier, for instance, to individuals having several, potentially conflicting citizenships. As I shall show in Chapter 4, one can be legally empowered to approach district, local, national, regional, and international courts for a variety of remedies, one can be represented in a variety of legislatures and executives by a range of political actors, and one can empower and constrain those actors to act in one's best interests by taking up one's entitlements to access a variety of advocacy and accountability agencies.[254]

---

[254] None of this requires that one profess oneself to be (oddly) a citizen of a court or a legislature. Citizenship is constituted by a bundle of legal rights (and obligations), held against definite authorities that are capable of discharging their circumscribed responsibilities to meet those rights. One would not be a citizen of the International Court of Justice (ICJ) because the 'bundle' is insufficiently dense and variegated; one could however be a global citizen in virtue of a stronger United Nations that guarantees certain political rights in conjunction with remedies provided by the ICJ. I leave on one side the question of just how 'dense and variegated' this legal complex has to be for one to qualify as a citizen.

It is quite possible that our allegiances to such institutions, actors, or movements will contingently conflict with each other—just as it is quite possible that our daily principles will contingently conflict. (For example 'never tell lies' and 'protect the lives of the innocent': what if the murderer comes to our door and asks if we are sheltering the child whom he hopes to murder?).[255] The possibility of contingent conflict need not undermine our overall patriotic allegiance either to principles or to institutions, representatives, and fellow citizens. Indeed, in the case of institutions, representatives, and fellow citizens, it may be easier to determine where the stress should fall (easier, that is, than in the case of individual moral principles): some institutions will have the requisite capabilities and competencies to elicit and respond to certain judgements and actions of citizens, while others will not.

Yet it is sometimes claimed—in a last-ditch attempt to rescue the neo-Hobbesian motivational paradigm—that people are prepared to die for their country but not for causes and communities that attach to, say, 'universal humanity' rather than nations and states. This is patently false. People do risk and find death for such communities and causes: from United Nations representatives and personnel operating in dangerous contexts where their own countries have limited interests, to activists of the 'anti-globalisation' movement from Seattle to Davos to Genoa, to campaigners on both sides of issues of nuclear disarmament, environmental degradation, and the justice of war. These brave agents do not necessarily come from the most affected communities nor are they necessarily insensitive to the needs and values of those communities for whom they risk their lives. To the contrary, such campaigners and vulnerable communities often can and do actively value one another's way of life or practices (as Miller would put it), partly because they have learned to do so through extra-state engagement. And they do not share a national community. Of course, those prepared to die for non-national, non-state communities and causes are a hardy few. But how many people would be prepared to die for their country *without* the economic incentives and nation-statist education that drives so many young people to enlist? In any case, the implausible extreme standard for citizenship of 'preparedness

---

[255] For sustained Kantian accounts of conflict and consistency in acting on duties—accounts that seek to avoid the extreme conclusions of Kant, such as the conclusion that one should never lie, even to the murderer at the door—see B. Herman, *The Practice of Moral Judgement* (Cambridge, MA: Harvard University Press, 1993) and O. O'Neill, *Towards Justice* and 'Instituting Principles: Between Duty and Action', in M. Timmons, ed., *Kant's Metaphysics of Morals: Interpretive Essays* (Oxford: Oxford University Press, 2002c).

to die', and its erroneous application, would render very few people citizens of states: How many of us are brave enough to risk death for *any* grand community or ideology? Does this relative lack of courage necessarily make us non-citizens or worse citizens in other respects?

Yet I have argued that, as soon as we adopt any more plausible standard, multiple motivations—including universalist motivations—stand a better chance of generating the loyalty, solidarity, and responsibility that Miller maintains are necessary for a stable political order. A Responsive Democratic configuration is not only *morally* rationally compelling to ideal individuals, because it best respects their basic freedom and equality, by satisfying the principles of justice (Chapter 1) and democracy (Chapter 3), but also *prudentially* more compelling to actual individuals in that these diverse powers and opportunities allow various motivations to come into play rather than merely accommodating (and regularly repressing and distorting) them in what little room is left by nationalism.

Is Responsive Democracy messier than a nation-state system? In one sense, yes: Responsive Democracy reflects some of the complexity of multiple motivations and allegiances. In another sense, no: the messiness of real motivation is compatible with a consistent set of principles and is better channeled institutionally, allowing citizens to play a specific, limited, yet crucial role within a definite division of political labour, enshrined and contestable in terms of a clear Charter of Obligations. Is Responsive Democracy more likely as a result to be just and democratic on an ongoing basis? Yes.

9.5. Who Counts as a Citizen?

I have sought to establish that, where citizens' input into political processes is limited and in large part indirect, individuals would not necessarily be less in control of their public lives, nor would individuals be less likely to see their best interests judged and pursued in a responsible fashion. In light of this argument, scale and multiplicity no longer seem irremovable barriers but rather potential boons for democracy. The critic may now be forced to produce a last trump card: 'Fine, perhaps citizens would have more effective means of control and motivation in your kind of scheme, but the scheme could not get off the ground for one simple reason: it will be impossible to work out who counts as a citizen.' This common criticism is based on a serious misconception.

Nothing in the *concept* of the state could ever tell us which specific territorial boundaries to draw: existing states and citizenships are historically contingent configurations—albeit configurations that are (implausibly) supposed to meet certain abstract criteria (e.g. shared nationality). Similarly, *nothing* in the *concept* of Responsive Democracy tells us which specific boundaries to draw: no amount of analysis of the concept of multiple citizenships can deliver us from historical contingency, and that is no embarrassment. The issue is which abstract criteria apply and whether their application helps resolve debates and disputes over the bounds of extant authoritative institutions. Given the focus on effective discharge of functions that underlies Responsive Democracy, this issue is resolved by answering not an ontological or metaphysical or historical question (e.g. about the dimensions of the ethnos or the history of a territorial border) but rather by answering an empirical forward-looking question: *In what ways can existing political units be transformed and extended so as to include more citizens, improving the capabilities and control exercised by those citizens?* That is, how can the institutions be modified so that those who hold office pursue the best interests of more persons whom they potentially affect, in a manner that is more responsive to those persons?

The theory I have presented denies that there is an inevitable tension between scope (including more people), efficacy (producing outcomes in their best interests), and citizen control (increasing their capacities to empower and constrain representatives). Adopting Responsive Democracy as an orienting ideal, the next and final chapter illustrates how the apparent tension can be dissolved in specific cases. I discuss four major extant global institutions in turn and show how each can and should be transformed and extended, increasing scope, efficacy, and citizen control. It is a singular virtue of Responsive Democratic theory that it demands this kind of concrete and entirely forward-looking practical reasoning.

It is time, then, to determine which concrete political institutions and strategies responsive democrats have most reason to promote in the current, non-ideal world. Here there have been important political changes since Diogenes: humanity does now as a matter of fact live with global institutions. The United Nations and its specialised agencies, the World Bank Group, the World Trade Organisation, numerous international courts and arbitration panels, and many other institutions (all tied to an array of international legal covenants), make authoritative decisions that affect the lives of almost everyone, and regularly claim to do so on everyone's behalf. These institutions are global in reach. But they are severely limited also in their density, strength, autonomy, and reliability. As presently constituted, it is no wonder that most of them are notoriously unresponsive. For these reasons, we are now world *subjects*, not world *citizens*. Can we realistically hope for more? In the next chapter I show that, with the help of a normative theory—Responsive Democracy—and some political imagination, we can begin gradually to move beyond such subjection.

4

Transforming Global Institutions
Four Concrete Cosmopolitan Proposals

It is obvious that between theory and practice there is required, besides, a middle term . . . providing a transition from one to the other . . . an act of judgement by which a practitioner distinguishes whether or not something is a case of the rule; and since judgement cannot always be given yet another rule by which to direct its subsumption (for this would go on to infinity), there can be theoreticians who can never in their lives become practical because they are lacking in judgement . . . But even where this natural talent is present there can still be deficiency in premises, that is, a theory can be incomplete and can, perhaps, be supplemented only by engaging in further experiments and experiences . . . In such cases it was not the fault of theory if it was of little use in practice, but rather of there having been not enough theory, which the man in question should have learned from experience . . .

> Kant, 'On the Common Saying: That may be
> correct in theory but it is of no use in practice', 275

[C]ontemporary globalization has not only triggered or reinforced a significant politicization of a growing array of issue areas, but has also been accompanied by an extraordinary growth of institutionalized arenas and networks of political mobilization, surveillance, decision-making and regulatory activity across borders. This has enormously expanded the capacity for, and scope of, political activity and the exercise of political authority. In this respect, globalization is not, nor has it ever been, beyond regulation and control. Globalization does not prefigure the 'end of politics' so much as its continuation by new means. The prospects for 'civilizing' and 'democratizing' contemporary globalization are thus not as bleak as some suggest.

> Held et al., *Global Transformations*, 444

Prelude: Philosophy and Institutional Design

Political philosophers are regularly blamed for providing grand theories but almost no indication of how their ideas would (even ideally) be realised in concrete institutions, let alone how their ideas could be realised prudently through the messy business of politics. There is something in this accusation. Members of the discipline often become mired in the analysis of concepts, even while they claim to say something about how to approach the empirical phenomena broadly called politics. While the free intellectual division of labour means that any thinker is quite entitled to choose the focus of his or her projects, a philosophy for political action that is at no point grounded in and applicable to present empirical reality is partial and ultimately unsatisfying. It is a philosophy that does not take proper account of the significant interpretive play that depends on context, the susceptibility of political ideas to use and abuse, the practical concerns of existing agents, and the possibilities open to those who have the power to effect change. All four elements are central to understanding and orienting politics.

In this chapter, I try not to err on the side of ignoring actual political institutions, actors, or action: the focus is almost entirely on how the theory of Responsive Democracy presented in previous chapters can guide and be implemented in political practice. I propose some significant, illustrative reforms to: (1) the jurisdiction of the International Criminal Court; (2) the jurisdiction of the International Court of Justice; (3) membership in, and decision procedures of, the United Nations General Assembly and Security Council; and (4) structures and methods of corruption control by Transparency International.

My aim is to illustrate how the theory of Responsive Democracy could prove revealing and useful in considering the mandates of and reforms to distinct *kinds* of institution: a criminal court concerned with certain egregious crimes, a court with more multifaceted jurisdiction, a 'legislature' and its accompanying 'executive', and a potential advocacy and accountability agency. Each set of reforms also illustrates a distinct aspect of the overall pluralisation of authority that, I argued in previous chapters, would improve inclusion and representation in the global political system.[256]

---

[256] Establishing an effective International Criminal Court would introduce a new locus of authority—thereby expanding subsidiarity. Extending the jurisdiction of the International Court of Justice would strengthen an existing locus of authority—thereby better distributing subsidiarity. Altering membership and

But why focus on institutions, their redesign and reform? How can such complex institutions be approached in an analytically tractable way? The answer to the first question should come as no surprise. The theory of Responsive Democracy is subject to special pressures to take account of the empirical constraints on and potentials of global political institutions. Chapter 1 argued that global justice is best practically achieved through functionally delineated, plurarchic political institutions rather than through a nationalist and/or statist order. Chapter 2 argued that feasibility constraints on institutions and on persons' cognitive capacities together eviscerate the deliberative democratic project for societies of any significant size; we cannot place almost all hope in 'civil society' or 'the public sphere' to do the lion's share of the work of democratic governance—we must look to structures that secure thicker forms of representation. Chapter 3 argued that democratic representation is best achieved by introducing certain institutional preconditions: more types as well as levels of authority must be established, such that the representatives who hold office in those authorities are mutually empowered and constrained to make informed and capable judgements as to the public's best interests—partly by taking into account the judgements of the public—and to act responsibly on those judgements. In short, the weight placed on institutions in the theory is so great that I take it that I am obliged to offer at least a sketch of some just and democratic basic global institutions.

The ambitious scope of this argument leaves me open to an accusation opposite to that levelled at most political philosophers: that I have said too much, too briefly. I have discussed too many institutions and I am prescriptive without having provided a rich empirical description of the present circumstances or the history of each institution. Of course, the proof of the pudding is in the eating: either I have found an analytically tractable route through these disputed areas of analysis or not. But as an initial reply, let me make four connected points.

decision procedures in the United Nations would bring in more types of representatives—that better check and balance one another. Restructuring Transparency International would produce improved types of advocacy and accountability agencies—to serve as a necessary supplement to representatives checking and balancing one another. Other issues of application that demand further attention include the use of force for humanitarian intervention, democratising conditions on loans and aid from Bretton Woods institutions, as well as immigration and emigration (all explored briefly in Chapter 1). Each topic is a necessary and fruitful area for future research on cosmopolitan justice and responsive representation.

One, it is part of my argument that these kinds of institutions could be systematically connected, and could become responsive and effective, through a specific functional division of labour—together with related forms of cooperation, conflict, and communication. A classic case of 'the Spinoza problem': everything is and must be connected to everything else. There is no option but to discuss some institutions in tandem.

Two, the problems to which my argument respond arise in large part from a common pattern of misconceptions and misallocations of powers—that is, nationalism, statism, territorialism, deliberativism— evident in the present design and functioning of political institutions. The remedies that I present also fit a certain pattern.

Three, given the sheer scale and complexity of global institutions and politics, the argument is inevitably suggestive rather than exhaustive, a set of *illustrations not demonstrations*. I do not offer a confident eighteenth-century-style 'peace plan' or blueprint. I do not even wish to claim that my proposals for institutional reform are all original or can only be identified and justified from the perspective of Responsive Democracy. (Far from it: insofar as I wish to speak to actual politics, it seems fortunate that several of my proposals overlap with or draw on proposals from a variety of other perspectives.) Although a number of my proposals do have unique elements and derivations, I mainly wish to show that the theory of Responsive Democracy systematically enables us to identify and/or develop proposals—in a variety of domains—that are consistent in their underlying justifications and complementary in their effects.

Four, if at some point other writers or actors—or I—have more space and ability to develop, revise, and apply the theory, I shall be extremely interested to see the results. Until then, I shall try to sail between the Scylla of silence and the Charybdis of sweeping overview. All too aware of sirens of hubris that lie in wait, I shall nail my colours—if not myself—to the mast.

1. Jurisdiction of the International Criminal Court

There can be no peace without justice, no justice without law and no meaningful law without a Court to decide what is just and lawful under any given circumstance.

Benjamin Ferencz, Nuremberg prosecutor[257]

---

[257] International Criminal Court, www.un.org/law/icc/general/overview.htm

1.1. Improving the Quality of Regulators

I have argued that universalist constraints on the exercise of political power can and should become less uneven in their empirical reach—by design and not by chance. The greatest determinant of improvement on this score is the development of institutions that are able to introduce and enforce those constraints—authorities that thereby restrain and empower each other as well as other actors. While the Westphalian system of states was dominant (again, reports of its death are greatly exaggerated), *global* moral and legal constraints on power were not entrenched as fundamental, evident, and feasible considerations in and across daily procedure and action. State and corporate actors in particular were formally and often substantively obliged to obey strict rules at home, but they enjoyed near-total licence in most places abroad. From human rights abuses to exploitative labour practices to pollution, it was legally defensible for governments as well as companies to deny almost all responsibility for actions that directly affected people in distant countries. Some of these powerful actors behaved with restraint; most did not.

It would be wrong to claim that all this has changed. But, as many commentators have noted, the domestic laws of states as well as international law have increasingly shifted away from such laxity.[258] Here I focus *not* on how international law should be reconceived to become cosmopolitan law, as others have done at length,[259] but rather on the important and growing nexus of global judicial institutions that make, interpret, and apply such law. Some twenty international judicial bodies now exist.[260] The more than 210 international judges who

---

[258] Held et al., *Global Transformations* is a useful gateway to this literature. In addition, N. Klein's *No Logo* (London: Flamingo, 2001) chronicles some causes and effects of these changes more incisively than does much of the academic literature.

[259] See D. Held, 'Law of States, Law of Peoples: Three Models of Sovereignty', *Legal Theory*, Vol. 8 (2002), 1–44 and T. M. Franck, *Fairness in International Law and Institutions* (Oxford: Clarendon, 1995). For a critique of entirely fairness-based approaches to conceptualising cosmopolitan law, see J. Tasioulas, 'International Law and the Limits of Fairness', *European Journal of International Law*, Vol. 13 (2002*b*), pp. 993–1023.

[260] I individuate international judicial bodies as bodies that are permanent, composed of judges not selected by the parties to the dispute, who adjudicate legal disputes between two or more agents on the basis of predetermined rules of procedure, whose decisions are made on the basis of international law, and whose decisions are accepted as legally binding by the core United Nations or one of its sixteen specialised organs. (This definition in good part follows C. P. R. Romano

serve on these bodies are recognised in international law as acting as 'final arbiters on everything from the death penalty and responsibility for genocide, to the rights of gays in the armed forces, paid leave for part-time workers and restrictions on the use of genetically modified organisms'.[261] Yet the geographic reach and the scope of competence of these institutions as well as—partly for this reason—of international social and legal norms more generally are still highly limited and uneven. Drawing on the theory of Responsive Democracy, I want to consider how the two most prominent examples of these judicial institutions could be reformed to improve this situation. I shall argue that, in our non-ideal world, the International Criminal Court and the International Court of Justice can and should obtain expanded and compulsory jurisdiction within certain domains of law, over all persons, regardless of citizenship or country of origin.

One main, often-expressed objection here is that entrenching such powers would have one of two effects: either such Courts will be effective, in which case actors will constantly challenge and bypass lower-level courts, producing excessive concentration of judicial power at the global level; or such Courts will be unable to cope efficiently and sensitively with the multiple claims that arise—resulting in tardiness, patchiness, and abuse in the execution of international law—which would undermine the doing of justice. If accurate, this objection counts against my view that it is feasible to position authorities at multiple levels such that the resulting institutional formation is just, stable, and efficient.

However, as will become evident, this objection is conceptually and empirically inaccurate. There is a great need for a 'residual' or 'failing whom' jurisdiction, whereby actors can approach or appeal to global courts in respect of a limited but crucial set of claims. Arguments to the contrary are disingenuous because they ignore the

of the Project on International Courts and Tribunals; see www.pict-pcti.org/matrix/matrixintro.html and C. P. R. Romano, 'The Proliferation of International Judicial Bodies: The Pieces of the Puzzle', *New York University Journal of International Law and Politics*, Vol. 31 (1999), 709–51.) A less strict definition would, on my calculation, take the figure to thirty-nine. The latter figure includes international criminal tribunals, permanent international arbitration and administrative tribunals, international inspection panels, and international statutory human rights bodies—including the UN Commission on Human Rights—but still excludes non-statutory bodies such as international industry bodies.

[261] C. Booth and P. Sands, 'Keep Politics Out of the Global Courts: International Judges Must Be Independent and Representative', *Guardian*, 13 July 2001.

seriousness of this need and misdiagnose the feasibility constraints on meeting it institutionally. There is no evidence of a slippery slope to a world state or anything like it. On the contrary, the danger is that, insofar as they lack genuine universal residual jurisdiction in a few crucial domains of law, these Courts will be unable to check the concentration of power in states. It is this danger that can and must be obviated.

1.2. Justifying and Establishing the Court

We can begin by recalling the argument that persons, and not states, ought to be the epicentre of moral concern equally in international as in domestic law (Chapter 1). Yet the application of principles of right generally requires judicial authorities that are able to try and convict those who violate those principles egregiously. And it is undoubtedly the case that many individuals are the victims of national governments and national courts who flagrantly violate the principles of current international law—let alone cosmopolitan principles of global justice. Since there are no adequate moral or prudential reasons for halting the scope of justice at the borders of any state, or for allowing any 'national government' or 'national court' to decide exclusively on the fate of persons within that state, justice evidently requires a judicial authority (or authorities) that can safeguard the human rights of individuals against national governments and national courts where necessary.

The practical implications of this requirement for effective (global) judicial institutions are nowhere more evident than in the debate over the United States of America's refusal to sign and ratify the Rome Statute of the International Criminal Court. The ICC is the first standing international body tasked with investigating and prosecuting war crimes, 'acts of genocide and egregious violations of human rights'.[262] The ICC will investigate and prosecute such crimes only if national courts are unwilling or unable to do so.

The United States nevertheless made attempts to rewrite the Statute of the Court so as to exempt US citizens from investigation

---

[262] One hundred and twenty states voted to approve the text of the statute in Rome on 17 July 1998. Despite vigorous lobbying from the United States, only seven states declined; there were twenty-one abstentions. Before the Court could be set up, sixty states needed to ratify the treaty. One hundred and thirty-nine states signed the treaty by the 31 December 2000 deadline; sixty-seven states ratified by 15 May 2002, bringing the statute into force as of 1 July 2002. See www.un.org/law/icc.

and prosecution pursuant to such egregious acts.[263] On meeting firm resistance, the United States then proposed that decisions to authorise investigation and prosecution by the ICC should always go through the Security Council—on which the United States has a veto. Although this attempt too failed, the United States did succeed in obtaining, through the Security Council, a one-year exemption from prosecution for UN peacekeepers and personnel, including those hailing from the United States.[264] Thereafter, the United States set about obtaining from other states—one by one—agreements not to extradite US peacekeepers or personnel to the court.[256] Many countries, confronted with determined 'encouragement' from the United States, reluctantly signed the agreements.

The United States' main objection was that the treaty in theory gives every state that is party to the treaty, as well as the ICC itself, the right to try US citizens for grievous international crimes. This right was seen not only as an attack on the state sovereignty but also as unfair: Since the country performs a significant portion of the world's 'peace-keeping' and 'peace-making', its peacekeepers and other personnel would be vulnerable to prosecution more often and in greater absolute numbers than would the nationals of any other country. Further, given the strength of anti-US sentiment, driven in part by its hegemonic position in global affairs, its peacekeepers and personnel (and perhaps especially its political office-holders) would be peculiarly exposed to politically motivated prosecutions.

I shall show that these arguments fail.[266] The aims of the United States in respect of the ICC are unjustifiable—and are not even in the

---

[263] The official reasons for the United States' efforts are articulated in a statement by David Scheffer, Ambassador at Large for War Crimes Issues and Head of the US Delegation at the Rome Conference, to the Senate Committee on Foreign Relations, *Hearing on the United Nations International Criminal Court Before the Senate Committee on Foreign Relations*, 105th Congress (Washington, DC: United States Government, 1998).

[264] This was achieved by threatening to withdraw US peacekeepers and support from current and future United Nations peacekeeping missions. See S. Schmemann, 'U.S. Links Peacekeeping to Immunity from New Court', and 'U.S. Vetoes Bosnia Mission, Then Allows 3-Day Reprieve', *New York Times*, 19 June 2002a and 1 July 2002b, respectively.

[265] See C. Marquis, 'U.S. is Seeking Pledges to Shield Its Peacekeepers from Tribunal: Romania and Israel are First to Sign Agreements', *New York Times*, 12 August 2002.

[266] At present, the major practical issue in respect of this institution is its basic mandate—that is, its very scope and justification—and not its formal structure and functioning. I engage in this debate because the Court can be seen a crucial

interests of US personnel and peacekeepers. My argument emphatically does not imply support for critics who find fault with every action or inaction of the United States; nor does my argument imply support for critics who insist that the world's only superpower has no special obligations and should exercise no special legal powers whatsoever. I wish to establish only that the aims of the US on this one issue are indefensible and misguided, and to indicate a better way to approach the establishment of an effective Court.

There are, it seems to me, four decisive arguments for rejecting the US claims about the ICC. First, a closer look at the present ICC statute reveals that the Court must effectively defer to states: the Court can only act where the signatory state whose nationals are in question is not 'willing or able' to investigate or prosecute a case.[267] Any state, including the United States, can assert its superior right merely by instituting proceedings in its own courts. While some poor and weak states might be 'unable' to assert this right, that is hardly true of the United States, which lacks neither substantial resources nor a robust legal system. Meanwhile a state can only be found 'unwilling' to prosecute if a panel of ICC judges, and an appeal panel, finds that the national proceedings were a sham—that is, failed three tests that any barely decent legal procedure can meet.[268] Given these clear rules of competence and precedence, it seems that the US administration is mainly concerned *not* with avoiding prosecution elsewhere but rather with trying to avoid prosecution *in its own courts*. Whether that is because the US administration has no faith in those courts' capacities, or because it views those courts as excessively political, this is hardly likely to prove a publicly defensible position—especially for an administration that, from the very start, has made extensive use of those domestic courts.

Second, the prospect of 'rogue' prosecutors pursuing political agendas through the ICC—targeting top officials such as the US President—is rendered miniscule by the checks and balances incorporated into the

advance away from more statist modes of thought about international order towards more cosmopolitan governance. In this sense, an ICC that is widely regarded as legitimate is itself the greatest reform needed.

[267] B. S. Brown, 'U.S. Objections to the Statute of the International Criminal Court: A Brief Response', *New York University Journal of International Law and Politics*, Vol. 31 (1999), 885–91, at 878.

[268] That is, if the national proceedings are designed with 'the purpose of shielding the person concerned', are conducted neither 'independently' nor 'impartially', or are delayed in a way 'inconsistent with an intent to bring the person concerned to justice' (Article 17 (2) of the Rome Statute).

Statute. In addition to states' superior rights to prosecute their own nationals, a three-judge Pre-Trial Chamber at the ICC supervises decisions concerning admissibility and rules on requests for orders or warrants from the prosecutor. Here there must be evidence not merely of technical violation, but of grave and extensive violation, for prosecution to go forward.[269] Further, since in practice at present the ICC needs the support of the UN Security Council for investigation and enforcement of a range of decisions, 'the United States has little reason to fear frivolous international prosecution. It would be both futile and irrational for the ICC to provoke an indispensable patron'.[270] Since only the UN Security Council can initiate cases before the ICC without the consent of state governments whose citizens are parties to the case, the five permanent members of the Security Council are in fact the most likely source of 'political' prosecutions. The real danger seems to be not injustice against powerful states, but victor's justice that serves such states.[271]

Third, insofar as the range of action of the United States and its nationals is narrowed, so that they cannot commit serious crimes with impunity, it is narrowed in the right way. The responsibility not to commit war crimes, genocide, and egregious violations of rights is a *negative* responsibility—to refrain from certain extreme abuses of power. It is not at all unfair or onerous to treat an agent (the United States) with more power as having negative responsibility in the exercise of that power, and to hold it to account for failing to act responsibly. Cosmopolitan justice draws a firm line in respect of those responsibilities. The moral priority accorded to persons over states, and the political priority accorded to the rights of persons over the sovereignty of states, implies that—as recognised in much recent interpretation of international law—no state 'has a legitimate interest in shielding its nationals from criminal responsibility for genocide,

---

[269] Article 17 (1) of the Rome Statute. The US did manage to add two words to the definition of war crimes within the Statute, which further limit the chance of prosecutions for harming civilians: 'collateral damage' is now defined as damage that 'would be *clearly* excessive in relation to the concrete and direct *overall* military advantage anticipated' (Article 8 (2), emphasis added).

[270] Brown, 'Objections', 883. It is unclear whether this illusory 'patron' will indeed turn out to be 'indispensable': the second Bush administration did not miss many opportunities to demonstrate its deep antagonism to the court, but the court continues to establish itself with the support of other states and powerful actors.

[271] On how international courts may well do better in avoiding victor's justice than do domestic courts, see R. Goldstone, *For Humanity: Reflections of a War Crimes Prosecutor* (New Haven, CT: Yale University Press, 2000); also M. Ignatieff, 'The Right Trial for Milosevic', *New York Times*, 10 October 2000.

crimes against humanity, or serious war crimes'.[272] Indeed, one can go further and insist that no cause is just—and no response is 'proportional' to the just objectives sought—if it necessarily involves perpetrating grave and extensive (criminal) actions of this kind against numerous innocent persons.[273]

Fourth and finally, there is the consequentialist argument that the possibility of prosecution will deter the United States from undertaking peace-making and peacekeeping missions. To this there are three consequence-sensitive replies: A greater degree of caution before and during intervention would probably be a good thing—reducing the propensity to 'political' interventions by the United States itself.[274] The danger of being held solely responsible, after failing to consult and convince, might restrain tendencies towards US unilateralism, and even encourage the United States to operate and cooperate a good deal more under the auspices of the United Nations.[275] Lastly, and most importantly for US peacekeepers and personnel themselves, the existence of an effective ICC is highly likely—as the US administration acknowledged earlier in the process of establishing the Court—to 'reduce the need to send US troops around the world in the aftermath of such atrocities'.[276]

In light of these arguments, the Statute of the ICC appears—if anything—excessively statist, and the Court's powers could be modified in a cosmopolitan direction. Most noticeably, the assumption that national courts have precedence is not the best primary criterion for allocation of cases. Rather, the primary criterion should be which

---

[272] Brown, 'Objections', 871.

[273] On arguments for and the limits of proportionality, see M. Walzer, *Just and Unjust Wars: A Moral Argument with Historical Illustrations* (New York: Basic Books, 1977).

[274] Might the US stay out of situations where its intervention is badly needed? If there exists a sufficiently high risk that the United States would commit grave and extensive international crimes against civilians in the course of its interventions, the United States would be quite correct to stay out. It is unclear how any deontological account of morality worthy of the name could avoid drawing this line.

[275] Where the prospect of prosecution produces less intervention by the United States, that may well be justified to avoid greater harm; and where it does not prevent peace-making and peacekeeping, these interventions are likely to be of a better kind. See R. Falk, R. Wedgwood, W. L. Nash, F. A. Gerges, and G. Lopez, Roundtable on 'The New War: What Rules Apply?', *Ethics and International Affairs*, Vol. 16, No. 1 (2002), 1–26.

[276] I cannot pursue this empirical-predictive argument here; see Brown, 'Objections'; quotation is at 890.

court is most likely to give the defendant a fair (and not merely a decent) trial, as well as best protect witnesses, parties, and judges from intimidation and attack.

This revised principle for allocating institutional obligations can be justified on the basis of arguments presented in Chapter 1. There I showed Rawls and other liberal statists are mistaken to regard the interests of any individual as limited to minimally decent treatment by his or her own state. The state system provides less than optimally not only for the fuller range of individuals' interests but also for individuals' minimal liberty rights; thus there is good reason to reject a statist allocation of institutional obligations. Moreover, cases brought before domestic courts in illiberal legal systems may meet formal tests of impartiality in the *application* of the law even while the law itself is discriminatory—based, for instance, on a 'common good conception of justice' that still treats women and minorities unequally in crucial respects. This is likely to cause such domestic courts to view the violations of women's and minorities' rights as less serious than violations of men's and majorities' rights. Meanwhile, in liberal states, it is not uncommon that violations of the rights of foreigners and immigrants are taken less seriously than violations of the rights of citizens.

None of these points implies that the ICC should replace domestic courts; indeed, given the current Statute, the Court can only review the decisions of domestic courts, and only in cases concerning 'grave and extensive' violations of rights. Rather, I am suggesting that existing requirements that domestic legal processes be 'independent' and 'impartial' should over time come to be stringently interpreted by the Court, not in terms of a minimal threshold of decency but rather in terms of whether the ICC itself is better able to offer a fair trial in accordance with international law, as well as better able to access and protect the parties involved. Initially, in its infancy, the Court may have to be more circumspect in revising or overturning the verdicts of national courts, but—as with the US Supreme Court's pivotal decisions at the height of the civil rights movement—the Court's determination to interpret legal protections increasingly widely could encourage significant changes in state rulers' and state courts' treatment of individuals.

2. Jurisdiction of the International Court of Justice

2.1. Standing Before the Court

If the failings of statism are subtly evident in the Statute of the ICC, they are extensively evident as a threat to global justice in the case of the International Court of Justice. The cosmopolitan remedies needed here are consequently more substantial. I will consider particularly the revealing issue of which actors have 'standing before the court' (*locus standi in judicio*), that is, have the right to appear before the ICJ and argue a case.[277] And I will argue that the theory of Responsive Democracy helps identify good reasons and feasible ways to expand the range of relevant actors who have standing before the Court, as well as to expand some of the forms of petition and remedy that may be considered by the Court. These changes are also likely to make the Court more effective and relevant to global governance than it has been to date.

According to the ICJ Statute, the Court has jurisdiction in all legal disputes submitted to it concerning '(1) the interpretation of a treaty; (2) any question of international law; (3) the existence of any fact which, if established, would constitute a breach of an international obligation; (4) the nature and extent of the reparation to be made for the breach of an international obligation'.[278] This competence appears broad but is in fact strictly constrained at other points in the Statute: where binding decisions are to be made, '[o]nly states may be parties in cases before the Court' and all states that are parties to the case first have to agree to submit their dispute to the Court.[279] The Court may give advisory opinions on 'legal questions referred to it by duly authorised international organs and agencies'; but these opinions are non-binding and the actors that qualify to petition the Court in fact are heavily restricted to 'five organs of the United Nations and sixteen specialised agencies of the United Nations family'.[280]

Given the range of actors that now participates in global governance, this specification of the two kinds of actors (states and UN bodies) relevant to the Court is undoubtedly narrow. In previous chapters, I have shown that there are no *principled* grounds to restrict the moral concern shown to individuals by making representation in political and judicial bodies an exclusive prerogative of states or state-based organisations. States are not, nor should they be, the primary political agent for bearing international obligations. The remaining objections

---

[277] More strictly, according to the *Butterworths Dictionary of Legal Words*, the entitlement of a person or organisation to bring a judicial review action to challenge administrative action which is justiciable or to bring a merits appeal (www.butterworths.com.au).

[278] Article 36 (2) of the Statute of the International Court of Justice, www.icj-cij.org. This Statute was annexed to the Charter of the United Nations and signed in San Francisco on 26 June 1945.

[279] Article 34 (1) and Article 36 (1).

[280] Article 65 (1).

to opening up the Court to petition from actors such as individuals, intergovernmental organisations (IGOs), and non-governmental organisations (NGOs) are *pragmatic* ones: that such an expansion of jurisdiction will overwhelm the Court's capacities, and that states will never accept such a broadening of the rights of petition. These objections are belied by strong comparative and inductive evidence to the contrary.

The main impediment to the ICJs credibility in global politics and its effectiveness in applying international law is in fact that the Court is seriously *under*-utilised. While on average the European Court of Human Rights decides on around sixty cases a year, and the US Supreme Court decides about 100, on average the ICJ renders judgements annually on a grand total of four cases.[281] Mark Janis summarises his study of the Court's caseload as follows:

The central truth about almost one hundred years of practice is that neither states nor international organisations want to use the International Court [the ICJ and its precursors] very much. This is due in large measure to a perfectly rational desire on the part of [state] government officials and [state-appointed] international civil servants neither to lose political and administrative control of disputes nor to embarrass other states and organisations . . . [282]

Comparing this record with that of the two post-1945 European regional law courts,[283] Janis finds that rights to individual petition make a stark difference: '[These] very reasons . . . are turned on their heads when individuals are involved. Private parties do not have political control and indeed often wish to reverse political and judicial decisions already made. Moreover, individuals often have little fear about embarrassing governments and international organisations'.[284]

All the cases before the European courts, bar one, were brought by individuals and not by states.[285] While other causal factors are also significant, this inclusiveness and impact have undoubtedly made the

---

[281] M. W. Janis, 'Individuals and the International Court', in A. S. Muller, D. Raic, and J. Thuranszky, eds., *The International Court of Justice: Its Future Role After Fifty Years* (The Hague: Martinus Nijhoff, 1997), 208–12. The figure for the European Court is taken from 1990–4 (in the decades before that, the average annual number of cases was seventeen); the figure for the ICJ is taken for 1946–94, during which time there was no dramatic acceleration.

[282] Ibid., 209.

[283] Namely, the Court of Justice of the European Communities and the European Court of Human Rights.

[284] Janis, 'Individuals', 209.

[285] Ibid., 211–12.

European courts far more credible and relevant to European govern-ance than the ICJ is at present to global governance.[286]

Recall, further, my argument that global institutions could avoid being 'swamped' by individuals' claims if certain pragmatic threshold mechanisms—such as ombudsmen—were introduced that could win-now out, agglomerate, and advance relevant claims of individuals. In 1989, the Court of Justice of the European Communities introduced a mechanism of this kind, a 'Court of First Instance', that decides on the admissibility of some cases to the Court of Justice, and is empowered to render judgements itself in a range of other cases.[287] One similar pro-posal for the ICJ would see three layers rather than two: a 'five judge Committees to decide the admissibility of individual complaints', a sep-arate Chamber for inter-state complaints (and, potentially, complaints where large non-state actors are the parties), and a 'full thirty judge Plenary Court' to whom appeals could be referred if appropriate.[288] This could be complemented by the 'greater use of chambers, assessors, or special masters'.[289] This combined proposal has the virtue of recog-nising that disputes that involve individuals generally require rather dif-ferent procedures of resolution than inter-state disputes and disputes involving large non-state actors; it may also allow for definite allocation of responsibility while avoiding inflexibility.

There also is little prospect that granting rights of petition to *IGOs* will undermine the Court. Paul Szasz's survey of the possible types of litigation that IGOs might bring to the Court reveals that—largely because IGOs are creatures of or dominated by states—both states and IGOs tend to have good reasons to consider political and administra-tive resolutions of conflicts (disputes over interpretation of treaties, 'turf wars', and so on) superior to judicial ones.[290] But why then should IGOs (beyond the United Nations) be allowed access to the Court at all?

The answer is that such rights of petition would go some way to rectifying a fundamental imbalance in the powers of different levels of

---

[286] On the degree and impact of the former, see L. N. Brown and T. Kennedy, *The Court of Justice of the European Communities*, 5th edn. (London: Sweet & Maxwell, 2000).

[287] D. Lasok and J. Bridge, *Law and Institutions of the European Communities*, 5th edn. (London: Butterworths, 1991), 319–22.

[288] Janis, 'Individuals', 209.

[289] P. Szasz, 'Granting International Organisations Ius Standi in the Inter-national Court of Justice', in A. S. Muller, D. Raic, and J. Thuranszky, eds., *The International Court of Justice: Its Future Role After Fifty Years* (The Hague: Martinus Nijhoff, 1997), 169.

[290] Ibid., 171–83.

global governance. In the event of disputes with other authorities (within but also outside any particular state), states—if they are not 'failed states'—are often able to resort to self-help, forcibly imposing their own view about regulations on the actors within a territory, collecting taxes, arresting people, and so forth, but also importantly withholding cooperation. Evidently, this gives them relatively greater power in disputes with IGOs: consider, most damagingly, states' continual non-payment of assessed contributions to the United Nations during past decades. IGOs have few means to rectify this situation except by publicity that shames the default states into supplying the relevant funds. These powers are limited by the tendency of national legislatures, executives, and citizens to place a relatively low priority on such international obligations compared to domestic goals.[291]

However, the public argument by states to justify non-payment in fact tends to take a legal form: for example, that the state is supposedly not obliged to pay up because the IGO is wasteful and inefficient, or because certain parts of the national budget have absolute priority over the expenses of the IGO.[292] Granting IGOs standing before the Court would not, of course, remove either this tendency or the great inequalities in enforcement powers of states and IGOs entirely; but the ICJ could settle these legal disputes, undermining the often specious authority of states' side of the debate. Indeed, the mere prospect of very public litigation that results in defeat is likely to induce greater compliance by states.[293] And if and when states have a point, the Court could clarify and improve the situation by assessing and specifying which reforms are unfeasible, and in some cases which reforms can be reasonably required before funds are released. If the number of such disputes does escalate in time, and if such assessments prove especially complex, cases might be referred to an adjunct court similar to the European Court of Auditors.[294]

---

[291] Statistics on foreign aid provide compelling evidence: almost all states spend over 99 percent of their Gross National Product on 'looking out for their own'. The United States comes at the top of this league table of parochialism—with only 0.13 percent of GNP going to foreign aid. For measurements of the limited extent of development assistance, see the World Bank's *World Development Indicator 2000*, table 6.8 (www.worldbank.org/data/wdi2000). It is not apparent that the 'war on terrorism', begun in 2001, has changed this pattern substantially.

[292] See Szasz, 'Ius Standi', 176.

[293] One must not, however, ignore the perverse incentives that such public litigation creates (including, for instance, incentives to murder witnesses); see Section 1, above, and Section 4 below.

[294] Among other things, the Court of Auditors' reports 'draw the attention of the Community institutions and the citizens of Europe to the weaknesses in systems of procedures and controls which the Commission and the national

One way to strengthen the relative IGO position further is to remove the restriction that renders purely 'advisory' ICJ opinions on disputes involving such organisations. There is no moral justification for this restriction other than the spurious normative and prudential claims, defeated in Chapter 1, to the effect that state sovereignty must almost always trump other levels and loci of authority. Nor does such a claim seem easily sustainable in international law any longer.[295] Meanwhile, the damage that non-compliance by states does to international institutions—wreaking havoc with planning, as well as starving organisations' operations of necessary resources—should not be underestimated.

Whether *NGOs* should be granted rights of petition is a more vexed question, especially in the light of the massive recent proliferation in the number and motives of NGOs. It seems plausible that well-financed NGOs would indeed swamp the Court if granted full and equal rights of petition. NGOs can in any case play a pivotal role in financing individuals' applications to the Court, in effect putting their own claims to the test indirectly by supporting individuals' petitions.[296] This is not entirely a bad thing, since NGOs are a vital source of grass-roots information, funding, and argument (consider the Kurdish Human Rights Project, which has taken several compelling cases to the European Court of Justice). However, the overall problem seems to be that, whether included or excluded, NGOs threaten to develop an overwhelming presence.

A way out of this conundrum might be to grant certain NGOs a limited status as *amici curiae* ('friends of the court'),[297] where NGOs

authorities concerned must endeavour to overcome' (European Union Court of Auditors, www.eca.eu.int/EN/coa.htm).

[295] I. Seidl-Hohenveldern's study of the legal status of IGOs concludes: 'The personality of international organizations has become so similar to that of states that their exclusion from the full jurisdiction of the ICJ appears to be an unfair discrimination'. See his 'Access of International Organisations to the International Court of Justice', in A. S. Muller, D. Raic, and J. Thuranszky, eds., *The International Court of Justice: Its Future Role After Fifty Years* (The Hague: Martinus Nijhoff, 1997), esp. 189–203.

[296] There is a possibility that NGOs could form alliances with IGOs to make applications, but—leaving aside the obvious counterbalancing powers of state regulatory controls on NGOs—the prospect and problem of such alliances is small relative to the prospect of NGO alliances with individuals.

[297] '*amicus curiae* . . . a phrase that literally means "friend of the court"— someone who is not a party to the litigation, but who believes that the court's decision may affect its interest' (W. H. Rehnquist, *The Supreme Court: How It Was, How It Is* (New York: Morrow, 1987), 89).

may not be parties to a case but may submit briefs in support of one side or the other. This accreditation of NGOs would have to be governed by at least two considerations: (1) whether the NGOs central areas of competence and purpose are directly relevant to and affected by the Court's decision; and (2) whether those interest areas meet minimal standards of both permissibility of purpose and fairness of process. We do not lack for definite models of how this would work.[298] Again, there would be a need for a Court of the First Instance, and/or chambers and assessors, which interpret these kinds of qualification rather stringently.[299]

It is of course within the discretion of the Court to take as much or as little account of *amicus curiae* briefs as it deems appropriate. But it must also be possible for the Court to declare NGOs that constantly support the bringing of specious cases before them 'vexatious litigants', whereupon the NGOs in question must be barred from submitting briefs or funding individuals' applications in the future, and in severe cases must be subject to civil penalties for obstructing justice.[300] There is a real danger that such NGOs can then simply be set up under

[298] In the law of the United Kingdom, for instance, most NGOs fall under the rubric of 'charities', and Charity Law establishes standards of charitable purpose by designating and regulating four permissible kinds of public purpose: education, religion, relief of poverty, and public benefit. The point here is to rule out pernicious objectives (e.g. terrorism) and the use of organisations as instruments of one or two people, as well as to rule out a less extreme range of NGOs that have little helpful to add. (See the Scottish Charity Law Commission, www.charityreview.com, and the Liverpool University Charity Law Unit, www.liv.ac.uk/law/units/clu.htm#overview) As to determining whether a party's interests are affected, this difficult issue is considered by local and national courts all the time, and those courts have developed a range of tests of impact. At the global level, the difficulty lies not so much in finding some tests that are justifiable in principle but rather in making the empirical assessments of impact at a global level that such tests require. There is likely to be a larger grey area for international than for local and national courts, but some NGOs will obviously pass the tests and some obviously not. As in local and national courts, the tests could become more refined and capture more relevant factors over time. For an example of relevant tests, see Section 3, below, where I provide a list of criteria for admitting NGOs and other actors to the United Nations General Assembly. It is quite possible that this list could be modified to apply to *ius standi* in respect of the ICJ.

[299] It would also be important to secure disclosure of all financial contributions to individuals' cases before the Court, in forms that meet transparency requirements (see Section 4, below).

[300] An intimation of this approach can be found in Rule 37 (1) of the US Supreme Court: 'An *amicus curiae* brief that brings to the attention of the Court relevant matter not already brought to its attention by the parties may be of

a different name, or set up vexatious affiliates; it may then prove necessary to expose, bar, and penalise the major financial backers and office-holders who direct the activities of such vexatious NGOs.

Having established that there are good reasons and feasible ways to give specific forms of legal standing to a wide range of the actors now participating in global governance, the remaining question is whether states could be induced to relinquish their almost exclusive prerogative to petition the ICJ. The record here is more promising than one might anticipate. The European Human Rights Convention included two Articles (Articles 25 and 46) that permitted individual access to the European Court of Human Rights, yet states ratified the convention because these clauses were made *optional*, until specifically accepted by each member state: 'Those favoring state sovereignty believed states would never accept the optional clauses. Those favoring individual access believed states would accept them in time . . . in time the optimists proved right . . . 20 years after the signing of the convention, 11 states had accepted . . . [40 years after,] all 22 states had accepted both Article 25 and Article 46'.[301]

The forces ranged in favour and against wider access to the ICJ are certainly different from those relevant to this European Court, and it may take a number of years before all states are prepared to allow other agents access to the Court. Nevertheless, there are grounds for both hope and political action. States are being driven by current global transformations to acknowledge the powers and obligations of other authorities and actors, and to cooperate with some of them in international organisations (see Sections 3 and 4 below). There is an increasingly felt need for clear mechanisms to adjudicate conflicts over whether state- and non-state actors have met their respective international obligations. The ICJ already possesses a number of the actual capacities and formal powers necessary to provide this adjudication—a fact that is unlikely to go unnoticed, especially by many smaller states and by non-state actors. Much may be achieved by a coalition of these political actors, determined to create a standing legal forum for their claims. At the same time, the idea of clauses that render state support for an improved ICJ *optional* holds out the hope of progressive realisation of a more inclusive global legal order. These clauses would instantiate the principles of Responsive Democracy, by entrenching in international law a definite ideal that can orientate

considerable help to the Court. An *amicus curiae* brief that does not serve this purpose burdens the Court, and its filing is not favored' (www.supremecourtus.gov).

[301] Janis, 'Individuals', 211.

democratic political practice (including lobbying of states to sign on and ratify such changes) in the present.

2.2. *Funding of World Courts*

The so-called 'financial argument' against extending and strengthening the powers of world courts has attained great prominence. If sound, this argument does serious damage to cosmopolitan justice as a feasible ideal. I therefore conclude this section by indicating why the financial argument is misguided and indeed seriously misleading.

The annual cost of administering international justice at present is 240 million dollars; this figure drops dramatically to 100 million dollars if we exclude the European Court of Justice from the calculation.[302] Both figures represent 'an extremely small share of the overall cost of international cooperation', especially given the importance attached to, and costs borne to support, legal systems within states and localities.[303] This would be true even if the budgets of international judicial institutions totalled three or ten times as much. But the figures look particularly negligible when we consider, as I now do, the alternatives. That is, justice is likely to be far less selective, and far more efficiently pursued, where there are institutions with clear and permanent jurisdictions over certain crucial areas of global concern.

This is immediately evident if we consider the advantage of permanent courts over the ad hoc tribunals to prosecute individual perpetrators in Rwanda and the former Yugoslavia. For one thing, glaring selective injustices abound: some state governments agree to set up or cooperate with a tribunal, others do not; egregious crimes in some states attract the sustained international attention necessary to establish such a tribunal, others do not. For another, as the Rome Statute of the ICC recognises, ad hoc tribunals are actually more expensive than standing courts (such added expense also softens the political will required to make the tribunals work). Ad hoc tribunals are also more fraught with delays in being set up (leading to the 'disappearance' of crucial evidence, witnesses, and perpetrators).[304] Finally, tribunals are more inflexible—for example, the Rwanda tribunal only

---

[302] Project on International Courts and Tribunals (PICT), 'Funding of and Access to International Courts and Dispute Settlement Bodies [1997]', www.pict-pcti.org/publications/publications.html

[303] Ibid.

[304] United Nations, 'Overview of the Rome Statute of the International Criminal Court', www.un.org/law/icc/general/overview.htm

considers events that occurred prior to 1994, preventing it from prosecuting the murder of thousands of refugees since then.[305]

It should be added that the resource problems that beset present international judicial institutions are often not so much a matter of limited quantities as of inadequate forms of funding and of failures to develop and follow through non-state solutions. As discussed above, dependence on the political will of state governments—to provide funds on what is effectively an ad hoc schedule—damages the abilities of international judicial institutions to plan strategically and in turn to resolve disputes rapidly. The damage caused is immense: at a recent meeting of leading legal theorists and practitioners from international judicial institutions, those attending shared the view that 'length of proceedings ... [is] the most serious threat to the credibility of the international legal system'.[306]

Another immediate threat to credibility is the justified perception of unfairness in cases where poorer parties are excluded because litigation is prohibitively costly. There is a need to develop sources of funding for potential litigants that are less dependent on immediate decisions by states as well as less dependent on the agendas of NGOs. The ICJ Trust Fund established by the UN Secretary General in 1989, to provide financial assistance to developing countries, is a step in this direction (the Permanent Court of Arbitration has now established an equivalent), though it is for resource-strapped *states* only and would need to be expanded to include other actors and greater amounts of support. Another important step, especially on the way to including individuals as applicants before the Court, would be the establishment of a *pro bono* list of international legal practitioners, willing to provide some free advice and assistance to parties and to mediate in disputes. In time, this could be properly institutionalised: a number of practitioners have envisioned the establishment of an International Bar.[307]

---

[305] Time limitations in bringing such cases may be practically important in enabling people to begin to live together. A permanent Court can assess, however, whether an expansion of its ambit would endanger such coexistence—or perhaps stabilise and improve the situation.

[306] Project on International Courts and Tribunals, www.pict-pcti.org/activities/london.html. The complexity of the proceedings themselves is one reason for their length, but is, as I have argued, far from the only contributory cause.

[307] On 13–15 June 2002, the first 'Conference on the creation of the International Criminal Bar' was held in Montreal—jointly organized by the Bars of six countries (see Coalition for the International Criminal Court, www.igc.org/icc/index.html).

In the domain of global judicial institutions, then, there is no short-age of feasible strategies for change in the direction of cosmopolitan justice. These reforms, individually and collectively, are not peculiarly expensive—whether we define that notion relative to the costs of peace-making and peace keeping operations, the costs of establishing and maintaining international tribunals, or the far larger total costs (let alone benefits) of law-governed global cooperation.

3. Membership in the United Nations

The title of an important paper says it all: 'The necessity of reforming the United Nations and the impossibility of doing it'.[308] No one doubts that the organisation needs significant reforms if it is to fulfil its present responsibilities, let alone take on new responsibilities; yet, on sane assessment, the political and technical obstacles to extensive reform often appear insurmountable. Partly for this reason, I wish to develop an unconventional route to improving representation in the United Nations, and show that this route avoids much of the inertia and inequity that has attended and would attend statist and delibera-tive reforms.

I shall focus on the implications of the theory of Responsive Democracy for one vexed issue: UN membership; that is, who can and should represent persons' interests, and how they can and should make decisions, at the level of this global authority. Moreover, while I shall mention other UN organs and agencies, my argument concen-trates on the General Assembly and Security Council. Strictly speak-ing, there are four issues of representation for this 'core UN': composition, decision processes, competences, and relations to other organs. I emphasise the first two.

3.1. The Statist Dilemma

The participation of new actors on the international scene is an acknow-ledged fact; providing them with agreed means of participation in the formal system, heretofore primarily the province of States, is a new task of our time.

---

[308] R. Falk, paper presented at a conference at La Trobe University, Melbourne; cited in B. Brown, 'Summary: A Mid-Life Crisis for the UN at Fifty', in Thakur, ed., *Past Imperfect Future Uncertain: The United Nations at Fifty* (Basingstoke: Macmillan, 1998), at 247.

Thus begins Boutros Boutros-Ghali's *An Agenda for Democratization* of 1996.[309] But, years later, the facts about representation in the United Nations remain familiar and dispiriting. It is an organisation constituted by states; other actors have at best consultative status. The organisation is dominated by a few states—by design.[310] Binding decisions are not made by the 191 states in the General Assembly (the latter's decisions are strictly advisory) but rather by a select group of fifteen states on the Security Council.[311] The five permanent members of the Security Council each have a veto, ensuring that each often has more power than 186 other member states individually and collectively.[312] Indeed, shortly after Boutros-Ghali published this reformist *Agenda*, the United States blocked his reappointment as Secretary General (final vote: 14 for, 1 against). Consider only one compound effect of this skewed selection process: the Secretary General in turn appoints the heads of several UN subsidiary organisations (e.g. UNHCR, UNPF, UNDP, WFP) without any requirement for public

---

[309] Reprinted in B. Holden, ed., *Global Democracy: Key Debates* (London and New York: Routledge, 2000), quotation at 105.

[310] Indeed, the phrase 'We the people' at the beginning of the UN Charter was introduced to replace the original 'the high contracting parties [i.e. states]', avowedly as a public relations exercise by Eleanor Roosevelt to appeal to the many members of the American public who had previously spurned the League of Nations (see B. Brown, 'Summary', 261).

[311] The General Assembly does not pass binding laws of the kind enacted by national legislatures, but 'this does not mean that its draft treaties and resolutions are without meaning. Draft treaties . . . may become effective in law in the member countries when ratified by the national legislatures of those countries, and they may come to constitute [mostly customary] international law' (W. Gordon, *The United Nations at the Crossroads of Reform* (New York and London: M. E. Sharpe, 1994), 22). In this respect, the General Assembly has in fact had *more* influence on Security Council decisions than appears to have been anticipated in the Charter. For instance, Article 12 of the Charter states that 'while the Security Council is exercising in respect of any dispute or situation the functions assigned to it . . . the General Assembly shall not make any recommendation with regard to that dispute or situation unless the Security Council so requests'. This restriction is almost entirely ignored. In fact, the Assembly has passed several resolutions—for example on the Israeli–Palestinian conflict—that contradict resolutions of the Council.

[312] The term veto does not appear in the wording of the Charter, but Article 27 (3) reads: 'Decisions of the Security Council . . . shall be made by an affirmative vote of nine members including the concurring votes of the permanent members'— the only exception being that parties to a dispute must abstain from voting altogether (an exception that is also ignored in practice). On the veto and reform prospects, see B. Fassbender, *UN Security Council Reform and the Right of Veto: A Constitutional Perspective* (The Hague: Kluwer Law International, 1998).

advertisement of jobs or short-listing and screening by any selection panel—let alone a panel that is well-constituted.[313]

If these facts are not in dispute, if the United Nations does not instantiate a democracy of states—let alone a democratic body representing crucial interests of all persons—what is to be done? The most popular refrain from critics of the status quo, and especially from smaller member states, is emphatically 'abolish the veto' in the Security Council. This refrain is regularly followed by demands that the General Assembly be assigned powers to make binding decisions, in the manner of state legislatures. But these so-called remedies are hardly responsible unless it can be shown that the resulting institution is likely to be more justifiable than the status quo. And it is not at all clear which is worse: rule by the 'great powers' or—possibly, in the absence of any break on majority rule—rule by a coalition of largely illiberal and undemocratic states, often easily bribed by richer states.[314] (One shudders to think of what the consequences might be for women's rights in particular.) However, the alternatives are not limited, as is often presumed, to 'great powers' statism and 'majoritarian' statism.

3.2. Deliberative Solutions and Why They Must Fail

In the nascent literature on cosmopolitan global democracy, several alternative institutional designs for improving representation in the core UN have been mooted. Consider three typical proposals:

1. David Held recommends the creation of 'a UN second chamber (following an international constitutional convention)', consisting of territorial actors other than states, with both chambers to be superseded in the long-term by a 'global parliament ... connected to regions, nations, and localities'. One version of this proposal envisions each territorial level appointing representatives; another version envisions direct global elections where representatives have territorial constituencies (a model closer to the European parliamentary elections).

---

[313] On distortions in appointment procedures, see H. Kovach and S. Burall, *Global Accountability Project* (London: One World Trust and Charter 99, 2001), esp. 8.

[314] Majoritarian statism, like great powers statism, has an inbuilt propensity to descend into rule by bribery by the rich. Since tiny and poor states have a formal vote equal to the largest and richest states, and since each of the latter can expend a small percentage of their resources to make a massive difference to each of the former, or install highly punitive tariffs and subsidies, richer states are often in a position to make 'offers you cannot refuse' to poorer ones. Proponents of abolition of the veto have not found a plausible way out of this quandary.

The Security Council remains, but it is expanded to 'give develop-ing countries a significant voice and effective decision-making capacities'.[315]

2. Daniele Archibugi recommends that delegates to the General Assembly 'must represent both government and opposition'; fur-ther, 'one or two delegates' from each country must be directly elected (quite how these two demands are to be harmonised is not clear). Meanwhile, the Security Council is to be opened up to 'regional organisations such as the European Union', and a 'con-sultative vote' is to be given to 'representatives of civil society'.[316]

3. Johan Galtung recommends nothing less than five Assemblies: a General Assembly for governments (UNGA), a People's Assembly directly elected by all the individuals of the world (UNPA), a Corporate Assembly for corporations, (UNCA), a Local Authorities Assembly (UNLAA), and a Council of Non-Governmental Organisations (CONGO). The last three would have consultative and coordinating roles—articulating 'concerns', entering into 'dialogue', and dispensing context-sensitive 'advice'. The General Assembly 'would head the executive organ'. Only the People's Assembly would be 'the ultimate sovereign . . . [and] would function like any other parliament, making laws, budgets and appointments'.[317]

Leaving aside copious, capacious questions about how these propos-als might be interpreted and implemented, what can be said about the value of each as a general approach to UN reform? I would not be discussing these approaches if I did not think that they represented some imaginative advances against more nationalist and statist models of UN membership. But these inventive proposals nevertheless suffer two serious limitations.

[315] D. Held, 'Democracy and Globalisation', in D. Archibugi, D. Held, and M. Kohler, eds., *Re-imagining Political Community: Studies in Cosmopolitan Democracy* (Stanford, CA: Stanford University Press, 1998), at 25.

[316] D. Archibugi, 'Principles of Cosmopolitan Democracy', in D. Archibugi, D. Held, and M. Kohler, eds., *Re-imaging Political community: Studies in Cosmopolitan Democracy* (Stanford, CA: Stanford University Press, 1998).

[317] J. Galtung, 'Alternative Models for Global Democracy' in Holden, ed., *Global Democracy: Key Debates* (London: Routledge, 2000), at 156. The idea of a Global Parliament or People's Assembly has been developed further by R. Falk and A. Strauss in 'On the Creation of a Global People's Assembly: Legitimacy and the Power of Popular Sovereignty', *Stanford Journal of International Law*, Vol. 36, No. 2 (2000), 191–219. Their proposals are innovative, but run into similar problems to the three models I discuss here.

First, despite a purported thoroughgoing cosmopolitanism, each proposal is intrinsically territorialist—and in some crucial respects statist—in its own way. Held seems to draw constituencies only in terms of different territorial levels, even while his Security Council admits more developing *countries* and remains solely an organ of states.[318] Archibugi wants the government as well as the opposition from *state legislatures* to be represented, and/or for there to be intra-*state* elections for one or two delegates from each state. 'Civil society' on his model has merely consultative powers to the Security Council, while only regional organisations—collections of proximate states—can gain full entry. Galtung's conception of the General Assembly confers executive power on state governments, and only state governments (which might cause one to doubt that a People's Assembly in fact would be 'the ultimate sovereign'). Moreover, when it comes to specifying how the People's Assembly will be appointed, Galtung presents an unnecessarily distortionary 'general formula . . . that each state should have the right to one representative per million inhabitants'.[319]

Second, more disturbingly, all these recommendations to increase the *size* and internal *plurality* of the United Nations are not accompanied by adequate accounts of how to improve the *quality and efficiency* of process and decision. This is most evident in the Galtung proposal: he claims that the 'totality would not be that complicated' yet goes on to estimate a people's assembly consisting of 'about 6,000 representatives'; 'ideally', each representative is elected against other candidates, after an extensive 'debate on key global issues'.[320] Chapter 2 demonstrated the absurdity and deep practical dangers of such purported inclusion: the consequences would be covert domination by an unresponsive

---

[318] Held has been careful, however, to distinguish short- and long-run objectives; moreover, his interpretation of international law itself does not seem to be intrinsically statist (see Held, 'Law of Peoples'). It is therefore unclear whether he envisions the Security Council withering away with the advent of a global parliament and of cosmopolitan international law.

[319] Galtung, 'Alternative', 158. Chapter One provided several arguments for considering this formula unnecessarily distortionary. In addition, one might be worried about the levels of corruption that might be found in global institutions if 40 percent of People's Assembly members were elected from the pool of politicians best known to citizens of China, India, and Indonesia. These three countries come in at 57, 71, and 86—out of 91—on Transparency International's *Corruption Perceptions Index 2001*, and in at 58, 72, and 96—out of 99—on it's *Bribe-Payer's Survey 2000* (Berlin: Transparency International, 2001 and 2000 respectively). I shall suggest that there are better ways to identify constituencies and select representatives.

[320] Galtung, 'Alternative', 158.

hegemon or by a minority (to improve brute efficiency), extremely poor decisions (due to a gross lack of information and understanding), bureaucratic paralysis, or indeed all of the above. Merely adding participants and participation rights is a recipe for parliamentary gigantism and for marginalising disadvantaged individuals all the more.

Similarly, one of the few things that can be said in favour of the current structure of the Security Council is that it sometimes (but only sometimes) allows for swift decisions in the face of urgent dilemmas; simply adding representatives of many more countries to the Security Council—as Held suggests—may do something to improve brute inclusion in decisions but only at great cost to expeditious action.[321] Further, it is not clear that developing states that become members will on the whole look after one another's interests rather than using newly acquired power largely to compete against other developing economies or political foes.[322] Archibugi's suggestion, that regional organisations simply be added to the Security Council along with states, also founders on the problem of gigantism. If, on the other hand, inter-state regional organisations were *replacing* the existing states as members of the Security Council, the effect would be limited since it largely shifts statism up a level, largely retaining the initial demarcation of states. In short, none of these deliberative proposals justifies any realistic hope that all individual persons will be much better represented than in the statist status quo. Is there a more convincing alternative?

3.3. How to Include Non-State Actors

Clearly, there is a place for territory-based representatives in the United Nations; but that should not be confused with assigning them an exclusive or even a hegemonic place. The route to including other actors in a just, democratic, and prudent fashion can be found in my accounts of plurarchic sovereignty (Chapter 1) and responsive representation (Chapter 3).

---

[321] I take it that Held has in mind something more significant than the expansion from 15 to 24 that is commonly mooted; in any case his Security Council would still consist of 24 *states*.

[322] This argument is sometimes offered by the 'great powers', which is disingenuous given their demonstrated willingness to use the veto to achieve parochial ends and create deadlock where urgent action is sometimes needed. I shall suggest that there is a better alternative than both gigantism and great powers domination of the Security Council.

In my discussion of sovereignty, I sought to establish that tasks of governance should be understood and allocated on functional rather than territorial lines. Political authority can then be understood as legitimate power over kinds of human practice and resources, only some of which are best regulated within territorial demarcations. Territorial authority is *derivative*—one potential form of effective authority that may be better or worse than others (e.g. syndicalism). I went on to argue that non-state actors—such as IGOs and NGOs, as well as local and regional territorial authorities—are sometimes better placed than states to operate decisively over crucial functions, and should be formally empowered to do so. Multiple levels and types of authority can and should be combined along with states in a pluralistic basic structure, where each authority has a different set of capabilities and clearly defined responsibilities, and each is compelled to cooperate and communicate with the others to meet its responsibilities. That structure—if it is to be balanced, effective, and stable— also requires advocacy and accountability agencies that provide good quality information to citizens and authorities, as well as eliciting citizens' judgements and gaining a more responsive hearing for citizens.

But the immediate, serious question for my approach is this: 'Granted, the state system brings about intense conflict and exclusion, but at least we generally know whom to include—namely, in old international law, something like "whoever monopolises (legitimate) violence over a territory". On what grounds would your pluralised system include some non-state actors and not others?' Although this question is vexed, although I do not have any complete solutions, it is not without answers. I began to provide some answers by developing a theory of representation.

The cornerstone of my theory of representation—as I have stressed repeatedly—is the idea that, while a democratic system requires *agents* who act as representatives, the primary question for a democracy is whether the *system* as a whole operates so as to be properly responsive to the public. Each member of the public need not and should not have a single representative individual or party or governmental authority that advances *all* his or her politically relevant interests. Some of a person's interests might be advanced by one agent, some by another, and some indirectly and even unintentionally through the interaction of representatives and institutions within a complex division of labour. Democracy does not require that I can point to one individual or body as my true representative. Rather, it requires that institutions of governance operate so as to maintain a systematic causal connection between members of the public having certain interests and—in part through eliciting of citizens' judgements, but largely through institutions that check and balance one another—those interests being identified capably and pursued responsibly.

Thus the criteria for inclusion of actors as representatives must de-emphasise one-to-one representation and instead focus on what combination of actors produces the highest level of systemic responsiveness overall to the best interests and judgements of the public. We ask three basic questions: Which actors are of a kind and quality such that they will best be able to fulfil relevant governmental functions and cooperate with other authorities that fulfil related functions? Does the inclusion of this or that agent improve the overall quality of information and capacities available to representatives (to judge the best interests of the public and respond to the public's active judgements)? Does the inclusion of this or that agent help enable and constrain representatives to act on those judgements rather than abusing their knowledge and power (to pursue their own divergent interests)? These basic questions constitute non-state, non-electoral bases on which relevant criteria for inclusion of non-state actors can be developed—the task to which I now turn.

3.4. A Representative Global Assembly

Each of the following criteria is complex and contentious (each covers topics that are the subjects of many books) and merits vastly more discussion than can be provided here. But the task of trying to supply such criteria—for sifting good from bad candidates—cannot be avoided by those who seek justifiable forms of global governance. That is, the idea of 'sticking with states' as the only candidates is arbitrary, excludes many individuals, limits the prospects for democracy, and—especially given significant changes in the nature of global interaction—is perilously imprudent. As in many other areas of life, then, the task to be confronted is large and messy, but the consequences of denial are far more troubling.[323] The criteria that I mention should therefore be understood as tentative starting-points for debate—indicating the broad areas in which candidates might have to pass thresholds of competence. Since candidates would have to meet most or perhaps all of these criteria to be selected, the criteria in

---

[323] Rawls repeatedly and rightly insists that, whether or not a political philosopher can remain agnostic about 'the good' in politics, he or she cannot plausibly refrain from participating in debate as to the best—and best use of—social and scientific knowledge available (Rawls, *Theory*, 20–2, 44–53, and 136–42).

combination can be imagined as the mesh of a sieve that separates out good from bad candidates.[324]

Nine criteria for distinguishing relevant practice-based actors for inclusion as representatives in the General Assembly seem promising:

1. *The Criterion of Basicness*: Is the organisation or practice concerned with basic human interests—especially basic needs and rights? The main issues of interpretation and application concern how to conceptualise, individuate, and weigh relevant practices and interests. Philosophers do well to note that—for all our legitimate qualms—there is a vast development literature that addresses these topics in practice, and one or another measurement is and has to be adopted for practical purposes.[325] A criterion of this kind would help to identify representatives of, say, widely shared environmental interests, while excluding representatives of, say, ballroom dancing (however, more general practices of sport and entertainment might well be included).

2. *The Criterion of Inclusiveness*: Does the organisation or practice have members or participants distributed over a sufficient number of social divides? The main issues here are what counts as a divide and who counts as a member. But there seems little doubt that, for instance, the under-represented interests of many women would come to the fore: problems of childbirth and childcare, infant mortality and morbidity, domestic violence and more. On the other hand, nationalisms that are couched in purely cultural relativist terms would not gain entry. This is not to preclude more general nationalist concerns being represented; rather it is to maintain that, when it comes to deciding on basic political structures, even identity-defining commitments must be subject to minimal universalist constraints on reasoning, otherwise that structure is unjustifiably coercive.

---

[324] In constructing this list of criteria, I have found particularly useful M. Power, *The Audit Society: Rituals of Verification* (Oxford: Oxford University Press, 1997); Galtung, 'Alternative'; and O'Neill, *Autonomy and Trust* and *Question of Trust*.

[325] Consensus on well-grounded evaluations is far from impossible—as evidenced by the almost universal use of the *Human Development Report* as a touchstone for poverty relief. The *Report* is based primarily on Amartya Sen's capabilities approach to understanding and relieving poverty; while this conception can be debated, and may be replaced in time on the basis of argument or evidence to the contrary, one or another measure has to be adopted in the hope of saving and improving lives. If this is the case in respect of public policy, it seems all the more justified in respect of the basic structure.

3. *The Criterion of Distributive Subsidiarity*: Does the organisation or practice reflect some kind of global shared interest or could its activities and aims be pursued better via a lower level or different type of governance?[326]

4. *The Criterion of Democratic Control*: Is the practice or organisation structured such that the members are able to appoint, empower, and constrain those who hold major offices? Crucially, this does not always require elections but can be satisfied by demonstrating that the powers within the practice or organisation are distributed so as to check and balance one another, and to compel one other to elicit and take into account members' active judgements.[327]

5. *The Criterion of Permanence*: Does the practice or organisation have a proven record of successful action to satisfy specific basic interests? Is it likely that the practice or organisation's modes of addressing these interests will remain relevant in the longer term? The main issues here are the disputability of performance indicators, the lack of past performance by almost everybody in certain contexts, and the difficulty of prediction. All these issues are already central to a range of public policy debates.[328] This criterion would reduce the scope for the formation of organisations that are 'fronts' for other interests. Of course, it would also place a large barrier in the way of previously under-organised groups, but the solution—better organisation—does not lie in immediate UN entry.

6. *The Criterion of Non-Deception*: Are the practice or organisation's actual purposes and workings susceptible to, and robust in the face of, accessible and assessable disclosure of information?[329] Specifically, do they survive scrutiny and contestation by a range of advocacy and accountability agencies?

7. *The Criterion of Audit*: Does the organisation or practice's financial management survive scrutiny by independent accredited private auditors as well as accountability agencies such as Auditor Generals?

8. *The Criterion of Non-Dependence*: Does the organisation or practice receive funding and other essential support from a sufficient range of sources, such that it is not overly dependent on any one source or category of sources? Are those sources the kind of entities they purport to be, and are they legal? Do particular sources control

---

[326] See Chapter 1.

[327] See Chapter 3.

[328] See, for example, United Nations Development Program, *Human Development Report 2001* (Oxford and New York: Oxford University Press, 2001), chapters 3 to 5.

[329] See Chapter 3 and Section 4, below.

or dominate appointment of trustees and management? Since much company and charity law addresses similar problems, we are not without precedents and experience in this area.[330]

9. *The Criterion of Non-Partisanship*: Are the central figures in the organisation or practice likely to have serious conflicts of interest between their UN role and other roles? This criterion might be interpreted fairly strictly and substantively, barring—for instance—leading members of political parties and armed forces. Or, as in many parliaments, including the British House of Commons, it might be interpreted more loosely and procedurally, requiring extensive declarations of interests and abstention from decisions where those interests are directly at stake.

This list is hardly exhaustive or definitive; it is the merest of beginnings and requires extensive expansion and modification. What it does show, however, is that we do not necessarily lack rational grounds on which to admit some actors and not others.

Given the abstract criteria above, how would the membership of the resultant Assembly pan out? Since so many issues of interpretation and application remain to be resolved, I will spare no more than a few paragraphs on such wild speculation; but let me at least indicate what sort of structure might prove justifiable.

Quite a number of states would do fairly well out of the list of criteria above. However, for example, (1) satisfying the criterion of inclusiveness would probably increase the role of regional organisations; (2) criteria of distributive subsidiarity and democratic control would probably increase the role of local authorities; and (3) criteria of non-deception and democratic control would place conditions on entry that infuriate some state rulers, even while providing incentives to rule more responsively.[331]

Other actors that might do well in satisfying the nine criteria above would include some international NGOs. The emphasis here is on *some*: NGOs, like corporations, can be very powerful and yet scandalously unaccountable—let alone responsive.[332] Professing high moral purpose and independence (that slippery term) and often

---

[330] See, for instance, D. Morris, 'Political Activity and Charitable Status: In Search of Certainty', *The Exempt Organization Tax Review*, Vol. 23, No. 2 (1998), 247–60; and J. Warburton and A. Cartwright, 'Human Rights, Public Authorities and Charities', *Charity Law and Practice Review*, No. 6 (2000), 169–83.

[331] See Chapters 1 and 3, and Section 4, below.

[332] See O'Neill, *Question of Trust* and *Autonomy and Trust*.

operating in under-regulated social contexts, many NGOs are able to avoid scrutiny of their actual motives and activities, their financial probity and sources of support, as well as their appointment and decision procedures. Also notably difficult to resolve is the problem of the nature and quality of 'democracy' within NGOs (let alone TNCs).

However, recent theory and practice suggest that entrenching democratic norms—of a kind relevant to these organisations—is far from impossible, as was once supposed.[333] Corporate codes of conduct, audits, 'stakeholder' models of operation, 'managerial democracy', 'corporate governance', and similar ideas are all in vogue as legitimating creeds. We should not be sanguine about how much adequate justification and actual implementation is going on.[334] But requiring NGOs that wish to gain significant entry to the United Nations to meet the criteria above would focus attention on developing ever better mechanisms of this kind; it would also create incentives for organisations to move in this direction. International NGOs that meet such criteria—where they have distinctive, established competences in judging and pursuing important interests of many citizens—merit a place at the table of governance no less than states.[335]

These non-state actors would not, however, have a separate assembly, or merely consultative powers. Instead, they would be part of a single

[333] See McMahon, *Authority and Democracy*; Power, *Audit Society*; and Held, 'Cosmopolitan Social Standards'.

[334] See S. P. Sethi, 'Corporate Codes of Conduct and the Success of Globalization', *Ethics and International Affairs*, Vol. 16, No. 1 (2002), 89–106; M. Winston, 'NGO Strategies for Promoting Corporate Social Responsibility', *Ethics and International Affairs*, Vol. 16, No. 1 (2002), 71–88; and Klein, *No Logo*.

[335] There is a danger that several of the criteria above would exclude a disproportionate number of actors from the developing world, thereby increasing the dominance of the developed world in international affairs. One limited remedy might be to give particular weight to the criterion of inclusiveness—prioritising organisations that cross many social divides. Achieving better representation for the developing world will be an ongoing problem nevertheless: insofar as the make-up of representative bodies should be sensitive to whether actors are capable and constrained to act effectively, actors who are already powerful and operating under established regulatory regimes will continue to have a distinct advantage. A similar problem arises for *any* theory that takes into account present socioeconomic and institutional reality, even as it aims to express an adequate normative stance in response to that reality (see Tasioulas, 'International Law', 1–3). It might be said, in favour of the theory of Responsive Democracy, that it provides a basis for an unusual approach to reducing this problem: according to the theory, it might be justifiable to admit actors from the developing world to the Assembly who fail to meet a few criteria, *if* it can be shown that the inclusion of those actors improves overall responsiveness.

Global Assembly of about 600 representatives (rather than 6,000) of territorial as well as non-territorial actors. Anything much larger, I have argued, would dramatically damage the quality of analysis, debate, and decision. So one could imagine a Global Assembly (again, this is highly speculative) consisting of representatives of states, regional and inter-governmental organisations, local authorities, trade unions and professions, NGOs, perhaps TNCs, and perhaps practices that have only limited formal status—for example, practices associated with rearing children. Let me stress again that this is a very long-term ideal vision; the next two sections explain why and how such a vision is orienting in the short- and medium-term.

Each Assembly member would *not* represent *one* state or non-state agent. That would be impossible since, in almost every category of representative, even applying the tests above quite strictly, there are far more agents than there could be places in the Assembly (e.g. there are now at least 25,000 NGOs devoted to environmental issues alone). Rather, the agents who satisfy the tests above could, in each category, select persons to represent them—a process similar to that adopted by the 1,600-member Council of Non-Governmental Organisations, when it appoints 'consultative' representatives to the Economic and Social Council of the United Nations. Admission to CONGO takes place, however, through a far less stringent process of accreditation.[336]

---

[336] I said that the actors who are admitted would far outnumber the number of representatives 'in almost every category'; the category that is an exception is that of states. One hundred and fifty places for states would mean that most states—or indeed all that met the criteria above—could be represented directly. I have maintained that this approach to inclusion is not advisable, even if it is feasible. East Timor having an equal vote to the United States is a recipe for the US bribing and cajoling East Timor, or for East Timor forming alliances with a brute majority of other states that may well provide small populaces with excessive sway over global political decision. Rather, states could and should be represented, first, in terms of the extent to which they meet the criteria above, and second, proportionally to their capacity to bear crucial international obligations—such as their preparedness to contribute to UN upkeep and operations (which is already a criterion for admission to the Security Council). Smaller states would have to be combined into groups sufficient to elect at least one representative per group, and larger states would be subject to a cap on the number of representatives that they can appoint. This proportionality would create some distortions in generating equal responsiveness to individuals' interests; but these distortions would be reduced and could even be counterbalanced in governance as a whole by the absence of the current veto and the presence of other kinds of representatives—perhaps significantly outnumbering states.

3.5. A Representative and Effective Security Council

One idea for a more representative Security Council is for each category of actor within the General Assembly to appoint a proportionate number of it own delegates. Given a maximum of, say, twenty four delegates, states would still have many delegates, but there would also be space for delegates from regional and intergovernmental organisations, local authorities, trade unions and professions (and perhaps corporations), NGOs, and non-formalised practices. Each appointment might require a two-thirds majority election within the relevant category and a simple majority across the categories, or reliance might be placed on syndicalist methods of appointing the senior role-players within each category.

A range of possibilities for limiting powers of veto would then open up. For instance, a veto might apply when three categories of actors unanimously vote 'no'. On this non-statist model, significant circumscription or even abolition of veto powers would not inevitably lead to domination by a majority coalition of illiberal and anti-democratic states, by hegemonic rich and powerful states, or—as in some of the present UN's decisions—by a fitful combination of the two.

The obvious Realist response to this sketched ideal is the following: The Security Council was established in the first place *not* to be representative but to be effective in maintaining global security. The Council was and is the realist element to the UN's design, preventing the organisation from meeting the same fate as the League of Nations.[337] The idea was that the major military and economic powers—victorious after Second World War—should have greater say in decisions, and be insulated against external meddling, such that they would continue to support the organisation over time in the ways that matter. It was seen as crucial that the actors represented in the Security Council have extensive capacities and 'willingness to contribute to, and [to show] consistency in support for, peacekeeping and UN political and economic activities'.[338]

---

[337] The League adhered to the 'principle of unanimity as the regular mode of voting, thus granting *all* member states a "right of veto" ', producing much inertia in the face of threats to peace and security (Fassbender, *Veto*, 10–11). The League Council did give some legal expression to the hegemony of the 'Principal Allied and Associated Powers' who won First World War, but—the Realist argument goes—not enough.

[338] United Nations Open-ended Working Group on the Question of Equitable Representation on and Increase in the Membership of the Security

This much is largely true. But the Realist typically goes on to insist that non-state actors would not be able to make and keep the peace, since they have neither the resources nor the standing armies necessary to do so. This last claim is confused. Indeed, in a dramatic irony of grand historical proportions, it is the so-called Realists who have most misunderstood the implications of realistic constraints of power and stability. States are not now, nor are they ever likely to be, the only 'powers that be'. It is accurate to say that non-state actors generally do not have military capacities or capacities to tax; but it is entirely false to think that these are the only kinds of capacities that count in making and keeping the peace. Other relevant kinds of capacities can be exercised—sometimes decisively—to motivate conflicting parties to reduce hostilities.[339] This is not to deny that military might is important, but rather to insist that factors such as economic incentives and social suasion play a necessary complementary role, and sometimes even a greater role, in making and keeping the peace.

Examples are not hard to find and speak for themselves. The war in Angola was fuelled in large part by trade in 'conflict diamonds', and some of the most effective action to curb hostilities was agreement by the TNCs that are the world's major diamond sellers and purchasers to refrain from trade in these diamonds; Global Witness, an international NGO, played a central role in bringing about this agreement.[340] Similarly, the strongest incentives and proposals to resolve the conflict between Azerbaijan and various Armenian factions (in Nagorno-Karabakh province) came from large oil and gas companies who needed to transport their goods across the Caucasus.[341] Leaving aside TNCs and NGOs, regional organisations that have no standing armies of their own have nevertheless been pivotal in producing

Council and Other Matters Related to the Security Council, 'Annex to the Report [of 15 September 1995]' (New York: United Nations, 1995), 458.

[339] See Virginia Haufler, 'Is There a Role for Business in Conflict Management?' in C. Crocker, F. Hampson, and P. Aall, eds., *Turbulent Peace: The Challenges of Managing International Conflict* (Washington, DC: United States Institute of Peace, 2001); for a more partisan view on corporate capacities for peace-making, which emphasises the benefits to businesses of involvement, see J. Nelson, *The Business of Peace: The Private Sector as a Partner in Conflict Prevention and Resolution* (London: Prince of Wales Business Leaders Forum, 2000).

[340] Global Witness, 'Conflict Diamond Report', www.one.world.org/globalwitness/reports; and Winston, 'NGO Strategies', 83–4.

[341] See R. Forsythe, *The Politics of Oil in the Caucasus and Central Asia: Prospects for Oil Exploration and Export in the Caspian Basin* (Oxford: Oxford University Press, 1996).

greater security—for example, brinkmanship by the Organisation for Security and Cooperation in Europe played a significant role in lowering the intensity of the simmering conflict in Crimea.[342]

It is not realism, then, but false idealisation to treat (great power) states as the sole agents of global security. States have played an important role *alongside* non-state actors in reducing and resolving conflict. Different kinds of actors have brought—and could bring further—different capacities and experiences to bear, and there is an evident need for those actors to better coordinate their immediate responses and their ongoing efforts. Several kinds of power can and should be represented in decision-making structures that aim to create and maintain peace.

Something closer to the Responsive Democratic sketch above promises on these grounds to be a less dangerous, more realistic ideal. Of course, to serve as an adequate orienting ideal, my speculative sketch would have to be dramatically extended, and that in turn depends on developing the criteria for inclusion articulated above. But I now complete my discussion of the United Nations by arguing that even this initial list of criteria and this institutional sketch provide guidance on feasible action to reform the core UN.

3.6. *Immediate Strategies for Reform*

If one wants to feel dispirited about how much all this talk of abstract criteria and ideal models achieves, one can always turn to the vast three volume history of UN reform subtitled 'new initiatives and past efforts'.[343] Since the 1950s, the UN has undergone a series of management, structural, and policy reviews; there have been many proposals, some have been adopted, and a few implemented—but the central structural problems have not gone away.[344] Indeed, due to the complex outcomes of previous efforts, each new round of reform becomes more, not less, difficult to carry out. In their influential study of UN reform, Erskine Childers and Brian Urquhart ultimately

---

[342] See G. Sasse, 'The Crimean Issue', *Journal of Communist Studies and Transition Politics*, Vol. 12, No.1 (1996), 83–100; N. Mychajlyszyn, 'The OSCE and Regional Conflicts in the Former Soviet Union', *Regional and Federal Studies*, Vol. 11, No. 3 (2001), 194–219.

[343] J. Muller, ed., *Reforming the United Nations: New Initiatives and Past Efforts* (The Hague: Kluwer Law International, 1997).

[344] There have been five major rounds of reform in the UN Secretariat alone (1953–6, 1964–6, 1974–7, 1985–6, 1992–4).

ascribe the limited progress in reform so far to (what I have distilled into) six main factors:[345]

1. Neglected implementation—each round of reform deals with many similar or identical issues to the last, largely because of poor institutional memory within the United Nations and a lack of political will from states.
2. Piecemeal reform—negotiation processes leave only slivers of what were originally integrated recommendations, so new initiatives are hobbled or unsustainable because necessary supporting structures could not be agreed.
3. Mechanistic change—alterations to organisational structure have only 'moved boxes' on the organisational diagram, at most shifting control without attending sufficiently to how organs and agencies will interact.
4. Poor appointments—states often make indifferent choices of senior officials, due in part to resistance to effective UN powers, and in part to strict appointment quotas that emphasise nationality far more than competence.
5. Inadequate staffing—states and senior officials often overlook needs for better staff, training, and job descriptions, in large part due to UN budget constraints and to UN posts being used as patronage rewards.
6. Dysfunctional coordination—functions are often allocated away from the most effective repositories, to organs or agencies favoured by major funding states; meanwhile, separate functions are not orchestrated to be sufficiently mutually reinforcing, each with clear powers and terms of reference.

Clearly, these problems include many dilemmas that lie beyond the question of representation and require a compendium of solutions.[346]

---

[345] E. Childers and B. Urquhart, 'Renewing the United Nations System [1994]', reprinted in J. Muller, ed., *Reforming the United Nations: New Initiatives and Past Efforts* (The Hague: Kluwer Law International, 1997), esp. III.38/30–40.

[346] There is no shortage of compendia that tally and enumerate hundreds of needed and possible reforms. The solutions range across diverse areas, from managerial improvements such as improved recruitment criteria and meeting schedules, to major restructuring such as redefining relations between UN organs, consolidating the UN budget, and creating or removing agencies. For 'compendia of compendia', see Muller, ed., *Reforming* and P. Taylor, S. Daws, and U. Adamczick-Gerteis, eds., *Documents on United Nations Reform* (Aldershot: Dartmouth, 1997).

My concentration on bringing non-state actors into core UN authority structures is one part of this larger picture. Nevertheless, the ideal theoretical approach above casts the larger picture in a different light, making it necessary and possible to identify some strategic ways to widen membership so as to alleviate these six problems.

The UN Charter imposes no formal requirements and provides no formal means for the General Assembly or Security Council to consult with NGOs, IGOs, TNCs, local authorities, professions, trade unions, and other actors. Since, in the short to medium term, there is a low likelihood of significant amendments to the Charter, other routes need to be found by which the appropriate kinds of non-state actors can gain increasing sway in the core UN, and in so doing also move it in the direction of further reforms. The most promising routes are through bodies that feed strongly into General Assembly and Security Council decisions. I shall illustrate these routes by considering how NGOs in particular could increase their presence in UN bodies and how this would improve judgement and efficiency within the United Nations.

One promising entry-point for NGOs is through the currently underused Economic and Social Council of the UN (ECOSOC), tasked with coordinating and overseeing several major UN agencies. According to Article 71 of the UN Charter, ECOSOC 'may make suitable arrangements for consultation with non-governmental organisations which are concerned with matters within its competence'. In practice, this vague permission has been used to justify a formal process of accreditation, with the result that over 1,600 NGOs now have consultative status in one category or another.[347] Criteria for accreditation have been developed and refined, various NGOs' consultative statuses have been formally and informally upgraded, and it is possible to chart a steady increase in NGO impact overall.[348] (As mentioned above, one should not make the mistake of thinking such impact is invariably benign.) Since ECOSOC in turn makes recommendations that are taken up, though not often enough, by the General Assembly and Security Council, accreditation can become an important route to policy-formation by NGOs. But ECOSOC

---

[347] Professions and NGOs take leading roles in major initiatives of the UN Educational, Scientific and Cultural Organisation (UNESCO), the Children's Fund (UNICEF), the World Health Organisation (WHO), and the Food and Agriculture Organisation (FAO). Meanwhile, the International Labour Organisation (ILO) has long included trade unions in its tripartite structure. See Childers and Urquhart, 'Renewing', 167–88 and 207–8.

[348] Ibid., 167–71.

presently under performs and is underused; over 20 of the most powerful NGOs have therefore bypassed it altogether, and now regularly meet with the members of the Security Council, directly. Such informal accreditation is a vital step. Far from accreditation arousing the crushing antagonism of powerful states, many states have in fact smoothed the path to formal NGO inclusion, recognising particular capacities that NGOs could contribute to governance in a range of areas.

However, the process of inclusion ought not simply to be a game of increasing numbers and status. As Childers and Urquhart point out, 'NGOs working in a given issue-area can . . . consolidate their analyses and proposals in order to mount an effective representation, given that they outnumber by many thousands the number of [State] Delegations at any UN body'.[349]

More generally, improved political judgement and efficiency within the UN requires an emphasis on better communication and coordination between NGOs themselves, between NGOs and other non-state actors, and between NGOs and UN organs as well as states. Much of this consolidation of NGO influence can be achieved too without obtaining formal endorsement from a majority of states in the General Assembly or Security Council.

To see the effect that such coordination might have, one has only to consider the ways in which NGOs and other non-state actors could produce improvements in UN reform itself. As I pointed out, many of the failures of reform can be traced to a serious informational deficit within the United Nations: a lack of institutional memory, failed integration of mutually reinforcing reform proposals, and too little attention to monitoring and evaluation of reform implementation. Major states and bureaucrats are likely to be relatively attached to the statist status quo, and the institutional inertia and clientelism that underpin these deficiencies.

In contrast, non-state actors in several domains are better placed, and subject to stronger incentives, to access contextual information (their 'business' success and survival depend upon it) and to create and maintain quality information databases on pertinent social issues. For instance, NGOs, TNCs, and local authorities have more developed expertise at information management and publicity within difficult 'failed states' and 'grey markets' than do most state representatives or UN bureaucrats. Non-state actors also tend to be less concerned with diplomatic imperatives to avoid embarrassing states and bureaucrats. Finally, non-state actors are not necessarily driven—as most state

---

[349] Childers and Urquhart, 'Renewing', 207.

representatives are—to place a relatively low priority on international obligations compared with domestic goals. The latter two propensities have led state governments, for instance, to 'continuously reduce the portion of main UN system public information budgets', indefensibly, from an early 12 percent to less than 5 percent.[350]

This is not to deny that non-state actors have their own all-too-evident flaws and biases that sometimes lead them to disregard, suppress, or mismanage information. But it is to suggest that non-state actors, by very reason of those different competences and propensities, could begin to check the operations of states (and be checked in turn), producing an overall increase in 'horizontal responsiveness'. Of course, horizontal responsiveness cannot stand alone as a solution. Too much information, from too many sources, can overwhelm our cognitive capacities and defeat communication just as effectively as too little. The solution to this kind of problem—I have argued—does not lie in restricting information sources and flows, but rather in establishing strong advocacy and accountability agencies. These agencies would improve vertical as well as horizontal responsiveness, by providing relevant information to political actors and eliciting and advancing relevant claims of citizens.

Mechanisms of this kind do exist within the UN, but have been under-appreciated by potential champions and undermined by those who have much to lose from the successful operation of such mechanisms. For instance, the Internal Audit Division and Central Evaluation Unit are thoroughly under-funded and under-staffed. Meanwhile—and here it is difficult not to have a feeling of 'déjà vu all over again'—the Joint Inspection Unit is effectively appointed by the very states it is supposed to inspect. These deficiencies are by no means necessary characteristics of such 'guardians of the guardians'.[351]

There is, as I argued, a need to coordinate the work of all these actors and bodies. Again, the UN system contains mechanisms that could well be adequate to the task. The most important of these is the Advisory Committee on Administrative and Budgetary Questions (ACABQ), which can be mandated to maintain a comprehensive data bank of all significant restructuring and reform decisions, and to monitor present debates so as to provide crucial background information.

---

[350] Ibid., 169.
[351] Ibid., 205. The European Union Court of Auditors is one good example of a more robust accountability agency—even though it is still somewhat hampered by states with parochial interests in protecting poor audit regimes (see European Court of Auditors, www.eca.eu.int/EN/coa.htm).

Childers and Urquhart argue that the ACABQ is already capable of issuing prospective 'Reform Impact Reports' that assess whether there are serious lacunae in 'packages' of reforms finally agreed to by states in negotiations.[352] Each report, along with recommendations and necessary adjustments, could be delivered directly to the General Assembly prior to its voting on reforms. When reform packages pass, the ACABQ can then be tasked with delivering a yearly report on delays and inadequate implementation.[353]

There is more to say about the many feasible routes to inclusion of non-state actors and—partly as a result—reform of the United Nations itself. I could have discussed, for example, the successful routes that non-state actors have found, and could pursue, to impact on state delegations and on appointments to major UN posts.[354] I could have discussed how proposals to include the European Union in the Security Council have been seriously debated in various forums by the permanent member states.[355] It might be possible to argue, for instance, that if the EU were at some point to gain entry to the Security Council, it would be difficult to exclude other regional organisations, such as the Association of South East Asian Nations (ASEAN) and the African Union (AU).[356] These would be important steps in the right direction; but this is not the place to pursue these speculative and strategic questions.

I hope to have said enough to show that, in reforming the United Nations, we need not rely on the statist status quo or on deliberative

---

[352] Childers and Urquhart, 'Renewing', 184.

[353] In the longer term, Childers and Urquhart call for the establishment of an Intergovernmental Board of the UN System (under Articles 22 and 58 of the UN Charter), made up of heads of principal organs and agencies, which is tasked with engendering coherence and efficiency in the UN system.

[354] Some TNCs are worryingly effective—above all because there is limited quality control on their constitution and limited accountability for their actions. Section 4, below, discusses some important remedies.

[355] Taylor et al., eds., *Documents*, 567. Although eventually rejected (Britain and France vociferously opposed the likely loss of their special status) the very idea of a regional organisation gaining entry to the Security Council was utterly impolitic to express only a few years ago. If and when the European Union achieves higher consistency in its internal operations and foreign policy, and establishes a highly trained armed force, the plausibility of such objections is likely to weaken further, widening the realistic possibilities for UN reform.

[356] On opportunities and problems that arise if and when regional organisations have a greater role, see U. Adamczick-Gerteis, 'Annex: The Pontignano Conference on Aspects of UN Reform: Discussion', in P. Tayler, S. Daws, and U. Adamczick-Gerteis, eds., *Documents on United Nations Reform* (Aldershot: Dartmouth, 1997), esp. 560–3.

dreams of brute inclusion. By placing emphasis on a constrained plurality of powers, including high quality coordination and communication mechanisms, we can begin to envision a representative and effective Global Assembly and Security Council. Such ideals, though distant, can and do help to identify a range of immediate, beneficial reforms to the United Nations itself and to the wider structure of global governance.

4. Unbundling Transparency International

The emphasis has been on checking the abuse of political power, not economic power. Cosmopolitan international politics has developed few, if any, systematic means to address forms of economic domination... At stake... is the entrenchment of revised rules, codes and procedures—concerning health, child labour, trade union activity, environmental protection, stake-holder consultation and corporate governance, among other matters—in the articles of association and terms of reference of economic organisations and trading agencies... within their very *modus operandi*...

Held, 'Corporate Practice', 70 and 73–4.

4.1. Transparency or Communication?

Strong institutions are central to entrenching regulatory rules as fundamental, unavoidable, evident, and feasible considerations in and across systems of daily interaction and decision. But there is often a catch-22 in politics: reform and rejuvenation are most badly needed in contexts where the rules are heavily skewed and flouted; yet in those contexts it is precisely the agents with powers to effect change that are the very enemies of fairness, effectiveness, and change. In these situations, secrecy is doubly pernicious. It is an invaluable aid to such ill-motivated powerful actors, and it prevents others from seeing what reforms are needed and how they might be undertaken. In the discussion that follows, I suggest that there are remedies to this problem but these must be understood in less simplistic and optimistic terms than are popular at present; I then show that some institutional remedies do work and some could work, including at the global level; and finally, I suggest some ways to extend and coordinate these institutional remedies.

Consider the now-ubiquitous call for 'transparency', broadly defined as 'a process by which information about existing conditions, decisions and actions is made accessible, visible and understandable' by institutions and office-holders, where that information is 'relevant to evaluating those institutions' and office-holders.[357] While secrecy involves deliberately hiding or fudging one's motives, modus operandi, and actions, transparency involves deliberately and accurately revealing them. Although a mantra of many policy-makers, firms, organisations, and activists, transparency's nature and limits are rarely rigorously understood. Much confusion is produced by a failure to make one crucial distinction: transparency is the key virtue of information systems, but it is far from sufficient for genuine communication.[358] That is, transparency involves providing information, yet information on its own achieves very little when there is no definite audience able to assess and act on that information: 'Transparency merely lets people see streams of facts. It neither enables people to *do* anything about those facts, nor conveys any understanding of their meaning'.[359] Worse still, merely publicising (reams and reams of) information can stoke or mask disinformation, misinformation, and apathy in the audience.

The key virtue in communication, on the other hand, is the rejection of deception. Deception can be produced by too little disclosure of information but can also be produced by too much disclosure, by disclosure of the wrong kind, or by disclosure at the wrong time. Crucial facts and meanings can be 'buried' in lengthy technical documents (e.g. insurance consent forms), or amidst news of a major political event (e.g. the budget). Well-timed releasing of information about leaders can also produce 'scandals' that distract or detract from more central issues about competence and probity. More indirectly, a range of true 'facts' can be provided without specifying pivotal causal connections between them, thereby undermining any possibility of knowing the meaning and implications of those facts. In all these instances, information is accessible but it is far from properly *assessable* by its purported audience.[360]

---

[357] This definition combines the definitions supplied by the International Monetary Fund Working Group on Transparency and Accountability and by A. M. Florini in 'Does the Invisible Hand Need a Transparent Glove? The Politics of Transparency', paper presented at The Annual World Bank Conference on Development Economics, 28–30 April 1999; see 4–5 of the latter for both definitions.

[358] The following discussion of communication owes much to Onora O'Neill's work, including *Question of Trust* and *Autonomy and Trust*.

[359] Florini, 'Transparent Glove', 6.

[360] See A. Kuper and J. Kuper, 'Serving a New Democracy: Must the Media "Speak Softly"?—Learning from South Africa', *International Journal of Public Opinion Research*, Vol. 13, No. 4 (2001), 355–76, for a more empirical explication

Such 'deception' may or may not be intentional. People may be 'deceived', for instance, as part of outright manoeuvres to secure political advantage, or may be 'misled' by unknown distortions in an institutional framework or process, or for that matter by pure coincidence or honest misunderstanding or just by being overwhelmed. What complicates things is that people can also be misled as a function of modifications of (or refusals to modify) institutional frameworks and processes, for which particular agents can sometimes be held responsible. The individualist model of A 'not lying' to B is in this respect quite deceptive itself. Rejection of deception by representatives is a more complex commitment and activity than it might seem.[361]

For now, note an important limitation on the large claims made for transparency. It is hailed as improving the efficiency and legitimacy of corporations, organisations, markets, and governments, and also the fairness of outcomes from almost all institutional interactions.[362] This could be true in large part, but only if some other conditions—other constraints on power—were in place; otherwise the recipients of information could use it to inflict unjustifiable harm.[363] Transparency can be a positive bad where it enables strong or malevolent agents to expose and abuse the vulnerable. Thus transparency has to be embedded in other regimes of governance ensuring that the information provided is both not deceptive and used to protect and benefit vulnerable agents.

of how agents can approach understanding their audience and then use that understanding to make information accessible *and* assessable.

[361] Broadly, (1) the agent who is to disclose the information must be not just willing but able to provide information; (2) that agent must reasonably expect that the target audience is willing and able to distinguish relevant from irrelevant information when evaluating his or her or its performance, and to understand and act on that information; and (3) any inability to satisfy either of the two previous requirements must not be the result of that agent's actions to alter institutions so as to avoid scrutiny, or of a similarly motivated refusal to take feasible remedial action.

[362] See, for example, International Monetary Fund, *How to Enhance the Transparency of Government Operations* and *World Economic Outlook* (Washington, DC: International Monetary Fund, both 1998).

[363] Secrecy, not transparency, is the key refuge for many human rights organisations operating in the face of highly repressive regimes; more mundanely, it is why lax libel and privacy laws allow tabloids to heedlessly ruin innocent people's lives. More generally, secrecy is not necessarily a bad. For instance, one may have a legitimate claim to a limited 'private' sphere about which others have limited knowledge, and firms may at times have a claim to keep 'trade secrets' on which their business depends. My focus, however, is on the pernicious kinds of secrecy that allow actors, and especially representatives, to deceive and injure and escape the control of the public, on whose behalf they are supposed to act.

My account of representation directs us towards some critical dimensions of, and solutions to, this challenge. If transparency and other regulatory norms are to be effective—reducing vulnerability to deception and injury—the audience must have the abilities, time, and powers to sift, scrutinise, and connect the most relevant facts. Yet—as I showed in Chapters 2 and 3—it is overly demanding in the extreme to expect the public to do so on many matters of public concern; and the media, judiciary, civil associations, and political parties are relevant but limited parts of the solution—and sometimes parts of the problem. There is a need for accountability and advocacy agencies that perform the difficult tasks relevant to embedding transparency. These tasks are not confined to auditing and the supply of statistics, but include: setting, measuring, and advocating definite standards and sanctions; monitoring, facilitating, and helping induce compliance; and—throughout—identifying and anticipating underlying causes and concerns rather than resting content with mere 'facts'.

If ensuring and coordinating all this seems demanding, that is because it is. With the above conceptual framework in view, however, I now want to discuss specifically transparency aimed at combating corruption, showing how a specific institution does in fact powerfully instantiate such global advocacy and accountability. I will also suggest some deep reforms to its structure and operations that will have to be undertaken if it is to ensure and coordinate the optimal achievement of its objectives.

4.2. Globalising Corruption Control

The 'invisible hand' of the market . . . depends heavily on the support of a thick 'glove' of rules, norms, and institutions, including governments. But too often, the glove is opaque, obscuring flows of information essential to the efficient and equitable functioning of both markets and the national and international institutions that regulate them.

Florini, 'Does the Invisible Hand Need a Transparent Glove?',1

Until 1993, anti-corruption strategies tended to rely on local or national politicians, judges, NGO cadres, and business leaders. There were no agreed—let alone 'independent'—measures of corruption (absolute or relative), no coordinating mechanisms for anti-corruption research and projects across various countries and institutions (and hence limited cumulated learning), and no advocacy organisations with the breadth and depth to build necessary coalitions to combat corruption effectively.

The reasons for these glaring lacunae are no surprise given the argument of the previous chapter. First, the World Bank's legal department and much of senior management were 'implacably opposed' to becoming involved in corruption control, since becoming involved in 'political' considerations would violate the Bank's *Articles of Confederation*.[364] Other multilateral agencies claimed similar limits to their mandates, or had any extension of their mandate vetoed by states anxious about what would emerge.[365] Second, national politicians and judiciaries often lacked the basis in (domestic as well as international) law as well as the official competence to perform corruption control functions; for instance, only one country, the United States, had criminalised bribery by its multinationals.[366] Companies could be prosecuted under the domestic laws of the country in which the offence took place but not at headquarters; in countries where corruption was rife, more often than not this would mean paying off the relevant minister, judge, or other public official.

Several aspects of this situation have begun to change with the advent of Transparency International, the 'one-issue non-profit organisation' founded in 1993 in response to these lacunae, dedicated to 'curbing both international and national corruption'.[367] The single most important decision by the founders of Transparency was to reject a purely juridical model for operations *and* to reject the pure 'exposure' or publicity model exemplified by Amnesty International and investigative journalists. It was recognised that (as I argued in more general terms in Chapter 3) success would depend on the organisation developing competences that overcame traditional political–juridical–civil society divides: if corruption crosses boundaries between states, governmental

---

[364] For an overview of the early history of Transparency International, by two of its leading figures, see F. Galtung and J. Pope, 'The Global Coalition Against Corruption: Evaluating Transparency International', in A. Schedler, L. Diamond, and M. Plattner, eds., *The Self-Restraining State* (London: Lynne Rienner, 1999). Objections of this kind from within the World Bank have now disappeared almost entirely.

[365] The so-called Asian Tiger states effectively vetoed the inclusion of corruption on the WTO's agenda at that body's first meeting; it is an important lesson of history that their economic collapse in 1997 was 'induced to a significant degree by corruption' (ibid., 265 and 281, n. 35); also see J. Furman and J. Stiglitz, 'Economic Crises: Evidence and Insights from East Asia', *Brookings Panel on Economic Activity* (Washington, DC: Brookings Institute, 1998).

[366] The US did so through the Foreign Corrupt Practices Act of 1977. A code of conduct for TNCs globally did exist, in the form of the International Chamber of Commerce's 'Rules of Conduct to Combat Extortion and Bribery', but was 'widely recognised as a toothless and unenforceable instrument' (ibid., 262).

[367] Transparency International, www.transparency.org.

functions, and forms of regulation, so too must the organisations that combat it.[368]

To this end, Transparency has developed non-partisan cross-national measures and analyses of corruption, captured in its annual 'Corruption Perception Index', 'Bribe Payers Index', and 'Global Corruption Report'.[369] Transparency has also promoted inter-governmental agreements to fight corruption—it played a leading role in producing the crucial 1997 OECD Convention Against the Bribery of Foreign Public Officials and other agreements[370]—and it actively monitors and lobbies for the implementation of these agreements by signatory countries. It has established National Chapters of the organisation in over seventy countries, which variously undertake projects, distribute sourcebooks, lobby, and provide advice on corruption monitoring and control.[371] Transparency also operates as the secretariat for the biannual Council of the International Anti-Corruption Conference (IACC), which brings together agents from throughout the private and public sectors who are involved in corruption control. While these indices, rules, mechanisms, and activities are nowhere near perfect, nor are they together more than a partial solution to the enormity of the problem of corruption, they do constitute a major advance on this central issue of governance.[372]

However, corruption control still depends largely on state governments' capacities and willingness to enforce such rules—inevitably selectively, especially where leading figures are themselves corrupt. Initially, it is not clear how much Transparency can do to remedy the

---

[368] Galtung and Pope, 'Global Coalition', 259.

[369] The CPI is a 'poll of polls' that 'captures the perception of thousands of international business leaders, risk analysts, and business journalists on the relative degree of corruption in more than fifty countries' (ibid., 275). It measures trends over time and relative positions of countries, not absolute levels of corruption in any one country.

[370] See, for example, P. Lewis, 'Straining Towards an Agreement On Global Bribery Curb', *New York Times*, 20 May 1997, and articles throughout the weeks of 21–7 May and 29 November to 5 December 1997.

[371] Galtung and Pope, 'Global Coalition', 268–74.

[372] So much so that it can be plausibly stated that '[all] the leading econometric work on corruption in recent years is based at least in part on the TI index' (ibid., 282, n. 55). Of course this might be due in part to econometricians' addiction to spurious accuracy. But the index has achieved some credibility in the face of scrutiny, proved a useful starting-point in other areas, and is a staple of policy debates on government reform. This is not to deny that many methodological problems concerning cross-country as well as diachronic (perception) measurement are still very much present.

situation of reliance on states for enforcement. One is tempted to say that as long as the ideology of privileging states predominates, Transparency's ability to bring pressure and sanctions to bear will remain rather limited. But here the ideas of non-statist structures of authority and responsive representation enable us to think in a more inventive and less dispirited fashion about how Transparency might act.

First and foremost, there is a form of statism in Transparency's approach that the organisation could do much to remedy. At present, its corruption indices only rate *countries* and *industries* within those countries. Transparency does not specifically rate IGOs, INGOs, and TNCs. Admittedly, this is a large task for a newly established organisation—there are now over 300 IGOs alone[373]—but it is not one that can be ignored in the future. After all, there is strong evidence of much venal corruption within such organisations; there can be unusually strong incentives to corruption within them (as in the UN, where—as I indicated—the quota system produces a pronounced tendency of state governments to use UN jobs as patronage rewards); and the effects of such corruption on human freedom and well-being can be devastating (consider the charges levelled at a previous High Commissioner for Refugees and a Director General of the World Health Organisation).[374]

A strong start can be made by evaluating a fairly small number of non-state actors who account for a large proportion of global aid, advocacy, regulation, and business: eight INGOs, nine IGOs, and ten TNCs.[375] The task would still be complex: for instance, Transparency would have to assess corruption (indeed largely corruption *perception*) both internal to these non-state actors and in their interaction with other agents. One model for this extended form of assessment can be found in the pilot 'Global Accountability Project' (GAP) of the One World Trust, a registered charity operating out of the British Parliament, which uses a so-called 'stakeholder analysis' to measure four dimensions of 'internal accountability' and four of 'external accountability' in these eight INGOs, nine IGOs, and ten TNCs.[376]

---

[373] Kovac and Burall, *Global Accountability*, 3.

[374] For a clear overview of corruption in the United Nations, from which these examples are culled, see G. Arnold, *World Government by Stealth: The Future of the United Nations* (London: Macmillan, 1997), chapter 15.

[375] For the methodology and process of public consultation by which these actors were selected, see Charter 99, www.charter99.org.

[376] The pilot stage of the project was completed by 2003. The concept of accountability is used too broadly in GAP, and its blueprint contains blunt, ill-advised phrases like 'the term "member" refers to member states' (Kovac and

Projects of this kind are indeed complex, but not prohibitively so, and the benefits could be immense. For instance, transparency is likely to have a peculiarly powerful effect on TNCs and INGOs, since—as Naomi Klein has recently demonstrated—the strongest 'brands' can be especially vulnerable to publicity as a form of sanction (no matter how well they 'manage the media').[377] Over time, exposure of leading actors can produce a positive 'herd effect' in the area of corruption, as it has domestically in many states: firms and organisations do not want any embarrassing surprises, and they do not want to have to play by the rules when competitors do not. Thus when major players incorporate anti-corruption regulations and practices across the range of daily operations, they tend to demand and ensure that business partners, affiliates, and competitors do the same: 'business men and women object less to political regulation and social reform per se than to the intrusion of regulatory mechanisms that upset "the rules of the game" in some particular place or country only . . . if they handicap companies' competitive edge in relation to enterprises from areas not subject to similar constraints'.[378]

Taking account of 'reinforcement' motivations and possible virtuous cycles in this way puts paid to a hoary old chestnut: that firms and organisations have almost 'no interest' in better regulation, or that there is almost always an overwhelming incentive to 'defect' from putative agreements.[379] These claims—and the language in which they tend to be couched—can only be maintained in a highly temporally constrained and motivationally impoverished view of the world, for which a single and inflexible iteration of the 'prisoner's dilemma' situation is the paradigm of human interaction. If it is in fact feasible to alter the situation itself, so as to reduce risk overall by cutting down on ambiguities of process and capriciousness of outcomes, then pivotal actors can be brought on board, producing a 'tipping' effect that brings most others on board too.[380] Thus when several banks and

Burall, 'Project', 4 and 15). The two fallacies perpetuated here are (1) that accountability, especially electoral accountability, can be coextensive with democracy; and (2) that only states can be major internal stakeholders in the UN and other IGOs.

[377] N. Klein, *No Logo*, 279–396.

[378] Held, 'Corporate Practice', 71.

[379] The pro-corporate press regularly warms up this poisonous chestnut for popular consumption; see 'Bribery and Business: The Short Arm of the Law', an otherwise remarkable special report in the *Economist*, 2–8 March 2002, 63–5.

[380] On 'tipping', a concept pioneered by R. Schelling—explaining when and why the breaching of a threshold of compliance results in near total compliance—see J. Rauch, 'Seeing Around Corners', *Atlantic Monthly*, Vol. 289, No. 4 (2002), 35–46.

information services were persuaded of the usefulness of corruption assessments for calculating risk, they incorporated Transparency's assessments into their investment ratings (upon which numerous other actors in turn depend), effectively making Transparency's indices and analyses daily components of the international financial architecture.[381]

4.3. New Agents of Transparency

It should come as no surprise that Transparency International is not strictly or predominantly about transparency. Extensive and non-deceptive measurement, analysis, and publicity certainly help in curbing corruption, but they constitute only some aspects of the necessary means to that end. Transparency International has been successful where others have failed because its main method is, as its Mission Statement proclaims, 'mobilizing a global coalition to promote and strengthen international and national integrity systems'.[382] Almost everything depends on mobilising and changing the background conditions of power and constraint, and in particular on *other* key actors being appropriately responsive to relevant information. Thus Transparency has had to convince the business sector (e.g. that corruption impinges on property rights and increases risk), professions (e.g. that it damages professional standards in law and accounting), NGOs (e.g. that it erodes human rights and environmental protections), local authorities (e.g. that it reduces budgetary allocations from the state), state governments (e.g. that it corrodes legitimacy), and more. Some of its successes are startling, as with its impact on the banks and financial architecture mentioned above—agents and structures that are among the most powerful and pervasive sources of sanction and reward.

There are two kinds of effect here: deterrence and reassurance. 'While deterrence is about preventing someone from failing to abide by a standard, reassurance enables an actor to prove that he or she is abiding by the standard' (Florini, 'Transparent Glove', 7).

[381] There is an especially large, lengthy, and complicated debate over whether corruption lowers costs: one side contends that it smoothes interaction and distributes benefits from complex deals; the other claims that it corrodes efficiency, competitiveness, and security because rules and punishments are applied quite arbitrarily. The latter side has increasingly won out, in governing and financial institutions at least.

[382] Transparency International, 'Mission Statement', reprinted in R. Martin and E. Feldman, *Access to Information in Developing Countries* (London: Commonwealth Secretariat, 1998).

But consider the demands placed on an organisation that aims to engender a political coalition of this kind. Are they compatible with robust independence? Drawing on the functional designation of powers approach developed in Chapter 1, it is evident that Transparency is at present fulfilling three functions that may not be entirely compatible: standard-setting and measurement, investigation and publicity, and coalition-building. While these functions may work synergistically over time, in time there will also be conflicts of interest if one organisation attempts to fulfil all these functions. For instance, working with major companies to combat internal corruption may lead to there being less political will *within* Transparency to expose wrongdoing by those companies, or less psychological orientation to develop standards and measurement that count heavily against those companies' interests.

Recognising this, Transparency has rightly taken a position in respect to a number of such conflicts of interest and focus. For instance, it restricts national chapters from undertaking 'investigations of individual cases of corruption' because this would 'undermine TIs efforts to build coalitions that can strengthen anticorruption systems'.[383] But each time Transparency chooses one horn of a dilemma, it cannot but create some systematic slack on the other horn. (For instance, Transparency could not fulfil its coalition-building aims at the same time as committing to exposing all persons or firms who are pivotal promoters of corruption; a statutory authority might do the latter while leaving Transparency to do the former.) As two leaders of the organisation put it, 'If there is a criticism that can be made of TI, it is that it tries to do too much, not too little'.[384]

One can, of course, simply shrug one's shoulders regretfully. Or one can recognise that Transparency is only the beginning of what is needed—institutionally—to deal with the spectres of corruption and pernicious secrecy. Transparency International may in time come to specialise in, say, coalition-building, leaving standard-setting and measurement to other credible ratings agencies, and leaving independent investigation and publicity to organisations such as Global Witness. There is no shortage, of course, of non-governmental organisations that could take up the slack: in the domain of corporate responsibility alone, for example, the Fair Labour Association, Social Accountability International, SA8000, Multinational Monitor, Corporate Watch, and Global Exchange all have a significant presence and effect.[385] A carefully managed pluralisation and coordination of such agencies could create clusters of power from which pressure and sanctions could be brought to bear in order to give regulations teeth.[386]

But here we need to be wary. Nothing guarantees continued high levels of quality, independence, and effectiveness from these NGOs. Furthermore, there is a real concern that we will have too many different institutions performing one or another task, none of them doing it in the same terms or doing it well. On an optimistic scenario, the needs of investors and other actors to make decisions based on accurate information will allow quality and non-partisanship to win through. On a pessimistic scenario, a critical mass of corporate wrongdoers, say, will pick and choose between NGOs whose ratings are more or less favourable to them; in turn, the prominence and ostensible legitimacy of such regulative NGOs will come to depend on how much support is offered by this group of cynical and rapacious firms.

There are several ways out of this conundrum, all potentially compatible but none of them easy. One is to ensure better coordination, scrutiny, and cross-referencing of advocacy and accountability organisations' activities—for example, by establishing regular forums in which they can learn from and cross-reference one another's measurement

---

[385] The need for coordination of the strategies of these organisations for promoting corporate, NGO, IGO, and governmental responsibility cannot be responsibly ignored—and has received much attention at the World Social Forum and other major conferences. These strategies include social auditing and reporting, litigation, selective purchasing laws, government-imposed standards, moral stigmatisation and shaming, and economic pressure tactics such as boycotts and disinvestment. For an evaluation of their effects and prospects, see Winston, 'NGO Strategies'.

[386] The likely gains might appear to be offset by the creation of more spaces in which corruption could flourish and by the difficulty of building even more extended coalitions against corruption; but, as I have argued, this impression is false. Auditors precisely safeguard against fraud and swindles by instituting complex cross-checks within firms and organisations, to be carried out by multiple, definite, and identified agents at specific times. (Internal and external auditors must of course check one another: in the infamous Enron case, Andersen was checking itself.) This internal pluralisation is best practice because it tends to work. Where it does not, those responsible are more likely to be identified. While the guilty parties can and will try to shift the blame, they can more easily be brought to task for not fulfilling specific duties within the division of labour. All of which is far more effective and just than holding agents to account for failing in a more ill-defined, agglomerated, and amorphous responsibility to, say, 'fight corruption nationally'.

techniques and ratings. Another route is for these organisations to avoid too much reliance on one funder or category of funders. However, these routes may well not be enough; a crucial way to move towards the optimistic scenario—I argued in Chapter 3—is to recognise, and compensate for, the limitations of non-statutory authority.

This implies not the replacement so much as the supplementing of NGO powers—with official regulators who can exercise formal powers of investigation, access state-controlled information banks, be constrained by clear professional codes of conduct, and be appointed by substantially non-partisan commissions of appointment. Sticking with the example above, it may be necessary to establish international ombudsmen, operating out of the UN system and reporting to the Secretary General, who are empowered to investigate individual cases of cross-border corruption. There also needs to be much careful thought about whether standard-setting and measurement should become the province of a quite autonomous statutory body under the United Nations Development Program—similar to the office that produces the *Human Development Report*.

I do not believe that we have enough information or knowledge at this point to come down in favour or against these proposals; but that is precisely the point. The possible configurations of advocacy and accountability agencies merit careful attention, such that they come to facilitate optimal scrutiny of states as well as other non-state actors. Transparency International has made remarkable progress in moving corruption control beyond the state; but corruption control that is predominantly orchestrated by NGOs is likely to be only one stage in the much needed evolution of institutions of advocacy and accountability.

All I hope to have shown here is that, by focusing on reforming and extending such institutions, it is possible and practicable to mobilise immense power behind the effort to establish definite, comprehensible, and widely followed shared moral and legal standards in the global domain. Serious engagement with the problem of corruption, encompassing a plurality of institutions globally, and their communicative interactions, has just begun. Yet corruption is only one area in which we have good grounds to believe that the so-called 'democratic deficit' within great and global institutions is *not* irremediable.

Conclusion: Responsive Democracy

In all very numerous assemblies, of whatever characters composed, passions never fail to wrest the sceptre from reason. Had every Athenian been a Socrates, every Athenian assembly would still have been a mob.

Madison et al., Federalist, No. 55

1. Ten Dimensions of Theories of Global Justice and Democracy

The extended argument of the previous chapters began with abstract questions about the moral status of persons and ended with some concrete proposals for reforming current global institutions. A single text is a small torch for illuminating this long path—the path of a liberal theory of justice and democracy that is neither statist nor territorialist nor deliberative. I see no reason to punish the careful reader by recapitulating each step in the argument. Instead, I shall bring out the distinctive features of Responsive Democracy by contrasting this theory with the theories of Rawls, as the exemplar of liberal statism, and Habermas, as the exemplar of deliberative democracy. This comparative approach enables me to provide a broader perspective on why the ideas underlying Responsive Democracy might in a few crucial respects make for a more coherent and felicitous theory than these leading alternatives. The approach also allows me to elaborate on how various features of Responsive Democracy are connected and to cast light on some areas left under-explored. The murkiest and most unsettling of these areas is, of course, the relationship between justice and democracy.

Normative theories of justice and democracy can be understood and compared in terms of ten dimensions that are rarely kept sufficiently distinct in the literature:

1. *Sources of Normativity*: What facts about persons and their societies give rise to normative claims (to moral concern and political inclusion)?
2. *Moral Scope*: How widely should the boundaries of normative concern be drawn? (Who counts morally and how?)
3. *Political Scope*: On which of these normative bases should persons be included under institutions of governance? (Who counts politically and how?)
4. *Spheres of Governance*: To which spheres of human life should those institutions extend their activities, and from which spheres should they be excluded?[387]
5. *Political Interests*: Towards which human ends, within permissible spheres, should governmental activities be directed, and in what order of priority?
6. *Constraints on Governance*: Which means to those ends are unjustifiably coercive and may not be used?
7. *Political Judgement*: How is it possible to identify those ends and their relative priority, along with the permissible means to achieve them?
8. *Political Discretion*: How and to what extent is it possible to empower office-holders in institutions to access and act on these judgements, while limiting office-holders' capacities to pursue their own divergent interests?
9. *Political Participation*: To what extent and in what ways can and should non-office-holders make political judgements and decisions, as well as control the actions of those office-holders and institutions?
10. *Sites of Governance*: At which levels and loci of power should governing institutions be situated so that they are stable, enabling office-holders and citizens to operate in these justifiable ways on an ongoing basis?

Each of these aspects comprises large, contested areas of moral and political thought. Rather than reviewing the nuances articulated in previous chapters, I shall simply highlight the main fault lines that I sought to uncover in the theories of Rawls and Habermas, and examine how the theory of Responsive Democracy works to avoid these fissures.

---

[387] I take this Humboldtian formulation largely from Geuss, *History and Illusion*, 88.

2. *Rawls and Liberal Statism*

(1) Rawls' theory of international law accords normative priority to political culture, territory, and order; for these to be maintained, persons need only be treated as cooperative members of their (ascriptive) associations and (thin) states—as reasonable and rational, not as free and equal. (2) All persons are included as deserving of this minimal respect, but international law is to be silent on legal and policy norms that instantiate more far-reaching respect for persons—including full liberties of speech and conscience. (3) These restrictions arise from Rawls' argument for 'toleration' of 'decent peoples'—an argument that fails to recognise the reasonable pluralism of individual persons. A number of oppressive and unequal restrictions on individuals' liberty are treated as permissible since they are merely aspects of doctrines that are legitimate organising principles for political orders, and are matters for states to decide upon in much the same way as individuals are left to decide upon aspects of their conceptions of the good in liberal societies.

(4) 'Decent' peoples are in fact states that extend their activities into spheres of life that liberals and democrats normally defend as sacrosanct—for instance, promoting a state religion and barring members of other religions from public office. Meanwhile, dissenters (including women who seek equal treatment, etc.) who cannot make their argument on the (religious, etc.) terms of the regime are stipulated to be unreasonable. (5) Rawls' nation-statist presumption about the demarcation of political membership obscures these and other ways in which the interests of persons and of peoples do not coincide, and rules out the possibility that other institutional configurations may *better* secure persons' minimal liberty rights *as well as* other important interests. (6) While Rawls does reject the unqualified sovereignty defended by Realists, the qualifications he places on sovereignty do not preclude an important range of abuses in the pursuit of the comprehensive ends of regimes.

(7) The ends and means of government (other than protection of minimal liberty rights and non-aggression towards other thin states) may be determined by a tradition or way of life, or more precisely, by rulers who owe their position to that tradition or way of life, and are not subject to democratic controls. A 'decent consultation hierarchy' requires these rulers to consult only minimally with groups that hold different comprehensive doctrines—that is, with the apparent leaders (rabbis, imams, etc.) who interpret the ends of all purported members of such groups. (8) This consultation does not provide sufficient

information and incentives to make rulers act to prevent mass famines, let alone other humanly caused events that are especially injurious to the poorest and most vulnerable individuals.

(9) While Rawls does elaborate on equality and liberty in a democratic state under the rubric of a 'principle of participation' and an 'idea of public reason', his specification of practicable mechanisms for securing representation in democracies consists only of free and fair elections, no gerrymandering, and reducing the effect of some inequalities of wealth that impact on elections (for instance, he endorses campaign finance reform in the United States).[388] In illiberal and undemocratic 'decent' states, participation is a rather strong word for the limited, distorted, highly mediated action permitted to many individuals. (10) In the face of current global transformations, Rawls' Law of Peoples continues to presume unitary and territorial sovereignty, places few restrictions on what states may do to their own members, and requires few outlets for dissent (even the dissent of majorities). For these reasons, an international state system underpinned by the Law of Peoples is unlikely to generate the ongoing moral and prudential endorsement necessary to render it stable.

Perhaps it is misleading in any case to describe Rawls' theory as a democratic theory rather than simply as a theory of justice—despite some of the avowals central to *Political Liberalism* and *The Idea of Public Reason Revisited*. His conception of international justice regards a range of undemocratic states as legitimate and he has no significant account of actual democratic representation and participation. We should say rather that he has a theory of liberal constitutionalism within some states—which, as it stands, has little plausibility beyond states—and that he has no theory of liberal democratic politics either within or beyond states.

3. Habermas and Deliberative Democracy

(1) For Habermas, we are speaking animals: we lay claim to moral and political inclusion because we are able to participate in practical

---

[388] Rawls' fullest discussion of actual political representation—alas, perfunctory—is to be found scattered in *Theory*, 221–43 (see also *Idea Revisited*). Here he confines himself to some commonplaces in the political science literature, and to elucidating which kinds of attitude, speech, and action are reasonable and compatible with his background framework of justice. To be fair, actual representation was not one of his main preoccupations; to be bold—given later developments and claims in his theory—there are grounds to believe it ought to have been.

discourses—discourses that are at once rational and 'located within the horizon of shared, unproblematic [background] beliefs'—which make it possible for normative claims to be redeemed through acceptance by all other participants. (2) He considers the scope of moral concern to be more expansive than does Rawls, since Habermas's conception of practical reasoning treats all persons—and not merely citizens of liberal states—as ideally free and equal participants in a (potentially global) scheme of social cooperation. (3) However, by misconstruing the bases for political inclusion, Habermas too ultimately fails to locate all individuals at the epicentre of normative concern. The deliberative requirement that norms and commands be justified through a 'fully inclusive' 'real discourse' cannot be redeemed under conditions of scale and pluralism, since political judgements and decisions could never be prospectively validated 'in the consciousness of the political actors themselves'. (4) In particular, where many millions of persons are involved, it is impossible for any, let alone every, member of the public or ruler to attain an 'ideally extended "we" perspective' prior to political decision. Yet this is precisely the perspective that purportedly justifies extending political legislation into spheres of life normally treated as sacrosanct by liberal theory.

(5) If interests can only be identified and validated through a demanding participatory process that no institutional configuration can instantiate, this effectively rules out the possibility of judging interests. (6) Valid legislation and political decision in the interests of the public are rendered strictly impossible; interests that do appear to be validated are likely to be the interests of richer and more powerful agents who are able to gain a hearing for themselves and present their interests as those of the public—which is hardly a stable basis for protecting and advancing the interests of the most disadvantaged individuals. (7) Deliberative theorists are not short of institutional recommendations to avoid such dangers—they variously propose five kinds of institutionalised 'representation' that make political judgement and decision feasible—but none of the institutions they favour successfully models or mirrors inclusive and rational deliberation of any scope by the public themselves. Either the proposed institutions, such as deliberative polls and citizens' juries, model so-called deliberation in ways that violate core democratic principles such as free association, or they model deliberation in ways that allow a minority to be determinate over a majority for no reason. (8) Meanwhile, political representatives—who would in fact be able to cumulate necessary information and skills for making and acting upon judgements of the interests of the public—may contribute to and even lead discursive processes, but are not given sufficient discretion to judge and act separately from prior public endorsement.

(9) Habermas's requirements on participation fail to recognise the limits of human cognitive capacities (limits that would remain, even in utopia), assuming instead agents that are capable of simultaneously understanding and integrating the views of huge numbers of interlocutors, along with all information relevant to every important decision. Maximising participation, or seeking to mirror what the public would choose, often counts against informed, capable judgements and timely, responsible action by representatives in the interests of the public. (10) Unlike Rawls, Habermas is avowedly 'post-national' when specifying sites of legitimate coercive power and even recognises that it is representation that emancipates government from statism and exclusivist solidarity;[389] but his theory of representation is too thin to deliver such emancipation because his account of the role of representation is circumscribed by an overly demanding conception of participation.

Habermasian normative constraints on legitimate rule might rule out certain abuses of power, then, but they also prevent the *use* of power for worthwhile ends—ends for the sake of which democratic government is justifiably established. More concretely, deliberative theories vitiate the discretion required at the core of democratic representation— replacing the aspiration to systematic control over representative government with an ideal of direct and determinate involvement in government decision-making by the public. In the end, such commitments implicitly violate the principle of moral universality by endorsing an illusion: that inclusive moral and political concern, which is possible, is achieved by radically inclusive participation, which is not.

Habermas does not lack a democratic theory—far from it. What he does lack, ironically and despite initial appearances, is a theory of modern democratic representation under conditions of pluralism and scale. A thick theory of representation of the latter kind is indispensable to conceptualising justice and democracy, as he aspires to do, both within and beyond state borders.

4. Responsive Democracy: Underlying Ideas about Power and Knowledge

The argument of this book has been motivated by two underlying ideas about the relationship between power and knowledge. The first

---

[389] See J. Habermas, *The Postnational Constellation* (Cambridge: Polity, 2001); see the review by D. Runciman, 'What Constitutes a Superstate?' *London Review of Books*, Vol. 23, No. 14, 19 July 2001.

idea is that ideals can be most effectively orienting, and thus practical, only if they are not based on idealisations; that is, ideals must not assume predicates that could not be true of any human being or society. Political society will always involve people exercising discretionary power over one another *et in utopia*; in constructing a practicable ideal, we must recognise that deep asymmetries of power and knowledge are enduring features of social life. We are then able to confine ourselves to removing unnecessary and unjustified power relations, and to creating political institutions that identify power and knowledge differentials as well as channelling them to positive effect.

I take this idea to be a development of Rousseau's famous dictum that, in establishing the principles of legitimate government, we ought to be 'taking men as they are, and laws as they might be'.[390] Habermas falls short especially on the first part of the dictum: his theory requires psychological and coordination abilities that are beyond human reach. Rawls falls short especially on the second part of the dictum: his theory pays too much homage to culturalist, nationalist, and statist power relations.

Put in this way, the error common to Habermas and Rawls becomes clear: both are wedded to forms of idealisation. Habermas obscures *enduring* asymmetries of power by postulating impossible forms of knowledge and society; while Rawls obscures *existing* asymmetries of power—and their ill effects—by unnecessarily incorporating current social forms into the structure of governance, as justifiable permanent features of the social landscape.

Cosmopolitan global justice avoids idealisation above all by rejecting characterisations of sovereignty as intrinsically unitary and territorial, let alone grounded in nationalist sympathies. Instead, sovereignty can and should be dispersed horizontally and vertically, to multiple levels and loci of authority, each exercising distinct and determinate power over kinds of human practice and resources. Plurarchic sovereignty is, however, limited on functional grounds by needs for efficacious coordinated action and democratic inclusion—needs that give rise to Principles of Distributive Subsidiarity and Democracy. These principles constitute non-arbitrary reasons for drawing boundaries of sovereignty—boundaries that are historically contingent, but only in the permissible sense that they take account of the best current institutional means (including key institutional reform) to reach the ends of free and equal persons.

---

[390] Rousseau, *Social Contract*, Book 1, 49.

Yet at this point it was still unclear how these principles could be instantiated in large-scale, pluralist, and overlapping societies: How is it possible for office-holders in such a complex institutional configuration to make good political judgements as well as coordinate their actions? And how is it possible for citizens to exercise determinate influence and control over those political agents and processes?

The second underlying idea of the book holds the key to an ideal theory that avoids idealisation of rulers and citizens as well as institutions. It is the idea that we cannot attain a disinterested synthetic perspective that incorporates and locates the totality of political knowledge. Members of the public in particular do not need to have expert and extensive knowledge in order to be politically effective moral and political agents. Rather, authorities with different institutional capabilities and purposes can be situated such that they focus on different areas of governance and cumulate distinctive competencies at understanding and acting in those areas. Occupying professional office in these authorities does not make representatives superior to the public, but it does put representatives in a position to cumulate, check, and deploy certain kinds of power and knowledge to judge and act on the interests of the public. Representatives can also be situated such that they have good reasons not only to empower but also to constrain other representatives—in part by eliciting and conveying citizens' judgements—to act responsibly in fulfilling definite and dischargeable obligations.

However, I argued that these hopes are misplaced if we stick to the traditional separation of powers approach: Differentiation of tasks within ordinary legislative and executive institutions does limit the exercise of power by representatives, but it remains the case that scrutiny and sanction are largely internal to the regime and are still subject to the logic of professional politics (the modes of thinking, social ties, imperatives, and shared corporate agendas of politicians, political parties, and bureaucrats). The judiciary can and often does have greater independence, but in order to preserve that relative autonomy it must conform to a rigorous jurisprudential logic and a code of conduct that, although not ruling out some kinds of intervention, preclude the judiciary from offering new, non-remedial courses of action and engaging in certain much-needed forms of publicity, advocacy, and education.

Nor can we leave it to elections, 'the public sphere', or 'civil society' to avert the ill effects of asymmetries of power and knowledge: The vote is a blunt instrument for producing accountability, reliability, and receptivity. The purportedly deliberative public sphere is an impossible dream, dangerous to try to approximate in reality because overly intensive participation damages the quality of political judgement and inclusive concern for all. Elements of civil society at best provide partial and uneven constraints on rulers and at worst intensify political inequalities between rich and poor, powerful and vulnerable citizens.

I argued that these deficiencies could be offset in good part by strong, standing, and semi-independent accountability and advocacy agencies. Unlike members of the public, these formal agencies would have institutional resources and legal powers that enable them to accumulate expert knowledge and act skilfully in complex issue-areas; unlike rulers, they would not be directly subject to the imperatives of rule and re-election; unlike the judiciary, they could be proactive in addressing some underlying causes of wrongful action; unlike civil society, they would have statutory capacities to compensate for inequalities in political capabilities (between citizens, and between citizens and rulers) and to act as professional contesters in core areas of concern for less advantaged and less mobilised citizens.

My account of an extended division of political labour—which offsets the deficiencies of conventional institutions—also places weight on the idea of including more types of actors, such as NGOs, in formal structures of governance. We must go beyond the recognition that these actors can and should be the primary agents of justice where the state is weak or predatory. We must recognise too that some of these actors could contribute distinctive capabilities and perspectives to governance in many contexts, on an ongoing basis, improving the quality of political judgement. Careful inclusion of such actors (requiring that they pass thresholds of capacity, probity, etc.) would also introduce forms of power that constrain conventional authorities to act more responsibly and to elicit citizens' views—even while placing conventional political authorities in a better positions to scrutinise and sanction actors such as NGOs, as well as TNCs. I confirmed and elaborated these general claims about plurality by showing (among other things) that it would be beneficial to steadily pluralise authority within the United Nations General Assembly and Security Council.

An ideal—but not idealised—theory enables us to understand concretely how representatives could be made to act in the interests of the public, even while controlling one another as well as citizens, as Madison once hoped. In contrast, neither Rawls nor Habermas has supplied a thick account of actual political representation within and beyond states. Both liberal statist and deliberative theories offer accounts of democratic *constitutionalism* but are in an important sense *non-political*: they operate on hypothetical ideas of inclusion and cannot specify how to achieve actual real-time inclusion of the public in controlling rulers and political decision under conditions of scale and pluralism. Critics of Rawls and Habermas are not entirely misguided in the accusation that political philosophy of this kind has lacked a theory of politics and has consequently lacked credibility as guidance for concrete political action.[391]

The theory of Responsive Democracy, on the other hand, begins with an acceptance that no agent can grasp and act on all aspects of political knowledge. However, it is possible to establish a constellation of individual and institutional knowers with different foci and competences, who produce political decisions through structured negotiation of their variously coinciding and competing views of how to contend with social issues. This coordinating constellation can generate a plurality of *refined practical capacities* to understand and to communicate—capacities that improve our collective ability to *judge* how to act. As such, the theory of Responsive Democracy points beyond the theory of constitutionalism that predominates in contemporary analytical political philosophy, towards a liberal democratic theory of *politics*.

A great barrier to developing any such theory appears to be that liberalism and democracy do not always fit together terribly well. I do not wish to deny that contingent conflicts between the two do and would occur in actual institutional configurations. But I have suggested that the lack of conjunction between contemporary liberalism and democracy is to a large extent the result of a *statist* conception of liberalism and a fundamentally *electoralist* conception of democracy. As long as any single locus of authority (e.g. the state) appears to be the ultimate guarantor of justice, the obvious reaction is to construe justice above all in terms of protecting ourselves from this overweening power. As long as electoral processes appear to be the primary route to identifying the views and pursuing the interests of the public, the natural reaction is to construe democratic inclusion above all in terms of maximising participation for each individual (on the one hand) and ridding the demos of mechanisms that mediate between majority views and political decisions (on the other).

I do not wish to claim that majorities would and should not have determinate influence in certain respects; or that minorities do not need protection in other respects. But once we accept that political power need not be (and has never entirely been) located in the last

---

[391] For a forceful critique of this kind, directed against much current liberal political philosophy, see Dunn, *Cunning of Unreason*.

instance in one kind of authority, and once we accept that political judgement and constraints need not be derived in the last instance (and have never entirely been derived) from an electoral process, our liberal and democratic imaginations could coalesce to a significant extent. That is, the liberal—in seeking to protect the integrity and interests of individuals—asks which kinds of dispersal of authority are inevitable, which recommended, and which best avoided; the democrat—in seeking to take into account the views and pursue the interests of the public—asks which kinds of dispersed political processes are inevitable, which recommended, and which best avoided. I have suggested that the practical answers to these questions often coincide.

In marked contrast to neoliberalism and Realism, I view the liberal project as requiring the entrenchment of multiple levels and loci of authority, allowing for more individuals to be included in the scope of political concern, even while ensuring that authorities check and balance one another, protecting individuals from abuse by any one authority. In marked contrast to electoralist and deliberative theory, I do not associate democracy primarily with voting or with citizens directly generating political decisions. Rather, the democratic project requires the incorporation of multiple and often disjunctive positions and processes of judgement (elections are only one such necessary process), which serve to reveal and connect diverse aspects of the public's views and interests. More concretely, this text has offered an account of how non-state actors of several kinds, as well as advocacy and accountability agencies, might be advantageously included at several levels of governance, and how this whole constellation—framed by a Charter of Obligations—could be stable and relatively efficient.

This radically extended separation of powers answers to the liberal preoccupation with checking the wrongful use of power against individuals; but it *also* answers to the democratic preoccupation with producing political judgements that show rich and inclusive concern for individuals' interests and for their control over the use of power. For instance, the capabilities of citizens in this polycentric order to approach international courts and advocacy agencies improves protections and remedies against wrongful action by rulers, but these capabilities also increase democratic control in four ways: First, the possibility of appeal, and of obtaining professional assistance in contesting actions by rulers, in itself constitutes an increase in control over one's life; second, since a number of authorities are compelled to rely on citizens' judgements, as a resource of power against domination by other authorities, those who exercise power are more concerned to elicit and take into account citizens' views; third, the differentiation and specialisation of political labour improves the quality of our collective judgements as to which interests should have priority and how those interests should be pursued; and finally, advocacy agencies take up concerns and complaints of people who are not highly mobilised as a group, and in so doing these agencies—without requiring high levels of collective awareness from (often vulnerable) individuals—create a 'we' that is able to impact on governance.

In the world as it is, the institutional requirements contained in my theories of cosmopolitan justice (Chapter 1) and responsive representation (Chapters 2 and 3) can largely be met through the same political transformations (exemplified in Chapter 4). The pluralisation of institutions of justice and the pluralisation of representative institutions are complementary endeavours that together could create Responsive Democracy.

5. Ideals in Politics

Long before writing *The Social Contract*, Rousseau sought to explain why, with the establishment of government, 'men ran headlong into chains': they saw the advantages of political institutions but did not have the experience to foresee the dangers.[392] At the end of a bloody and disillusioning twentieth century, the tendency—in global politics in particular—was quite the opposite. We must see this tendency—to avoid new and stronger non-state formal institutions—in historical perspective: Fascist and hard-line communist regimes had brought home the dangers of centralised domination and negative bureaucracy; neoliberal orthodoxies of deregulation had successfully yet disastrously presented themselves as remedies to the overweening state. However, pessimism about institutional arrangements and innovation is just as pernicious as grievous optimism about the capacities of political institutions to harmonise human ends. In the absence of some new political institutions and significant reforms to current institutions, everything from the flow of capital to human rights abuse to political violence will go largely unchecked—leaving narrow state and corporate interests to set most of the terms for so-called social cooperation.

A stoic retreat from action in the political world is not a moral option. We are suspicious of institutions but we cannot live without a dense network of rules and patterns enforced by extensive institutional

---

[392] See M. Cranston, 'Introduction' to Rousseau, *Social Contract*, esp. 22.

configurations; this network can be extended and reconfigured to produce better effects. Politics is about social hope as much as it is about necessity, about developing worthwhile aspirations as much as about strategic action to achieve our aspirations: the point is to understand how each shifts horizons of possibility for the other. Differentials of power and knowledge are now perhaps larger than ever, and are not entirely avoidable, nor for that matter invariably destructive; to attempt to eradicate rather than manage these differentials however would be variously ineffective or disastrous. I have sketched linked theories of justice and representation that could guide our approach to these global dangers and opportunities.

We should not be under the illusion that the spectres of corruption, inertia, mismanagement, and other political evils can be eradicated, at any locus of governance. But neither should we ignore human capacities and social possibilities for systematically controlling the use, and limiting the abuse, of political power to achieve the ends of free and equal individuals. The purpose of a normative theory of constitutionalism and politics is to establish the principles and ultimate goals that should orientate institutional design and political strategies. If we are to be prudent, we must not lose sight of our ideals; rather, realism requires that we render our ideals specific and compelling.

Bibliography

Ackerman, B., 'Political Liberalisms', *Journal of Philosophy*, Vol. 91, No. 7 (1994), 364–86.

Adamczick-Gerteis, U., 'Annex: The Pontignano Conference on Aspects of UN Reform: Discussion', in P. Taylor, S. Daws, and U. Adamczick-Gerteis, eds., *Documents on United Nations Reform* (Aldershot: Dartmouth, 1997).

Allot, P., *Eunomia: New Order for a New World* (Oxford: Oxford University Press, 1990).

Archibugi, D., 'Principles of Cosmopolitan Democracy', in D. Archibugi, D. Held, and M. Kohler, eds., *Re-imagining Political Community: Studies in Cosmopolitan Democracy* (Stanford, CA: Stanford University Press, 1998).

Archibugi, D., D. Held, and M. Kohler, eds., *Re-imagining Political Community: Studies in Cosmopolitan Democracy* (Stanford, CA: Stanford University Press, 1998).

Arendt, H., *The Origins of Totalitarianism* (New York: Harcourt Brace & Company, 1973).

Aristotle, *The Politics*, Carnes Lord, trans. (Chicago and London: University of Chicago Press, 1984).

Arnold, G., *World Government by Stealth: The Future of the United Nations* (London: Macmillan, 1997).

Austin, J. L., *How to Do Things with Words* (Oxford: Clarendon Press, 1962).

Balakrishnan, G., ed., *Mapping the Nation* (London and New York: Verso, 1996).

Beitz, C., 'Cosmopolitan Ideals and National Sentiment', *Journal of Philosophy*, Vol. 80, No. 10 (1983), 591–600.

—— 'Cosmopolitan Liberalism and the State System', in C. Brown, ed., *Political Restructuring in Europe: Ethical Perspectives* (London and New York: Routledge, 1994).

Benhabib, S., 'Liberal Dialogue vs. a Critical Model of Discursive Legitimacy', in *Situating the Self* (New York: Routledge, 1992).

—— 'Introduction', in S. Benhabib, ed., *Democracy and Difference* (Princeton, NJ: Princeton University Press, 1997).

Benn, S., 'Interests in Politics', *Proceedings of the Aristotelian Society*, Vol. 60 (1960), 123–40.

Blair, T., 'A Superpower, But Not a Superstate', *Guardian*, 7 October 2000.

Bohman, J., *Public Deliberation: Pluralism, Complexity, and Democracy* (Cambridge, MA: MIT Press, 1996).

Bohman, J. and W. Rehg, eds., *Deliberative Democracy: Essays on Reason and Politics* (Cambridge, MA: MIT Press, 1997).

Booth, C. and P. Sands, 'Keep Politics Out of the Global Courts: International Judges Must Be Independent and Representative', *Guardian*, 13 July 2001.

Bosco, A., ed., *The Federal Idea*, 2 Vols. (London: Lothian Foundation Press, 1991 and 1992).

Brown, B., 'Summary: A Mid-Life Crisis for the UN at Fifty', in R. Thakur, ed., *Past Imperfect, Future Uncertain: The United Nations at Fifty* (Basingstoke: Macmillan, 1998).

Brown, B. S., 'U.S. Objections to the Statute of the International Criminal Court: A Brief Response', *New York University Journal of International Law and Politics*, Vol. 31 (1999), 855–91.

Brown, C., ed., *Political Restructuring in Europe: Ethical Perspectives* (London: Routledge, 1994).

Brown, L. N. and T. Kennedy, *The Court of Justice of the European Communities*, 5th edn. (London: Sweet and Maxwell, 2000).

Brown, S., 'The World Polity and the Nation-State System', in R. Little and M. Smith, eds., *Perspectives on World Politics* (London: Routledge, 1991).

Butterworths, *Butterworths Dictionary of Legal Words*, www.butterworths.com.au.

Carens, J., 'Aliens and Citizens: The Case for Open Borders', *Review of Politics*, Vol. 49, No. 2 (1987), 251–73.

Charter 99, www.charter99.org.

Chaucer, G., *The Canterbury Tales* (London: Penguin, 1992).

Childers, E. and B. Urquhart, 'Renewing the United Nations System [1994]', reprinted in J. Muller, ed., *Reforming the United Nations: New Initiatives and Past Efforts*, 3 Vols. (The Hague: Kluwer Law International, 1997).

Clark, J. D., *Worlds Apart: Civil Society and the Battle for Ethical Globalization* (Bloomfield, CT: Kumarian Press, 2003).

Cohen, J., 'Deliberation and Democratic Legitimacy', in J. Bohman and W. Rehg, eds., *Deliberative Democracy: Essays on Reason and Politics* (Cambridge, MA: MIT Press, 1997).

—— and J. Rogers, *Associations and Democracy*, (London: Verso, 1995).

—— and C. Sabel, 'Directly-Deliberative Polyarchy', *European Law Journal*, Vol. 3, No. 4 (1997), 313–42.

Connolly, W. E., 'On "Interests" in Politics', *Politics and Society*, Vol. 2, No. 4 (1972), 459–77.

—— 'Speed, Concentric Cultures, and Cosmopolitanism', *Political Theory*, Vol. 28, No. 5 (2000), 596–618.

Coote, A. and J. Lenahan, *Citizens' Juries: Theory into Practice* (London: Institute for Public Policy Research, 1997).

Dahl, R., *After the Revolution?* (New Haven, CT: Yale University Press, 1970).

Dahl, R., *Polyarchy: Participation and Opposition* (New Haven, CT: Yale University Press, 1971).

Davidson, D., *Inquiries into Truth and Interpretation* (Oxford: Clarendon Press, 1984).

Dreze, J. and A. Sen, *Hunger and Public Action* (Oxford: Clarendon Press, 1989).

—— —— eds., *The Political Economy of Hunger* (Oxford: Clarendon Press, 1995).

Dryzek, J., 'Political Inclusion and the Dynamics of Democratisation', *American Political Science Review*, Vol. 90 (1996), 475–87.

Dunn, D., and J. Uhr, 'Accountability and Responsibility in Modern Democratic Governments', paper presented at the annual meeting of the American Political Science Association, Washington, DC, 1993.

Dunn, J., *Democracy: The Unfinished Journey, 508BC to 1993AD* (Oxford: Oxford University Press, 1992).

—— 'Situating Democratic Political Accountability', in A. Przeworski, S. Stokes, and B. Manin, eds., *Democracy, Accountability, and Representation* (Cambridge: Cambridge University Press, 1999).

—— *The Cunning of Unreason: Making Sense of Politics* (London: HarperCollins, 2000).

Economist, 'Bribery and Business: The Short Arm of the Law', *Economist*, 2–8 March 2002.

Elster, J., 'Accountability in Athenian Politics', in A. Przeworski, S. Stokes, and B. Manin, eds., *Democracy, Accountability, and Representation* (Cambridge: Cambridge University Press, 1999).

Emmerich, Z., 'Architecture as a Social Contract', *Scroope: Cambridge Architectural Journal*, Vol. 11 (1999), 32–9.

European Union, www.europa.eu.int.

European Union Court of Auditors, www.eca.eu.int/EN/coa.htm.

Falk, R., 'The Necessity of Reforming the United Nations and the Impossibility of Doing It', paper presented at a conference at La Trobe University, Melbourne; cited in B. Brown, 'Summary: A Mid-Life Crisis for the UN at Fifty', in R. Thakur, ed., *Past Imperfect, Future Uncertain: The United Nations at Fifty* (Basingstoke: Macmillan, 1998).

—— and A. Strauss, 'On the Creation of a Global People's Assembly: Legitimacy and the Power of Popular Sovereignty', *Stanford Journal of International Law*, Vol. 36, No. 2 (2000), 191–219.

Falk, R., R. Wedgwood, W. L. Nash, F. A. Gerges, and G. Lopez, Roundtable on 'The New War: What Rules Apply?', *Ethics and International Affairs*, Vol. 16, No. 1 (2002), 1–26.

Fassbender, B., *UN Security Council Reform and the Right of Veto: A Constitutional Perspective* (The Hague: Kluwer Law International, 1998).

Fearon, J. D., 'Electoral Accountability and the Control of Politicians: Selecting Good Types Versus Sanctioning Poor Performance', in

A. Przeworski, S. Stokes, and B. Manin, eds., *Democracy, Accountability, and Representation* (Cambridge: Cambridge University Press, 1999).

Ferejohn, J., 'Accountability and Authority: Toward a Theory of Political Accountability', in A. Przeworski, S. Stokes, and B. Manin, eds., *Democracy, Accountability, and Representation* (Cambridge: Cambridge University Press, 1999).

Fishkin, J., *Democracy and Deliberation: New Directions for Democratic Reform* (New Haven, CT: Yale University Press, 1991).

—— *The Voice of the People: Public Opinion and Democracy* (New Haven, CT: Yale University Press, 1995).

Florini, A. M., 'Does the Invisible Hand Need a Transparent Glove? The Politics of Transparency', paper presented at the Annual World Bank Conference on Development Economics, 28–30 April 1999.

Forsythe, R., *The Politics of Oil in the Caucasus and Central Asia: Prospects for Oil Exploration and Export in the Caspian Basin* (Oxford: Oxford University Press, 1996).

Fox, G., 'The Right to Political Participation in International Law', *Yale Journal of International Law*, Vol. 17, No. 2 (1992), 539–607.

Franck, T. M., 'The Emerging Right to Democratic Governance', *American Journal of International Law*, Vol. 86, No. 1 (1992), 46–91.

—— *Fairness in International Law and Institutions* (Oxford: Clarendon Press, 1995).

Furman, J. and J. Stiglitz, 'Economic Crises: Evidence and Insights from East Asia', *Brookings Panel on Economic Activity* (Washington, DC: Brookings Institute, 1998).

Galtung, F. and J. Pope, 'The Global Coalition Against Corruption: Evaluating Transparency International', in A. Schedler, L. Diamond, and M. Plattner, eds., *The Self-Restraining State* (London: Lynne Rienner, 1999).

Galtung, J., 'Alternative Models For Global Democracy', in B. Holden, ed., *Global Democracy: Key Debates* (London: Routledge, 2000).

Genn, H., *Paths to Justice* (Oxford: Hart Publishing, 1999).

—— *Paths of Justice in Scotland* (Oxford: Hart Publishing, 2001).

Geuss, R., *The Idea of a Critical Theory: Habermas and the Frankfurt School* (Cambridge: Cambridge University Press, 1981).

—— *History and Illusion in Politics* (Cambridge: Cambridge University Press, 2001).

Giddens, A., *The Consequences of Modernity* (Cambridge: Polity, 1990).

Global Witness, 'Conflict Diamond Report', www.one.world.org/globalwitness/reports/conflict.

Goldstone, R., *For Humanity: Reflections of a War Crimes Prosecutor* (New Haven, CT: Yale University Press, 2000).

Goodin, R., 'Democratic Deliberation Within', *Philosophy and Public Affairs*, Vol. 29, No. 1 (2000), 81–109.

Gordon, W., *The United Nations at the Crossroads of Reform* (New York and London: M. E. Sharpe, 1994).

Grice, P., *Studies in the Way of Words* (Cambridge, MA: Harvard University Press, 1989).

Habermas, J., 'The Scientization of Politics and Public Opinion', *Towards a Rational Society* (Boston: Heinemann Educational, 1971).

—— *Legitimation Crisis* (Boston: Beacon, 1975).

—— *Communication and the Evolution of Society* (Boston: Beacon, 1979).

—— *Discourse Ethics: Moral Consciousness and Communicative Action*, C. Lenhardt and S. W. Nicholsen, trans. (Cambridge, MA: MIT Press, 1990).

—— *Between Facts and Norms: Contributions to a Discourse Theory of Law and Democracy*, W. Rehg, trans. (Cambridge: Polity Press, 1996).

—— 'Popular Sovereignty as Procedure', in J. Bohman and W. Rehg, eds., *Deliberative Democracy: Essays on Reason and Politics* (Cambridge, MA: MIT Press, 1997).

—— *The Inclusion of the Other: Studies in Political Theory*, C. Cronin and P. De Grieff, trans. (Cambridge, MA: MIT Press, 1998).

—— *The Postnational Constellation* (Cambridge: Polity, 2001).

Haufler, V., 'Is There a Role for Business in Conflict Management?', in C. Crocker, F. Hampson, and P. Aall, eds., *Turbulent Peace: The Challenges of Managing International Conflict* (Washington, DC: United States Institute of Peace, 2001).

Harvey, D., *The Condition of Postmodernity* (Oxford: Blackwell, 1989).

Held, D., *Democracy and the Global Order* (Cambridge: Polity Press, 1995).

—— 'Democracy and Globalisation', in D. Archibugi, D. Held, and M. Kohler, eds., *Re-imagining Political Community: Studies in Cosmopolitan Democracy* (Stanford, CA: Stanford University Press, 1998).

—— 'The Changing Contours of Political Community', in B. Holden, ed., *Global Democracy: Key Debates* (London: Routledge, 2000).

—— 'Globalization, Corporate Practice and Cosmopolitan Social Standards', *Contemporary Political Theory*, Vol. 1, No. 1 (2002*a*), 59–78.

—— 'Law of States, Law of Peoples: Three Models of Sovereignty', *Legal Theory*, Vol. 8 (2002*b*), 1–44.

—— A. McGrew, D. Goldblatt, and J. Perraton, *Global Transformations: Politics, Economics and Culture* (Cambridge: Polity Press, 1999).

Herman, B., *The Practice of Moral Judgement* (Cambridge, MA: Harvard University Press, 1993).

Hirschman, A., *The Passions and the Interests* (Princeton, NJ: Princeton University Press, 1977).

Hoffman, S., 'Dreams of Just World', *New York Review of Books*, Vol. 42 (1995), 52–7.

—— *Duties Beyond Borders: On the Limits and Possibilities of International Politics* (Syracuse, NY: Syracuse University Press, 1981).

Holden, B., ed., *Global Democracy: Key Debates* (London and New York: Routledge, 2000).

Ignatieff, M., 'The Right Trial for Milosevic', *New York Times*, 10 October 2000.

International Court of Justice, www.icj-cij.org.

International Criminal Court, www.un.org/law/icc/general/overview.htm.

International Monetary Fund, *How to Enhance the Transparency of Government Operations* (Washington, DC: International Monetary Fund, 1998*a*).

—— *World Economic Outlook* (Washington, DC: International Monetary Fund, 1998*b*).

Project on International Courts and Tribunals (PICT), 'Funding of and Access to International Courts and Dispute Settlement Bodies [1997]', www.pict-pcti.org/publications/publications.html.

Janis, M. W., 'Individuals and the International Court', in A. S. Muller, D. Raic, and J. Thuranszky, eds., *The International Court of Justice: Its Future Role After Fifty Years* (The Hague: Martinus Nijhoff, 1997).

Kaldor, M., *Global Civil Society: An Answer to War* (Cambridge: Polity, 2003).

Kant, I., 'Groundwork of the Metaphysics of Morals', in *Practical Philosophy*, M. Gregor, ed. and trans. (Cambridge: Cambridge University Press, 1996).

—— 'On the Common Saying: That may be correct in theory but it is of no use in practice', in *Practical Philosophy*, M. Gregor, ed. and trans. (Cambridge: Cambridge University Press, 1996).

Klein, N., *No Logo* (London: Flamingo, 2001).

Kovach, H. and S. Burall, *Global Accountability Project* (London: One World Trust and Charter 99, 2001).

Krasner, S., 'Power Politics, Institutions and Transnational Relations', in T. Risse-Kappen, ed., *Bringing Transnational Relations Back In: Non-State Actors, Domestic Structures and International Institutions* (Cambridge: Cambridge University Press, 1995).

Kuper, A., 'Rawlsian Global Justice: Beyond *The Law of Peoples* to a Cosmopolitan Law of Persons', *Political Theory*, Vol. 28, No. 5 (2000), 640–74.

—— 'Facts, Theories and Hard Choices: A Reply to Peter Singer', *Ethics and International Affairs*, Vol. 16, No. 1 (2002*a*), 125–26.

—— 'Global Poverty Relief—More Than Charity: Cosmopolitan Alternatives to the "Singer Solution"', *Ethics and International Affairs*, Vol. 16, No. 1 (2002*b*), 107–20.

—— and J. Kuper, 'Serving a New Democracy: Must the Media "Speak Softly"?—Learning from South Africa', *International Journal of Public Opinion Research*, Vol. 13, No. 4 (2001), 355–76.

Kymlicka, W., ed., *The Rights of Minority Cultures* (Oxford: Oxford University Press, 1995).

Lasok, D. and J. Bridge, *Law and Institutions of the European Communities*, 5th edn. (London: Butterworths, 1991).

Lewis, D., 'Scorekeeping in a Language Game', *Journal of Philosophical Logic*, Vol. 8 (1979), 339–59.

Lewis, P., 'Straining Towards an Agreement on Global Bribery Curb', *New York Times*, 20 May 1997.

Little, R. and M. Smith, eds., *Perspectives on World Politics* (London: Routledge, 1991).

Luban, D., 'The Romance of the Nation-State', in C. Beitz, M. Cohen, T. Scanlon, and J. Simmons, eds., *International Ethics* (Princeton, NJ: Princeton University Press, 1985).

Madison, J., A. Hamilton, and J. Jay, *The Federalist*, W. R. Brock, ed. (London: Phoenix Press, 2000).

Maier, C. S., 'Democracy since the French Revolution', in J. Dunn, ed., *Democracy: The Unfinished Journey, 508BC to 1993AD* (Oxford: Oxford University Press, 1992).

Manin, B., S. Stokes, and A. Przeworski, 'Elections and Representation', in A. Przeworski, S. Stokes, and B. Manin, eds., *Democracy, Accountability, and Representation* (Cambridge: Cambridge University Press, 1999).

Margalit, A., and J. Raz, 'National Self-Determination', *Journal of Philosophy*, Vol. 87, No. 9 (1990), 439–61.

Marquis, C., 'U.S. is Seeking Pledges to Shield Its Peacekeepers from Tribunal: Romania and Israel are First to Sign Agreements', *New York Times*, 12 August 2002.

Martin, R. and E. Feldman, *Access to Information in Developing Countries* (London: Commonwealth Secretariat, 1998).

McCarthy, T., *The Critical Theory of Jurgen Habermas* (revised edition) (Cambridge, MA: MIT Press, 1978).

McMahon, C., *Authority and Democracy: A General Theory of Government and Management* (Princeton, NJ: Princeton University Press, 1994).

Mill, J. S., *Considerations on Representative Government* (New York: Prometheus, 1991).

Miller, D., 'The Nation-State: A Modest Defence', in C. Brown, ed., *Political Restructuring in Europe: Ethical Perspectives* (London: Routledge, 1994).

—— *On Nationality* (Oxford: Oxford University Press, 1997).

—— 'Bounded Citizenship', in D. Miller, ed., *Citizenship and National Identity* (Cambridge: Polity, 2000).

Moellendorf, D., 'Constructing the Law of Peoples', *Pacific Philosophical Quarterly*, Vol. 77 (1996), 132–54.

Monk, R., *Ludwig Wittgenstein: The Duty of Genius* (London: Vintage, 1991).

Morris, D., 'Political Activity and Charitable Status: In Search of Certainty', *The Exempt Organization Tax Review*, Vol. 23, No. 2 (1998), 247–60.

Muller, A. S., D. Raic, and J. Thuranszky, eds., *The International Court of Justice: Its Future Role After Fifty Years* (The Hague: Martinus Nijhoff, 1997).

Muller, J., ed., *Reforming the United Nations: New Initiatives and Past Efforts* (The Hague: Kluwer Law International, 1997).

Mychajlyszyn, N., 'The OSCE and Regional Conflicts in the Former Soviet Union', *Regional and Federal Studies*, Vol. 11, No. 3 (2001), 194–219.

Nabokov, V., *Speak, Memory* (London: Penguin, 2000).

Neier, A., *Taking Liberties: Four Decades in the Struggle for Rights* (New York: PublicAffairs, 2003).

Nelson, J., *The Business of Peace: The Private Sector as a Partner in Conflict Prevention and Resolution* (London: Prince of Wales Business Leaders Forum, 2000).

Nussbaum, M. C. and A. Sen, eds., *The Quality of Life* (Oxford: Clarendon Press, 1989).

—— and J. Glover, eds., *Women, Culture and Development: A Study of Human Capabilities* (Oxford: Clarendon Press, 1995).

—— and Respondents, *For Love of Country*, J. Cohen, ed. (Boston: Beacon Press, 1995).

Ohmae, K., *The Borderless World* (London: Collins, 1990).

O'Neill, O., *Constructions of Reason* (Cambridge: Cambridge University Press, 1989).

—— 'Justice, Capabilities, and Vulnerabilities', in M. C. Nussbaum and J. Glover, eds., *Women, Culture and Development: A Study of Human Capabilities* (Oxford: Clarendon Press, 1995).

—— *Towards Justice and Virtue* (Cambridge: Cambridge University Press, 1996).

—— 'Political Liberalism and Public Reason: A Critical Notice of John Rawls, *Political Liberalism*', *Philosophical Review*, Vol. 106 (1997), 411–28.

—— *Bounds of Justice* (Cambridge: Cambridge University Press, 2000).

—— *Autonomy and Trust in Bioethics* (Cambridge: Cambridge University Press, 2002*a*).

—— *A Question of Trust: The BBC Reith Lectures 2002* (Cambridge: Cambridge University Press, 2002*b*).

—— 'Instituting Principles: Between Duty and Action', in M. Timmons, ed., *Kant's Metaphysics of Morals: Interpretive Essays* (Oxford: Oxford University Press, 2002*c*).

Otunnu, O. and M. Doyle, eds., *Peacemaking and Peacekeeping for the New Century* (Oxford: Rowman and Littlefield, 1998).

Persson, T., G. Roland, and G. Tabellini, 'Separation of Powers and Accountability: Towards a Formal Approach to Comparative Politics', Discussion Paper No. 1475 (London: Centre for Economic Policy Research, 1996).

Pettit, P., *Republicanism* (Oxford: Oxford University Press, 1997).

Pitkin, H., *The Concept of Representation* (Berkeley, Los Angeles, and London: University of California Press, 1967).

Pogge, T., *Realizing Rawls* (Ithaca, NY: Cornell University Press, 1989).

—— 'An Egalitarian Law of Peoples', *Philosophy and Public Affairs*, Vol. 23, No. 3 (1994*a*), 195–224.

—— 'Cosmopolitanism and Sovereignty', in C. Brown, ed., *Political Restructuring in Europe: Ethical Perspectives* (London: Routledge, 1994*b*).

Popper, K., *The Open Society and Its Enemies* (London: Routledge, 1945).

Power, M., *The Audit Society: Rituals of Verification* (Oxford: Oxford University Press, 1997).

Price, D., 'Choices Without Reasons: Citizens' Juries and Policy Evaluation', *Journal of Medical Ethics*, Vol. 26 (2000), 272–6.

Project on International Courts and Tribunals, www.pict-pcti.org/activities/london.html.

Protess, D. and M. McCombs, eds., *Agenda Setting* (London: Lawrence Erlbaum, 1991).

Przeworski, A., and twenty-one collaborators, *Sustainable Democracy* (Cambridge: Cambridge University Press, 1995).

—— 'Minimalist Conception of Democracy: A Defense', in I. Shapiro and C. Hacker-Cordon, eds., *Democracy's Value* (Cambridge: Cambridge University Press, 1999).

—— S. Stokes, and B. Manin, eds., *Democracy, Accountability, and Representation* (Cambridge: Cambridge University Press, 1999).

Rauch, J., 'Seeing Around Corners', *Atlantic Monthly*, Vol. 289, No. 4 (2002), 35–46.

Rawls, J., *A Theory of Justice* (Oxford: Oxford University Press, 1971).

—— *Political Liberalism* (New York: Columbia University Press, 1993a).

—— 'The Law of Peoples', in S. Shute and S. Hurley, eds., *On Human Rights: The Oxford Amnesty Lectures, 1993* (New York: Basic Books, 1993b).

—— *The Law of Peoples* (Cambridge, MA: Harvard University Press, 1999a).

—— 'The Idea of Public Reason Revisited', in *Collected Papers* (Cambridge, MA: Harvard University Press, 1999b).

Raz, J., 'The Morality of Obedience', *Michigan Law Review*, Vol. 83, No. 4 (1985), 744–54.

—— *The Morality of Freedom* (Oxford: Oxford University Press, 1986).

Rehg, W., *Insight and Solidarity: The Discourse Ethics of Jurgen Habermas* (Berkeley, CA: University of California Press, 1994).

Rehnquist, W. H., *The Supreme Court: How It Was, How It Is* (New York: Morrow, 1987).

Risse-Kappen, T., 'Structures of Governance and Transnational Relations: What Have We Learned?', in T. Risse-Kappen, ed., *Bringing Transnational Relations Back In: Non-State Actors, Domestic Structures and International Institutions* (Cambridge: Cambridge University Press, 1995a).

—— ed., *Bringing Transnational Relations Back In: Non-State Actors, Domestic Structures and International Institutions* (Cambridge: Cambridge University Press, 1995b).

Rogowski, R., 'Representation in Political Theory and Law', *Ethics*, Vol. 91, No. 3 (1981), 395–430.

Romano, C. P. R., 'The Proliferation of International Judicial Bodies: The Pieces of the Puzzle', *New York University Journal of International Law and Politics*, Vol. 31 (1999), 709–51.

Rousseau, J. J., *The Social Contract* (London: Penguin, 1968).

Runciman, D., 'What Constitutes a Superstate?', *London Review of Books*, Vol. 23, No. 14 (2001).

Saint-Exupery, A., *The Little Prince* (Ware: Wordsworth Classics, 1995).

Sandall, R., *The Culture Cult: Designer Tribalism and Other Essays* (Oxford: Westview, 2002).

Sandel, M., *Liberalism and the Limits of Justice* (Cambridge: Cambridge University Press, 1982).

Sasse, G., 'The Crimean Issue', *Journal of Communist Studies and Transition Politics*, Vol. 12, No. 1 (1996), 83–100.

Scanlon, T., *What We Owe to Each Other* (Cambridge, MA: Belknap Press of Harvard University Press, 1999).

Scarry, E., 'The Difficulty of Imagining Other People', in M. C. Nussbaum and Respondents, *For Love of Country*, J. Cohen, ed. (Boston: Beacon Press, 1995).

Scheffer, D., 'Statement of the Ambassador at Large for War Crimes Issues', *Hearing on the United Nations International Criminal Court Before the Senate Committee on Foreign Relations*, 105th Congress (Washington, DC: United States Government, 1998).

Scheffler, S., ed., *Consequentialism and Its Critics* (Oxford: Oxford University Press, 1988).

Scheufele, D. A., 'Deliberation or Dispute? An Exploratory Study Examining Dimensions of Public Opinion Expression', *International Journal of Public Opinion Research*, Vol. 11, No. 1 (1999), 25–58.

Schmemann, S., 'U.S. Links Peacekeeping to Immunity from New Court', *New York Times*, 19 June 2002*a*.

—— 'U.S. Vetoes Bosnia Mission, Then Allows 3-Day Reprieve', *New York Times*, 1 July 2002*b*.

Schmitt, C., *The Crisis of Parliamentary Democracy* (Cambridge, MA: MIT Press, 1986).

—— *The Concept of the Political* (Chicago and London: Chicago University Press, 1996).

Schumpeter, J. A., *Capitalism, Socialism and Democracy*, 3rd edn. (London: Allen and Unwin, 1950).

Scottish Charity Law Commission, www.charityreview.com.

Seidl-Hohenveldern, I., 'Access of International Organisations to the International Court of Justice', in A. S. Muller, D. Raic, and J. Thuranszky, eds., *The International Court of Justice: Its Future Role After Fifty Years* (The Hague: Martinus Nijhoff, 1997).

Sen, A., *Poverty and Famines: An Essay on Entitlement and Deprivation* (Oxford: Clarendon Press, 1981).

—— *Inequality Re-examined* (Oxford: Oxford University Press, 1992).

—— 'Our Culture, Their Culture', *New Republic*, 1 April 1996.

—— 'Human Rights and Asian Values', *New Republic*, 14 and 21 July 1997.

—— *Development as Freedom* (New York: Alfred A. Knopf, 1999).

—— and B. Williams, 'Introduction', in A. Sen and B. Williams, eds., *Utilitarianism and Beyond* (Cambridge: Cambridge University Press, 1982).

Sethi, S. P., 'Corporate Codes of Conduct and the Success of Globalization', *Ethics and International Affairs*, Vol. 16, No. 1 (2002), 89–106.

Shapiro, I., and C. Hacker-Cordon, eds., *Democracy's Value* (Cambridge: Cambridge University Press, 1999).

Shute, S., and S. Hurley, eds., *On Human Rights: The Oxford Amnesty Lectures, 1993* (New York: Basic Books, 1993).

Singer, P., 'Achieving the Best Outcome: Final Rejoinder', *Ethics and International Affairs*, Vol. 16, No. 1 (2002*a*), 127–8.

—— 'Poverty, Facts, and Political Philosophies: Response to "More Than Charity" ', *Ethics and International Affairs*, Vol. 16, No. 1 (2002*b*), 121–4.

Skinner, Q., 'The Empirical Theorists of Democracy and Their Critics: A Plague on Both Their Houses', *Political Theory*, Vol. 1, No. 1 (1973), 287–306.

—— 'The Italian City-Republics', in J. Dunn, ed., *Democracy: The Unfinished Journey, 508BC to 1993AD* (Oxford: Oxford University Press, 1992).

—— P. Dasgupta, R. Geuss, M. Lane, P. Laslett, O. O'Neill, W. G. Runciman, and A. Kuper, 'Political Philosophy: The View from Cambridge', *Journal of Political Philosophy*, Vol. 10, No. 1 (2001), 1–19.

Soper, P., *A Theory of Law* (Cambridge, MA: Harvard University Press, 1984).

South African Constitution, www.gov.za.

Sperber, D. and D. Wilson, 'Loose Talk', *Proceedings of the Aristotelian Society*, Vol. 86 (1986), 153–71.

Stokes, S., 'What Do Policy Switches Tell Us about Democracy?', in A. Przeworski, S. Stokes, and B. Manin, eds., *Democracy, Accountability, and Representation* (Cambridge: Cambridge University Press, 1999).

Suter, K., 'Reforming the United Nations', in R. Thakur, ed., *Past Imperfect, Future Uncertain: The United Nations at Fifty* (Basingstoke: Macmillan, 1998).

Szasz, P., 'Granting International Organisations Ius Standi in the International Court of Justice', in A. S. Muller, D. Raic, and J. Thuranszky, eds., *The International Court of Justice: Its Future Role After Fifty Years* (The Hague: Martinus Nijhoff, 1997).

Tan, K. C., 'Liberal Toleration in Rawls's Law of Peoples', *Ethics*, Vol. 108, No. 2 (1998), 276–95.

Tasioulas, J., 'From Utopia to Kazanistan: John Rawls and the Law of Peoples', *Oxford Journal of Legal Studies*, Vol. 22 (2002*a*), 367–96.

—— 'International Law and the Limits of Fairness', *European Journal of International Law*, Vol. 13 (2002*b*).

Taylor, P., S. Daws, and U. Adamczick-Gerteis, eds., *Documents on United Nations Reform* (Aldershot: Dartmouth, 1997).

Teson, F. R., 'The Rawlsian Theory of International Law', *Ethics and International Affairs*, Vol. 9 (1995), 79–99.

Thakur, R., ed., *Past Imperfect, Future Uncertain: The United Nations at Fifty* (Basingstoke: Macmillan, 1998).

Timmons, M., ed., *Kant's Metaphysics of Morals: Interpretive Essays* (Oxford: Oxford University Press, 2002).

Tolstoy, L., *War and Peace* (Oxford: Oxford Paperbacks, 1998).

Transparency International, www.transparency.org.

—— 'Mission Statement', reprinted in R. Martin and E. Feldman, *Access to Information in Developing Countries* (London: Commonwealth Secretariat, 1998).

—— *Bribe-Payer's Survey 2000* (Berlin: Transparency International, 2000).

—— *Corruption Perceptions Index 2001* (Berlin: Transparency International, 2001).

United Nations, 'Overview of the Rome Statute of the International Criminal Court', www.un.org/law/icc/general/overview.htm.

United Nations Development Program, *Human Development Report 2001, Making Technologies Work for Human Development.* (Oxford and New York: Oxford University Press, 2001).

—— *Human Development Report 2002: Deepening Democracy in a Fragmented World* (Oxford and New York: Oxford University Press, 2002).

United Nations Economic and Social Council, *Declaration of Human Duties and Responsibilities*, www.cdp-hrc.uottawa.ca/publicat/valencia/valenc1.html.

United Nations Open-ended Working Group on the Question of Equitable Representation on and Increase in the Membership of the Security Council and Other Matters Related to the Security Council, 'Annex to the Report [of 15 September 1995]' (New York: United Nations, 1995).

United States of America, Department of State, ed., 'Report of Rapporteur of Committee I/1 to Commission I', *The United Nations Conference on International Organisation: Selected Documents* (Washington, DC: Department of State, 1946).

—— Supreme Court, www.supremecourtus.gov.

University of Liverpool Law School, Charity Law Unit, www.liv.ac.uk/law.

Waldron, J., 'Minority Cultures and the Cosmopolitan Alternative', in W. Kymlicka, ed., *The Rights of Minority Cultures* (Oxford: Oxford University Press, 1995).

Walzer, M., *Just and Unjust Wars: A Moral Argument with Historical Illustrations* (New York: Basic Books, 1977).

—— *Thick and Thin: Moral Argument at Home and Abroad* (Notre Dame, IN: University of Notre Dame Press, 1994).

Warburton, J. and A. Cartwright, 'Human Rights, Public Authorities and Charities', *Charity Law and Practice Review*, Vol. 6 (2000), 169–83.

Warren, M., 'The Self in Discursive Democracy', in S. White, ed., *The Cambridge Companion to Habermas* (Cambridge: Cambridge University Press, 1995).

Weber, M., *Economy and Society: An Outline of Interpretive Sociology*, G. Roth and C. Wittich, eds. (Berkeley, CA: University of California Press, 1978).

Weil, S., *The Need for Roots: Prelude to a Declaration of Duties Towards Mankind* (London: Routledge, 1995).

Weinstock, D., 'Prospects for Transnational Citizenship and Democracy', *Ethics and International Affairs*, Vol. 15, No. 2 (2002), 53–66.

White, S. K., ed., *The Cambridge Companion to Habermas* (Cambridge: Cambridge University Press, 1995).

Williams, B., 'Consequentialism and Integrity', in S. Scheffler, ed., *Consequentialism and Its Critics* (Oxford: Oxford University Press, 1988).

Winston, M., 'NGO Strategies for Promoting Corporate Social Responsibility', *Ethics and International Affairs*, Vol. 16, No. 1 (2002), 71–88.

World Bank, *World Development Indicator 2000*, www.worldbank.org/data/wdi2000.

Wyatt, R. O., J. Kim, and E. Katz, 'How Feeling Free to Talk Affects Ordinary Political Conversation, Purposeful Argumentation, and Civic Participation', *Journalism and Mass Communication Quarterly*, Vol. 77, No. 1 (2000), 99–114.

Young, I. M., 'Together in Difference: Transforming the Logic of Group Political Conflict', in W. Kymlicka, ed., *The Rights of Minority Cultures* (Oxford: Oxford University Press, 1995).

Young, O. R., *The Intermediaries: Third Parties in International Crises* (Princeton, NJ: Princeton University Press, 1967).

Index